NO GUILT—
JUST TILT!

SOLUTIONS
TO BE A GUILT-FREE
WORKING MOM

Marci Fair

Testimonials for TILT

"Motherhood isn't always so zen, but how do you get to that peaceful place? Read *TILT*. I love how Marci is able to capture the moments of motherhood in a relatable and heartwarming way. *TILT* not only shares anecdotes, but offers solutions and insight from her experience raising 4 kids and weaves in wisdom from other moms who have been there too. It's more than a parenting book, but a tribute to our journey as moms, but not forgetting our journey as women."

Angela Chee
TV Host, Speaker, Media Coach, Founder, www.zenmediainc.com,
www.thezenmom.com

"Why settle for the ever elusive "balance" when you can live a *TILT*ed life, one that accepts the reality of family, work and imperfection? Through *TILT: 7 Solutions to a Guilt-free Working Mom*, Marci Fair gives us permission to let go of our guilt and accept who we are as mothers, making room for our dreams and ambitions on our own terms. From practical tools and advice to inspirational stories and quotes, *TILT* helps us change our perspectives and focus on what really matters in life."

Trish Morrison
Founder & CEO, MomCom Life, www.momcomlife.com,
@momcomaustin, @atxtrish

"This book is a treasure. I really love it. It has given me such joy remembering my very favorite time of life - raising my children. Today I am enjoying my wonderful grandchildren. Thank you for reminding me of my greatest life treasures. I am sending *TILT* to my children who thankfully understand how precious their children and these times are. Hang on to every treasured moment with your children!"

Mary Tennant
President, Keller Williams Realty International

"Marci Fair has taken real-world situations that so many Mom's face and applied very practical, useful solutions for overcoming the moments that make Mom's crazy... or *TILTed*! How wonderful it is to read an idea in *TILT* and then have the specific strategies for implementation of the idea. Sprinkled with the delightful musings of her children, it's a book that <u>all</u> women should read."

Cheryl Sadoti
Regional Director, Keller Williams Realty Southeast Region

"*TILT* is full of well over 100 practical, real-life tips busy moms like myself can use to improve their lives today. Everything from how to juggle less, how to manage what we choose to do, and how to have more fun as a family. I love Marci's children's quotes woven throughout the book and all the insightful quotes from so many women. Not only is *TILT* a great resource for working moms, it is a reminder of what really matters in our lives."

Diedra Sorohan
Managing Partner, O'Kelley & Sorohan Attorneys At Law, LLC

"Marci Fair, where were you twenty years ago? On reading *TILT*, I found myself thinking: Yep, "been there, done that," and wishing I'd had your 7 Solutions to a Guilt-Free Working Mom in the 90's. I was coping with what I'm sure most mothers feel when juggling work obligations with raising a family. Right (write) on, Marci. A great publication to have in any pediatrician's office."

Stefanie Brown
Regional Bank Private Banker, Vice President Community Banking, Wells Fargo Bank, N.A.

"Marci, this is so good I cried. I LOVE YOUR WRITING STYLE. It is engaging, interesting, and moving. Real life and real stuff. I am so proud of you for keeping the "quotes" of the children and incorporating them in the book. I ABSOLUTELY LOVED IT."

Mo Anderson
Vice Chairman of the Board, Keller Williams Realty International

"There are times I cannot get a good deep breath when I am not with my child. To power-through, it takes every prayer, every family member, every friend and regular reminders. *TILT* has reminded me to focus on the journey/not the destination, the quality/not necessarily quantity, and that I am not alone! This has repaired my spirit and lifted some of this weight from my heart. Thank you, Marci!"

Sue Ellen Burchfield
Vice President, Strategic Alliances, 2-10 Home Buyers Warranty

"Marci Fair has attained uncommon success as a mother, wife, and businesswoman -- and we are so fortunate to learn how she maintains this delicate sense of balance (and sometimes imbalance) with joy, humor, compassion, and grace. She brings a unique voice to the discussion of moms who can have it all, choosing to celebrate all that we have in common and how we can be better to ourselves, and better for our families and communities."

Antoinette Perez
Principal, ATP Inc., www.antoinetteperez.com

Why You—and I—Need to Read This Book

> "When I am a mom and have a purse, I will only put a pen in it (not a pencil).
> When you are a mom, you don't make mistakes."
> —Elle (age 8)

Well, if only it were that simple. She will realize soon enough that we all make mistakes and that we all need pencils. Life as a mom can often feel like one big mistake after another. We move at a rapid pace trying to keep our children in shoes that fit them, keep kid goop off our business papers, and get to all the places we are supposed to be with happy, well-fed children in tow. I am already exhausted and *TILT*ed way off balance just thinking about it.

There has to be a way to move through the parenting years with some fun, laughter, and love rising above the weight of the responsibilities. As a parent for over twenty years now, I have found several solutions for the *TILT* in our life and a lot more joy than I imagined possible. I have also found humor to be the best medicine.

If, like me, you're a mom who admits she makes mistakes along the way, yet is also looking to find the necessary humor in those interesting parenting moments, read on. Most of us have a few issues that make it a challenge to feel balanced in our lives; issues that make our ability to *TILT* even more important.

You know you are a mom who *TILTS* when...

- you quickly reach in your purse for your ringing cell phone but instead all your fingers encounter are cookie crumbs, a forgotten child's hairbrush, and a stowaway My Little Pony toy.

- "reading a book" actually means passing out on the bed from exhaustion with the book you finally opened lying next to you.

- you choose where you are going to eat out based on whether they have a diaper-changing table in the bathroom.

- you open your business folder for your important meeting and find the misplaced be-sure-my-child-rides-the-bus-home-today note that did not get to school that morning.

- you are excited when you get through the car-filled parking lot all the way into the store with all the kids alive *and* you remembered to bring your shopping list.

- you run out of candy on Halloween, but the doorbell keeps ringing with more trick-or-treaters, so you give away your one-year-old's candy, hoping he will never remember.

- you are excited to be able to go alone into the restroom stalls.

- you anxiously wait to hear the door open late at night to know that your teenager got home safely after being out with his friends.

- you can get yourself ready, make breakfast, do two loads of laundry, clean up the kitchen, get four kids dressed with their clothes on frontward, find that their book bags actually have a snack in them, stock the diaper bag with most of the essentials, have your briefcase ready to go, fill the back of your car with the dry cleaning and more for errands later, and it is only six-thirty in the morning.

All of those actually describe me. If any of them describe you, then we already have something in common. I wrote this book to help us, in seven practical, example-packed chapters, to find the strategies to help survive and find happiness in modern parenting. Along with my specific ideas, more than eighty other wonderful women share their thoughts and wisdom with you throughout the book.

After my oldest child turned eighteen, I became very thoughtful as we approached his time to leave for college. One day I asked him, "Your three sisters still have a few years at home with us before they go to college. From your eighteen years under our roof, would you give me any feedback, any suggestions of things I should think about in my parenting of them—from your experiences in our family?"

I have made many small and big mistakes along the way, so I waited quietly to hear his response. "Mom," he said, "I wouldn't change a thing." My heart melted.

The solutions in this book are working for us. I hope you enjoy reading them and using them for you and your family. On the days when I struggle with it all, I am reading the book right along with you.

About the Author

My name is Marci. My husband and I have built several successful businesses, and I run a children's charity that has served more than fifteen thousand children. I have four children aged nine to twenty. This is just one of the never-say-never stories of my life.

A portion of every book sale will go to Kares 4 Kids,
a children's charity benefiting children in need.
www.kares4kids.com

Kares
4 Kids

This book is written out of respect and love—

For my children,
May your lives be as richly blessed and full of humor as you have made mine.
"Courtney, that was so nice of you, but you did not have to buy me a ring."
—me
"I wanted to, Mom. Plus, it only cost $2.25."
—Courtney (age 9)

For Bryan,
Without you we would not have these four amazing children, and I would not have written *TILT*.
You are an intuitive life coach disguised as a dad, a business owner, and my soul mate.

For my parents, Marv and Mary Nance,
Thank you for always believing in me,
for supporting me above and beyond as a mom,
and for your unending love of us all.

Contents

Why You—and I—Need to Read This Book.. vii
About the Author xi
Contents.. xv
Foreword... xxi

Part I: What Is *TILT*?

Introduction: Living a *TILT*ed Life... xxvii
Guilt Is a Four-Letter Word...xxix
Balance Is Impossible: Learning How to *TILT* Instead xxx
Life Lessons and Best Ideas...So Far... xxxi

Part II: Balance Is Impossible

Chapter 1: Help Them Dream...Without Giving Up on Our Dreams · 1

"Mom, I want to grow up to tackle those boys playing football
who are trying to make touchdowns."
—Parker, age 4

Mom Quiz #1: Who Has Time for Dreams?.....................................2
All I Can Dream about Is Sleep 3
Dreaming Was What I Did B.C. (Before Children)..............................4
Dreaming for Ourselves—A Life-Altering Example of Leadership 6
Five Steps to Reconnect with Your Dreams 9
Helping Our Kids Dream—and Not Just through the Night 13
The Puzzle Pieces of Our *TILT*ed Lives: Fitting Our Objectives Together........20
Personal Profile in Mom Courage: The Happy Mom 23
Guilt-Free Tips – Ten Ideas to Help You Make Your Goals &
Dreams a Reality...25

Chapter 2: Leverage or Let Go—Dirty Shorts Can Be Worn Twice Sometimes · **27**

"Time to go to bed."
—me
"I don't want to; it must be morning time. Listen...Cock-A-Doodle-Do!"
—Elle, age 5

Mom Quiz #2: What Day *IS* It? 28
Why Is the Grass Always Greener?...29
Neck-Deep in Diapers...30
Be Aware and Survive the Five Years of Crazy...............................31
Five Ways to Keep Perspective—and Your Sanity 34
Live in Today—Don't Miss the Moments to Love and Connect....37
Time Management Tips for the Overcommitted 39
Time Management Mom Idea No. 1: Shop Online 40
Time Management Mom Idea No. 2: Manage Technology
Time Grabbers Now 41
Time Management Mom Idea No. 3: Learn When and How to Say No 43
Time Management Mom Idea No. 4: Build Leverage into Your Life.............45
Time Management Mom Idea No. 5: Use Time-Blocking
in Each Day 46
Time Management Mom Idea No. 6: Plan Over Time 48
Connecting with Your Kids Today—Making Time for Things That Matter.....51
Little-Kid Connections: Making the Ordinary Extraordinary 51
Big-Kid Connections 53
Don't Waste Time Feeling Guilty—Take Action Instead 58
Personal Profile in Mom Courage: Reconnect with Your Kids Every Day 62
Guilt-Free Tips – Nine Ways to Find Happiness in Today 63

Chapter 3: Expired in the Pantry and Other Tales of an Imperfect Motherhood · **65**

"Mom, the expiration date on this ranch dressing in the pantry was three years ago."
—Parker, age 16

Mom Quiz #3: Do You Think You Should...?....................................66
A Lot of Imperfect 67
Just When I Thought I Had It Figured Out: A Timeline 68
Staying Humble, Saying We're Sorry, and Forgiving Ourselves 70
Four Lessons in the Power of Humble Parenting...........................71

Choosing Carefully—Understanding Our 20 Percent 74

Parenting to Their Weaknesses—or to Their Strengths?................... 77

So How Do We Parent if We Cannot "Fix" Them?........................... 79

Focus on Their Strengths and Build Them.................................... 81

Making Mistakes: Losing Your Cool—It Can Happen....................... 82

Making Mistakes and Always Learning—Even in the Summer 84

Ultimately The Choices We Make, Make Us.................................. 85

Personal Profile in Mom Courage: I Am Doing Great Work! 88

Guilt-Free Tips – Eleven Ways to Overcome Mistakes and Live
With Imperfection.. 89

Chapter 4: Too Tired to Be Inspired · · · · · · · · · · · · · · · · · · 91

"Never underestimate the power of encouragement."
—Parker, age 8

Mom Quiz #4: We Are *Always* Inspired, *Aren't* We? 92

Hitting the Reset Button—Wow, I Needed That 93

Sources of Inspiring Strength 94

How Do We Keep Our Inspirations in Front of Us?...................... 106

Our Children's Chalkboard.. 107

When We Change Our Focus, We Change Our Life 110

Personal Profile In Mom Courage: A Lifelong Beginner 114

Guilt-Free Tips – Eleven Interesting Ideas for Inspiration........... 115

Part III: Memories Are Better

Chapter 5: Loving Your Family and Loving Yourself · · · · · · · · 121

"I love your cooking, Mom. You know, your Chinese and your pizza."
—Courtney, age 6

Mom Quiz #5: You Feel Loved When... 122

A Love Deeper Than I Ever Imagined.....................................123

Same Parents...Different Kids?! 124

As Our Children Change through the Seasons of Life, so Must We............128

Three Phases of Love..130

The Hardest Moments Are the Most Important Ones 131

Setting Boundaries Early: Out and About with Kids 133

Setting Boundaries beyond "Black and White": Elementary and Middle School..135
Surviving the Teenage Years: When They Need Us the Most......138
Ways to Guide Young Adults 139
Communicate, Communicate, Communicate...and Communicate Again....141
What Are Good Communication Skills?.....................................142
More Communication Tips for Problem Solving 143
Loving Our Family: Easy, Creative, Thoughtful Traditions That Connect Us...145
Lunchbox and Locker Surprises 146
Birthdays: Simple, Consistent, and Secret..............................147
Creative Connections: Making Traditions Special....................148
Loving Our Spouse..152
How Do We Love and Take Care of Ourselves? 154
Three Ways to Overcome Frustration with Time 159
Loving Our Family—and Being Loved in Return 160
Personal Profile in Mom Courage: Loving...and Being Loved 166
Guit-Free Tips – Ten Ways to Love Your Family and Yourself.....167

Chapter 6: Letting Them Grow Up and Giving Us Both Wings · **169**

"Honey, go clean up your mess."
—me to Courtney
"What mess happened?"
—Courtney, age 5

Mom Quiz #6: Are We Flying Yet? 170
Roots and Wings..171
Our First Gift: Roots 171
Our Second Gift: Wings..172
How Can We Achieve Both? 174
Let Them Succeed, but More Importantly, Let Them Fail 175
Guide Them to Find Their Own Solutions.................................180
Know That Consequences Are a Necessary Pain......................183
Choose Your Battles—They Don't All Matter............................184
Choosing the Battles That Matter 187
Friends—An Influence We Cannot Ignore 189
Decide Whose Homework It Is: Creating Self-Sufficiency 190
Know the Power of Extracurricular Activities............................193

What If They Don't Like Anything—or It Seems They Are Not Good at Anything?! 196

Set Standards That Empower 197

Before Our Children Leave: Creating an Eighteen-Year Plan 203

Writing Your Own Eighteen-Year Plan 205

Our Most Important Bequests 209

Personal Profile in Mom Courage: Give Them Wings..................213

Guilt-Free Tips – Ten Ways to Let Your Children Grow Up and Give Them Wings..214

Chapter 7: Wisdom from Women: Life Reflections from More Than 50 Wonderful Women · 217

"I do this ALL BY MYSELF...now you help me."
—Courtney, age 4

Mom Quiz #7: "Now I Do This All by Myself" 218

Mom Hazing to Mom Amazing...220

From Mom Hazing 221

To Mom Amazing...222

Where Can We Find the Best Mom Advice?...............................223

Being Ready for What Is Coming 225

How to Handle Coming-of-Age..226

Insights from Seriously Cool Moms Who Have Been There and Done That 227

If You Are Being Helped, Then Whom Are You Helping? 264

Personal Profile in Mom Courage: The Treasures of My Life 266

Guilt-Free Tips – Ten Resources for Mom-Wisdom—When in Doubt, Reach Out...267

Closing Thoughts: Our Purpose Is in Our Journey 269

Acknowledgments...273

Resources 277

Notes 279

Foreword

As a mother of six and a psychologist, author, nonprofit founder, and speaker, I know how easy it can be to feel *TILT*ed. Between the demands of kids, home, work, and keeping my relationship with my husband strong, it can be difficult to simply keep up. Then throw in other important relationships, hobbies, church and community responsibilities, and personal goals, and life can feel downright impossible! There have been plenty of times on my journey through motherhood when I have felt all alone, wondering how I might ever fulfill my dreams and live life to my fullest potential. But, over the years, I have learned it is not only *possible* to achieve my dreams for motherhood and career, it is the key to filling *me* with joy and raising *children* who live with joy and meaning, too. Marci shares the same positive message in her insightful book, *TILT*, encouraging us to ditch the guilt and "live on purpose as we raise our family."

First, *TILT* lets us know we are not alone. Not only could I completely relate to Marci's "mom quizzes" at the beginning of each chapter, they had me laughing and thinking, "Other people feel that way too?" And with stories and advice from over eighty amazing women from various stages of mothering life, Marci's book will also help *you* breathe a sigh of relief, knowing you're not the only one.

Second, *TILT* is full of tips to help working mothers see and do things just a little bit better. I have long believed, and agree with Marci, that balance is an impossible goal. From my perspective, it's more about making choices that matter. And Marci's idea to focus instead on the memories helps us remember what matters most. I especially adore the quotes she shares from her children as they have grown. They not only touched me and often made me laugh, they made me smile, remembering the "lessons" my own children have taught along the way.

Third, I love *TILT's* positive approach to raising families, helping us recognize the importance of what we do as mothers. Marci is right—the world often fails to value the role of motherhood. And the world needs more women to speak out and show mothers the importance of what they do every hour (and often, every minute!) of every day. *TILT* reminds us that when we focus on what matters most, we discover *we* are not only better, our children and families are too.

As my children have moved from diapers to dolls to college applications, I too have seen the need to *TILT,* the need for flexibility, the need to slow down and see what's most important, and the truth that while we might not be able to have it all *all* the time, we can have it all *over* time. *TILT* helps us discover the things that matter most and never let them go.

~Christina G. Hibbert, Psy.D.

Mother of six
Author, *This is How We Grow*
Clinical Psychologist; Founder, *The Arizona Postpartum Wellness Coalition*
Speaker; Singer-songwriter; Dark Chocolate & Nap Enthusiast
www.DrChristinaHibbert.com
www.facebook.com/drchibbert
www.pinterest.com/drchibbert
Twitter: @DrCHibbert

PART I
What Is
TILT?

INTRODUCTION:
Living a *TILT*ed Life

"I used to think heaven was in the clouds.
Then I rode on an airplane and realized it wasn't there.
Now I don't know where it is!"
—Elle (age 7)

I adore our children, and at the same time I have also always wanted to have a professional life. So when my oldest son was born, I tried every combination of child care to help achieve both goals. The stress and strain of seeking different solutions, along with our high-octane business life, was almost more than I could bear. Mentally, financially, and personally, mothering and loving our children was taking its toll. Facing many, many years of children at home, I did not know how I was going to keep all the balls I was juggling in the air and have any sanity left when it was done.

As the years progressed, I learned the hard way that life does not progress in a straight line. Life is more like being on a seesaw—some days are up, and many days are down. Finding the energy and the reason to push ourselves back up makes all the difference. We are, in fact, each here to experience, to learn, to grow from our mistakes, and to help each other. It would take me many challenging parenting years; many how-could-I-let-myself-be-outnumbered years; many late nights crying myself to sleep, wishing I could be a better mom, wife, and person, before I could begin to appreciate the *TILT* in our life, and it all started one crisp, cool fall afternoon...

I was driving our first child home from his preschool. A million thoughts were whirling around in my mind. Fiery orange, yellow, and red leaves were fluttering down off the tall hardwood trees through the breeze and swooshing aside as we drove along. I was deep in worried thought about all the responsibilities I had to deal with and all the unfinished work scattered across my office desk. In the middle of my haze, our four-year-old son commented, "Mom, the caterpillars better hurry up and eat—all the green leaves are almost gone."

I was not paying any attention to the beauty all around us. Frankly, beauty was the farthest thing from my mind. I had work to do, errands to run, groceries to buy, and a house to clean, as well as important professional objectives I needed to accomplish. Little-kid comments did not hold much merit. Or so I thought.

When I noticed the leaves and absorbed what he had said, I explained to my worried little boy that the caterpillars would be all right. I told him that they would have already eaten, and how they each had their own paths to becoming butterflies. Little did I know that day the impact that caterpillars, butterflies, and my children would have on me.

My husband and I were at just the beginning of our life together and had no idea yet how far off balance and *TILT*ed our world was going to become. I believed that my life should be organized and follow a fairly straight, predictable line. I did not know the truth yet, that my life would actually *TILT* from one extreme to another. On that particular fall afternoon, I didn't know that my husband and I would choose to bring four children into this world. I also had no idea that this future decision would push my sanity right back *out* of this world.

While our decision to grow our family was very deliberate as we thought about what would make our lives richer, the responsibility was overwhelming. I have had many moments when I wondered what I was thinking. Most of my short-term memory faded as I juggled too many diapers, too many pairs of mismatched socks, and too many crumb-covered pacifiers that had fallen on the dirty ground. From my disheveled existence and *TILT*ed point of view, I had fallen into a deep hole of major life responsibilities.

Then the very people whose existence put me in that hole were the ones who ended up pulling me out. As the children shared their kid-perspective wisdom with me as they grew, I began to write it down. I had to write down what they said immediately, or I would forget it. I scribbled their quotes on any scrap piece of paper, fast-food napkin, or toilet-paper square I could find. I tried to keep them all together and stuff them into a binder, hoping I would not lose them. I kept their words to reread, to reinspire me, and to make me laugh—and in the wild hope that I might actually organize them one day.

This is that day.

Guilt Is a Four-Letter Word

> "Mom, I wish you did not have an office at home, too.
> Then we could play together ALL the time!"
> —Elle (age 4)

Today—and this book—is the culmination of years of life, parenting, and children's quotes that I have listened to, written down, and learned from. The more I listened, the more I learned. Guilt that permeated me and pulled me down in my younger parenting years has changed, with careful planning and thought, into understanding and resolution. Guilt and worry about regrets in our lives can haunt us through our motherhood years. But feeling guilty is a choice. We can choose differently.

In fact, instead of having to shoulder the burden myself to resolve my *TILT*ed adult life, many of the answers to my frustrated questions were being handed to me by these funny little people I had surrounded myself with. I call these moments my *momoirs*.

It took me a little while to see the importance of those easy-to-miss moments when our kids share amazing perspective. But when I did, I realized some of their musings could actually become the heartfelt answers to our soul-searching questions—and perfect reasons why my life had been turned inside out.

Honestly, this clarity about my life goes in and out of focus. It depends on how many teachers I am trying to put gifts together for in honor of Teacher Appreciation Day. It depends on how many soccer games, wrestling matches, gymnastics meets, and track practices we are juggling to get our children to and from that week. It depends on whether all four children have outgrown their clothes at the same time and need something nice to wear to the Santa Brunch in three days. It depends on how much I am personally hoping to accomplish professionally that year.

In other words, my life can easily be overwhelmed with guilt and become out of focus. However, learning how to move with and plan for the up-and-down *TILT* of my life has changed the whole experience from fuzzy and frustrating to meaningful and purposeful.

Balance Is Impossible: Learning How to *TILT* Instead

"Mom, you are so easy to do jokes on!
You are always so busy, you cannot think straight."
—Elle (age 8)

After many frustrating years of trying to "do it all," I finally realized that balance is impossible—we are in constant motion, moving in and out of balance. So to strive for it is impossible, and to be hard on ourselves for never reaching it is a battle with no victory. Instead, we need to strive for positive action in the areas of our lives that matter.

I cannot be great at everything, but I can be pretty good at a few things that are important. The other things I have to let go of, at least for now. Some parenting responsibilities I am actually talented at, whether intentionally or not. Some I will never master.

I knew I could not live through twenty-nine years of children at home in frustration and disappointment over all I could *not* do. So, if I was going to be living out of balance, I had to create a plan that would still allow me to build a life I would be proud of. I had to learn to *TILT*.

I have realized that if I can build and foster my own dreams and mother each of my children within a big picture, then I am powerful. Here is what I *can* do:

I *can* strive for balance with them over time;

I *can* make memories with them that will last a lifetime; and

I *can* help them dream while I keep mine.

Here is how I do it.

Life Lessons and Best Ideas...So Far

> "Mom, do you know who Josephine Cochrane is?
> She saved your life by inventing the dishwasher!"
> —Elle (age 9)

The life lessons in this book are my *most significant lessons* so far—lessons that have absolutely shaped me and helped me understand my *TILT*ed life. They have shown up in the most unlikely of places and from the very children who have made my life so chaotic.

In my last twenty years of parenting with my husband, a few strong life ideas have revealed themselves. These truths bring clarity and meaning to my everyday life.

In the following chapters, I highlight the tips and tricks that have helped me the most. My ideas come from my experiences, as well as from my children's unexpected and unsolicited wisdom. This is a work in progress; I am a work in progress. So in my next, more enlightened decade, I might offer you other, even brighter, insights. But for now, with our first child in college, the second one to follow in one short year, one in middle school, and one in elementary, these are the current truths I live by. I am sharing them with you in the hope that you can *TILT* with them, too.

In these next ten years, all of our children will leave the house, go to college, and begin their lives out from under our roof. I want to look back on my twenty-nine years of kids in our home with satisfaction and pride that those years were thoughtfully lived and appreciated.

Our lives are sometimes *TILT*ed beyond any extremes I could have imagined before children. Yet they are also richer with love and laughter than I ever thought possible. I have learned how to shape and build happy, successful children as I reach for my own dreams in my *TILT*ed life. Balance is impossible; memories are better.

PART II
Balance Is Impossible

1

Help Them Dream...Without Giving Up on Our Dreams

"Mom, I want to grow up to tackle those boys playing football who are trying to make touchdowns."
—Parker (age 4)
(At age eighteen, Parker signed to play on the defensive line at the University of Dayton.)

Mom Quiz #1: Who Has Time for Dreams?

Check if anything below applies to you!

- ☐ I dream of sleeping more than five hours a night.

- ☐ I dream of a self-cleaning kitchen.

- ☐ I dream of going to work without kid gunk on my clothes that I have to pretend I never saw.

- ☐ I dream of actually getting to read one of those magazines I subscribe to.

- ☐ I dream of being respected when I choose my family over other pursuits.

- ☐ I dream of pretty flowers in the pot by my front door that do not die when I don't have time to water them for two weeks.

- ☐ I dream of being surrounded by my children at the end of my life, full of love and gratitude for the overwhelming number of blessings they gave me that, in my crazy years, I never imagined were coming.

All I Can Dream about Is Sleep

> "Chloe, why won't you wake up for school with
> all of these alarm clocks in your room?"
> —me
> "I like my Mom Alarm Clock better. It hugs me."
> —Chloe (age 10)

It was the middle of the night, and I was actually sleeping. As a mother of four children, this was no small miracle: no child needing a diaper change, no child tugging on me to help her make a grilled-cheese sandwich or asking me to sew the hole in her stuffed animal. Just a deep, peaceful, desperately needed sleep.

Bang! The bedroom door flew open and slammed against the wall. I leaped up from the depths of my pillow in instant fear. "Who is HURT? Is the house on FIRE?" No, neither of those. Instead, it was a little person flying to my bedside after a nightmare. For the first few nights of this, I was a calm and understanding mom. By the umpteenth time, I was so desperate for sleep that I could not function.

A few years later, after we had decided to have more children, another little one tiptoed through the door in the inky blackness to whisper gently in my ear, "Mommy, I am afraid. I had an awful nightmare!" I replied, "Come here and cuddle with me. I will keep you safe." Another sleepless night, but a completely different mothering experience. Every child is different. Every experience as a mom is different. I would never have guessed that before having my own children.

In our early-mothering, sleep-deprived years, it becomes almost impossible to think beyond the next feeding, beyond their next school week, or beyond the soccer season. Dreaming for ourselves is pushed aside almost out of necessity. We just try to get through our days, weeks, and children's birthdays without forgetting the cake and candles, or missing too many school programs, or dropping too many important professional obligations.

On top of the responsibilities, it feels like we can go from one emotional extreme to another. We experience the highest of happy moments to the lowest of mom exhaustion and self-doubt. Our life journeys as moms are roller-coaster rides, full of extreme turns and drops: extreme embarrassment at our children's inappropriate comments; extreme challenges, such as trying to keep everyone well fed with unexpired food; extreme pride in our children's accomplishments; extreme pain in their saddest moments; an extremely *TILT*ed, unbalanced act of juggling work and motherhood; extreme love so deep there are no words to describe it. But extreme can be exhausting. My first life lesson came when I realized that in my motherhood fog of trying to be everything for everyone, I was losing myself.

I adore my children, yet the day I realized I was no longer "Marci" was a defining moment. I was either introducing myself as "Parker's mom," "Courtney's mom," "Chloe's mom," or "Elle's mom." I knew then I had to be sure that Marci did not get lost in the process.

Dreaming Was What I Did B.C. (Before Children)

Beyond dreaming of sleep again, a significant theme emerged: reminding myself of the importance of continuing to dream for my life, too—not just for the lives of my children and family. In my new world of mothering, my inclination was to sacrifice myself to instead focus on my children. That was wrong.

Our individual lives are not meant to be lost in the extremes of motherhood or life. The definition of living a full life is very personal to each of us. And I believe that finding ourselves along the way and in the midst of it all is a critical part of our finding success and happiness in life. A full life for all of us includes reaching for our own personal life purposes.

Depending on your choices, your personal dreams for yourself might be put aside for a few years when your children are young. However, there are many ways to take the puzzle pieces of your life and fit them together during these years. As a result, we can each emerge from the *TILT* in our lives to continue on our own paths as we help our children along theirs.

In my early misguided belief in the juggle of motherhood, I thought sacrificing myself was the ultimate level of mom achievement. While letting go of sleep and some of the activities we would like to do might be a necessity at times, completely giving up on our dreams is not the real example we should set. We might have to move some of our individual dreams to another point in our lives, but we can take creative steps toward our goals in the meantime. Pursuing our dreams teaches our children that just as they are each here to fulfill their own life missions, we need to fulfill ours as well.

Our dreams for our lives can focus on many different objectives that are unique to each of us. Many of us want or need to work outside the home, some may aspire to charity efforts, and some may hope to further their education. According to the Bureau of Labor Statistics, in 2012 nearly 60 percent of married families had two breadwinners juggling child and household duties.[1]

A significant number of us in the workforce are trying to juggle it all. Interestingly enough, for those of us with professional dreams and goals, research demonstrates that the efforts to juggle both career and family life *are* worthwhile. Compared with mothers who work for financial reasons, and despite their heavier workload, career-oriented moms are more likely to describe their lives as balanced, healthy, and fulfilled. No matter the age of their children, these working moms are more likely to say having a job is a good thing.[2]

Whether or not your dreams include a career outside the home, thinking and dreaming about life goals when you are up to your eyeballs in sticky fingers and empty Capri Suns can feel a bit farfetched.

But it doesn't have to be that way. We can live on purpose as we raise our families. We can find fun and happiness along the *TILTed* journey. We can go after our goals and help our children achieve theirs. We can dream for more than sleeping through the night. In fact, the journey is that much richer with our children as part of it. The celebrations along the way are that much more fulfilling. The love during and at the end of the journey is that much deeper.

Dreaming for Ourselves—A Life-Altering Example of Leadership

> "In each of us are places where we have never gone.
> Only by pressing the limits do you ever find them."
> —Dr. Joyce Brothers

One of my favorite parenting poems, "When You Thought I Wasn't Looking," was written by Mary Rita Schilke Korzan. She shares example after example of how children observe our behavior more than our words. "When you thought I wasn't looking, I saw you hang my first painting on the refrigerator, and I immediately wanted to paint another one." Demonstrating the importance of thoughtfulness, "When you thought I wasn't looking, I saw you make my favorite cake for me, and I learned that the little things can be the special things in life." For caring for others, "When you thought I wasn't looking, I saw you make a meal and take it to a friend who was sick, and I learned that we all have to help take care of each other." For respecting our blessings, "When you thought I wasn't looking, I saw you take care of our house and everyone in it, and I learned we have to take care of what we are given."

For managing life, "When you thought I wasn't looking, I saw how you handled your responsibilities, even when you didn't feel good, and I learned that I would have to be responsible when I grow up." Truly demonstrating how important our actions are, "When you thought I wasn't looking, I learned most of life's lessons that I need to know to be a good and productive person when I grow up." Our actions speak so much louder than our words.

Know that, like our children, we will stumble a lot and often along the path. More than once I have shown up for a business meeting with two unmatched socks. But beyond the obvious desire to keep it together and do well in our professional lives, why else do we need to keep dreaming for ourselves? There are important reasons, one of which is to set a solid example for our children. In fact, by also having a professional life outside of the home—part time, full time, now or later—we are demonstrating to our children that we have a life's purpose as well. We are each here for a reason.

Dreams are not just made to come true; they are also made to inspire us along our journey.

Being a working mom doesn't mean we give up on our dreams. However, because of our desire to be the perfect mom, wife, daughter, and business-woman, we seldom take the time to work on our dreams and goals in life. Here are some tips to help you ignite your dreams.

Give yourself permission to dream.

Stop thinking you aren't good enough. Dreaming is like splurging, and we can feel guilty for thinking of ourselves. As moms and businesswomen, we function to serve others. It's very common to not humor ourselves with our own dream making. To really dream big, you have to step out of your day-to-day reality and let yourself indulge.

Be playful and inclusive!

Share your dreams with your kids. Let them see your passion. As a mom, don't you want your kids to see their dreams come true? Of course you do! It's a mom's most precious desire. So we must teach our family how to dream by living it. Encourage your kids to dream. Ask them what their dreams are. The younger your child, the more fun and limitless their dreams are. They will inspire you to dream bigger.

Know that planning is the enemy of dream making.

The older we get the less we seem to dream because we put up roadblocks as to why we won't be able to pull it off. Don't let the planner in you spoil your dream making. Eliminate guilty or negative thinking. Don't try to figure out how to pull off your dream—that will suffocate your excitement to dream big.

Avoid the "I wish I would haves."

These five words have haunted and inspired me to keep moving forward. I don't want to look back on my career and motherhood and say, "I wish I would have…" Think about being eighty years old. What stories do you want to tell your great grandchildren? You are creating those stories today.

Connect your personal dreams with your business dreams.

Let the two work for one another instead of competing against each other. If your dream requires a financial investment, then figure out what your career needs to do to support that. Your business dreams and your personal dreams can and should work together.

Think positive and take small steps.

Over twenty years ago my husband and I started dreaming about having a lodge in the New Mexico mountains. Sometimes the steps toward it were very small and time and money seemed to be our enemy, but no matter how small the movement we still pressed forward. We cut out tons of pictures, we searched for land online, we vacationed in New Mexico, then we finally bought some land right on the Red River (one criteria of our dream). I bought a "welcome to the lodge" picture that has been in my closet for two years. I can see it every day and smile as I think it will someday hang in our lodge. Our kids are excited and involved, and our "too big to ever happen dream" is slowly becoming a reality. Dreams are not just made to come true; they are also made to inspire us along our journey.

Linda Sasser
Mother of three
Founder and CEO, Impacting Leaders
www.impactingleaders.com
Facebook: Facebook.com/ILHappyHour
Twitter: Twitter.com/impactingleadrs
Blog: www.LeadershipWithSass.com

Dreaming for our own lives and striving to fulfill those dreams is an excellent example for our children to witness. Fundamental to any leadership position, including the critical role of parent, is to lead by example. We won't have to lecture our children half as much if we just lead the way by what we choose to do. They will hear more from our actions than from our words anyway.

Our kids observe us carefully. They watch us when we are in line at the grocery store with an overflowing cart and let the person with four items go ahead of us. They watch us when we have relatives or friends coming over to visit and how our words and actions line up. They watch how we treat our spouse. They listen to what we say about our friends and our business associates. They see when we are happy, but mostly they know when we are frustrated or upset. They are keenly aware of how we treat them.

If we want our children to be healthy, how will they listen to us if we do not build healthy habits into our lives? If we want them to have good relationships, be independent, and be happy, how will they believe us if we are not working on our own relationships? Whatever it is we want them to hold in high regard, how can we expect that out of them if we do not expect it first of ourselves?

We are each trying to be the best that we can be as we go along our journey, ever the juggler. Setting our own goals to succeed in our own dreams will not only focus our paths, but also teach our kids to do the same.

Five Steps to Reconnect with Your Dreams

> "The indispensable first step to getting the things you
> want out of life is this: decide what you want."
> —Ben Stein

So how do we get back to the basics and set our own goals? If you have lost sight of your own dreams along your mom journey, start with these five ways to reconnect.

1. Believe in yourself.

You believed in yourself when you were young. Maybe you thought you would grow up to be a teacher, an astronaut, or even your own version of Madonna. As high school happens and life happens, your belief in yourself can deflate. You have to remind yourself of this: there is no one else like you with your own special gifts to share. Repeat to yourself daily, "I am unique and special. There is no one like me. I have my own talents to make a difference." You can begin small, with quiet affirmations of who you are and who you can be, but do begin.

> "No matter what age you are, or what your circumstances
> might be, you are special and you have something to offer.
> Your life, because of who you are, has meaning."
> —Barbara de Angelis

2. Make alone time a weekly event.

Find some time alone—that may be late at night in the laundry room—to think just about YOU. I have to find that time creatively, so my alone time is in my mama-van or the sidelines during my child's practice or even when I am sitting on the plane on a business trip. I have my goals (which include my personal goals) in my iPhone task manager, so one thing I do is read them in those quiet moments to help me keep a positive focus. I also have some great, thought-provoking life books in my Kindle, so I can open them up on a moment's notice to be sure I have a good focus. Making some quiet alone time for yourself gives you that short breather to think, to refocus, to recharge, and to reconnect with a very important person—yourself.

3. Reintroduce yourself to you.

When we get so deeply involved in the lives of our children, it is easy to forget who we are. I went from being Marci, to being Parker's mom, Courtney's mom, Chloe's mom, and Elle's mom.

Reintroduce yourself to you: What do you love to do? What touches your heart? Look inside to rediscover the real you. What values drive your actions? Honesty, achievement, compassion, growth, spirituality, health, or fun could be values that inspire you in your life. There are many from which to choose.

This can be a difficult process that takes some real thought. Sometimes, to begin to reengage with who we are on a deeper level, it helps to think about this first:

- Imagine if you could have a conversation with yourself at the end of your life.

- What would your older self tell you today that really mattered over your lifetime?

- What would your older self tell you today to be sure you focused on and did?

- What would your older self tell you today about how to develop yourself to be the best version of you?

When you have identified some of the values that matter most, you are ready to begin your own goal-setting process. Choose the top three that matter the most. Write them in a journal. Then begin to intentionally focus on ensuring that those values are in your life.

4. Break your life down into buckets.

We have many buckets in—or facets of—our lives. Focusing on only one category can leave other important areas of our lives underserved. We are trying to live life as a whole, not in fragments. How do we break down our lives into smaller, more manageable pieces to focus on? What categories should we use to build a whole life picture? While there are many possibilities, I have found the following six to be the simplest, most comprehensive, and most critical: Relationships, Spiritual/Emotional, Health, Personal, Financial and Professional goals.

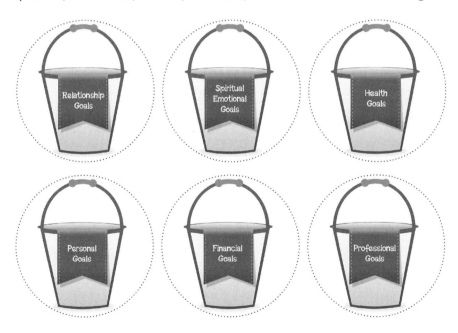

Instead of having goals that are all over the map or too disor-ganized to make sense, set only one goal (or two goals at most) in each area. Then focus on only those. For example, in health, you could set a goal to do one more thing than you are doing now—maybe exercise one more day each week or cut out drinking soda or choose to eat fast food one less day each week. Start small and build a solid base in each of these critical categories of living a whole life. More does not mean better—often brilliance is found in simplicity.

5. As we tell our kids, start small.

We can build over time. Small goals become small successes. If you are concerned with BIG, then start small to experience success. Success brings a sense of accomplishment that propels us to go for it again. A goal accomplished is a goal accomplished. Each one moves us forward.

Our lives are busy and full already. Our plates are full with music les-sons, business projects, diapers, critical decisions that will impact our peers at work, and plans to hopefully serve something besides chicken nuggets for dinner. Our heads are already swimming. But goals can give us the clarity and focus to keep our heads above water.

Is the process pretty? Usually not. Can it be hard to keep our focus? Yes. Is it worth it to try to live our best life and strive for our own dreams as well as our children's? Absolutely. We are each here to discover our own talents, to fulfill our own purpose, and to leave the world a little better because of our life.

Stop The Comparison Game—Be A First-Rate Version Of Yourself

A truth I wished I embraced a long time ago: stop the comparison game. I still need to be reminded from time to time. We aren't comparing apples to apples when we do that, and either way we lose. If we compare ourselves to the mom who was a former swimsuit model, we are going to end up feeling bad. If we compare ourselves to the workaholic mom who is never at any of her son's games, we are going to feel self-righteous.

I think Judy Garland said it best when she asserted, "Focus on being a first-rate version of yourself, not a second-rate version of someone else." This goes for all aspects of your life: stop worrying about the child's mom who makes her own party favors, or the mom who makes every family meal from scratch.

Guess what? There are things about YOU that are amazing gifts, and that can become extraordinary with intentionality and effort. Spend your energy there, instead of wasting it on comparing. Discover your God-given strengths and cultivate them. As you do, you set an amazing example for your children.

Rachael Bodie
Mother of two
Regional Director Leadership Development,
The John Maxwell Company

Helping Our Kids Dream—and Not Just through the Night

"I will not be a teacho when I gwow up; they have too many kids.
I will be a doctor; they only take care of one kid."
—Elle (age 4)

My first personal goal for my children was to get them to sleep through the night so I was not a lunatic from sleep deprivation. Once they became mobile, my goal was to keep them from sticking their fingers in things that would electrocute them. Then it was to get them potty-trained—which is every mom's third round of hazing. I was not so good at potty-training—maybe because it was more my goal than theirs.

As we work to have clarity about our lives, dreams, and goals, we set a great example for our children—not that we will perfectly achieve all our goals, but that we are reaching for them. The problem is this: as we struggle sometimes to determine our own dreams, how will we help our children discover theirs?

In my early mothering experiences, I felt certain that since I grew up dreaming of being a cheerleader, my daughter would also want to be one. I liked student council when I was in school; wouldn't she as well? My first instinct was to help our children dream...my dreams. I quickly found out that was not who they were. Our children are here for their own individual purposes. For each of us, our life mission includes discovering that purpose. Our mom responsibility is to guide our children toward their own self-discovery. This is a journey—not something discovered overnight.

So how do we know what our children's goals actually are? What's important to them? And how do we help foster their dreams by achieving these smaller goals? I always like to actually get down to their height—literally. Everything looks so different from down there. We forget that at their height, regular things can become threatening obstacles. For instance, the silverware drawer pulled out is in the perfect position for them to slam their face into it. So get down on the same level and try to think what is important.

Then simply ask them. When they are young, they will not have the words for it: "I'm just a kid, Mom..." "What *are* you talking about?" So maybe just listen to the problems they had that day and start there to define a small goal.

For the really little ones, their goal could be making a new friend to play with at recess. It is tough for young children to be out at recess with no one to play with; those times can result in some of the first feelings of rejection and worry. If that is an issue for them, or important to them, then focus on it as a goal. Maybe the goal is to make one new friend at recess in the next week. Then maybe invite the new friend over for a playdate. Set a reasonable, achievable goal so they have a little success early.

Once the small goal is set, give them ideas on how to accomplish it. Maybe they could find another child who is playing alone or looking for someone to play with. Maybe they could just run around with everyone and join in. Maybe they could start a fun game on the playground and invite a couple of the other kids to play with them.

Everyone's journey is different, so helping our children dream and set their goals will be a process unique to each child. Their goals will depend on what outcomes they want and by what age. For example, one of my daughters would like to be a college gymnast. For her to accomplish that, we know she has to progress through the team levels at a certain pace to be high enough when it is time to apply for college. Her goals will be uniquely hers in our family. So while we hold our children accountable to rules and desired results in their schooling, in the extracurricular part of their lives, their evolution will vary. In their younger years, just keeping them involved in an activity without quitting might be the objective.

As our children grow, with our support, they will spread their wings and experiment with different activities to find their interests. I am talking about healthy, legal kinds of experiments. Guiding them can be difficult, especially if they are interested in something we know little about. While it is sometimes worrisome as we try to help them in areas we are unsure of, it can also become quite a parenting adventure. As a mom, I have gained unexpected knowledge—such as how to earn a green belt in tae kwon do, what reeds are needed for a clarinet, what matters when judging a gymnast on the balance beam, who the forward is on a soccer team, what a takedown is in wrestling, and how to find the baseball in the woods when your child hits a grand-slam home run.

Depending on your family size, having another sibling help your younger child with solving a problem can work very well. In our family, we include our "big kids" in our younger ones' problem-solving sessions. They are built-in role models and only a few years away from the struggles the little ones are facing. Take advantage of those built-in coaching opportunities as you drive everyone around in your mama-van taxis, hang out together on the sidelines during a soccer game, or gather around the dinner table.

As we help our children through their development and dreams, we have many things to consider. One important issue: we don't want to hold them accountable to any "acceptable standard" of our own beliefs about what interests they should have or what they should become. When our children open up to talk about what they might want to do in life, they need us to openly listen and be their encouragement. They need a safe dream zone at home. Just like we do.

And don't forget to use your own business hat. Helping our children set goals is one of our most powerful parenting and teaching opportunities. Lucky for us, many of our professional goal-setting tactics apply.

Six Steps for a Safe Dream Zone at Home

1. Suggest easy, less-committed ways for your kids to try different things.

When there is a "season" of a couple months, ask if they want to try something out. One of my children is interested in being an artist. We have spent hours coloring at our coloring table. We took a beginning drawing class together one Saturday morning. The drawings we did together that day are hanging on the corkboard in her room. She sees them all the time as a little reminder of something she is striving for. She might illustrate books, become a graphic designer, or even get a degree in architecture. There is no way to know how it will play out yet, but in her little world, it shows her that we believe in her for her own possibilities.

2. Make mutual respect between family members a ground rule and do not discount early dreams.

Children will each have their own interests and dreams. We often serve as crossing guards to help one of them respectfully understand another one's personality without having a major head-on collision. By teaching them how to listen first, give everyone a fair chance to express their thoughts and ideas, they are learning the life skills of respecting their family and friends.

If you remember my son's quote at the beginning of this chapter, he told me when he was four years old that he wanted to "grow up and tackle those boys playing football who were trying to make touchdowns." After years of hard work and focus on that goal, he earned the opportunity to play football in college doing exactly what he told me at age four. Another one of our daughters told me, at age nine, that she was going to win first place in a gymnastics competition (which she had never done before). Well, she did it the next day.

We should not discount the possibility that our child's goal or dream could become a reality—regardless of how big it may seem. We have heard about famous people who knew their life passion early on: Taylor Swift started writing songs at age five, Gabby Douglas who won gymnastic gold medals in the 2012 Olympics, started gymnastics at age six. It is entirely possible that the young interests your children have could become a big part of their adult life. So let them dream and share in the possibilities.

3. Help your children write down their goals.

Depending on your child's age, the goal may only be verbal. For example, for young elementary children, simply discussing the goal on a regular weekly basis can help them remember it and focus on it. Once you think they are ready, help them write down a goal. It could be to get a certain grade on a class project. It could be to score a certain number of goals in a soccer game. It could be to have a lemonade stand to raise money for a sick friend. There are so many worthy goals a child could have.

4. Visualize the dream and achieve the goal.

Just as it is with adults, when our children have a goal they want to strive toward, they have a much greater chance of accomplishing it if they can see it. In other words, it needs to be written down and looked at regularly. Some people can look at a written goal to help them keep their focus. Others need something more visual, such as a vision board. Vision boards can be fun and engaging for your child. You can cut out photos from magazines related to the goal your child wants to achieve. Or you can print images off the internet that show the goal. If your son wants to make the baseball team, for example, photos of some of his baseball heroes might help him see himself accomplishing it. If your daughter wants to win the science fair, photos of other winning projects could help her. If your daughter wants to attend a certain college, photos of everything about that college could be on her vision board. The possibilities are only limited by your imagination.

5. Know that failure is inevitable and good.

The most important point to remember about goal-setting is that the teaching and learning come in the struggles to accomplish the goal. We know as adults that life is imperfect and riddled with issues and challenges—and rewards. Our children do not understand all that yet, but they will soon enough. We are equipping them for solving their problems later in life. They will set goals, and they will fall short of them. Our job is to be there to pick them up, give them a hug, then remind them how much we believe in them as they go off to try again.

6. Take it one step at a time.

Often the best way to tackle a big issue is deceptively simple: take one step at a time. Frustration can quickly build if a dream is too complicated for their age, if too many people around them tell them why they cannot succeed, or if disappointments along the way are pulling them down. How do we help them turn that tide? Take one positive step forward. It can be as simple as a phone call to a teacher or coach who could help them around their goal. It could be taking them to meet someone who will believe in them and help them. It could be researching online one step to move them in the direction they want to head. Taking action invigorates us all to take the next step. Take one simple step forward to give them the courage to then follow with the next step. Small steps now lead to big steps later.

Our children depend on us for our support and belief in them. If we believe they can accomplish their goals and dreams, they have a much greater chance of making them a reality. Parenting is picking them up and dusting them off when they fall down. It is applauding their positive movement forward. It is guiding them to self-discover what their gifts and possibilities are.

> Stretch Your Dreams:
> Only as high as I reach can I grow,
> Only as far as I seek can I go,
> Only as deep as I look can I see,
> Only as much as I dream can I be.
> (Karen Ravn, "No Limits but the Sky")

The Puzzle Pieces of Our *TILT*ed Lives: Fitting Our Objectives Together

> "Sometimes a dream is so destined to come true that it holds onto you long after you have let go of it."
> —Alicia Gonzalez
> www.247modernmom.com
> True story about the daughter she dreamed of for fifteen years, who finally arrived through an unexpected pregnancy.

In my twenty-five years of business development, I have learned many techniques to set and accomplish goals. Interestingly enough, the important skills we need as professionals and as parents are often the same: focus, integrity, service, discipline, determination, empathy, leadership, sacrifice, and communication. Often the tips for success or happiness are not a surprise—whether *they work* for us comes down to whether *we work* on them.

While we build plans around the different aspects of our lives (professional or financial, for example), it can be easy to not take our mom life or personal objectives seriously. For our family, we know we have to keep the house somewhat organized and hopefully clean, that the kids have to get to and from school with all they need, and that we must do our best to feed them healthy meals and not just what we can grab from the fast-food drive-through. Superficially, those activities do not necessarily inspire us. We might be inclined to first plan our business or financial goals and barely think about the big-picture goals for our personal lives or our lives as moms. Yet, in reality, those are two of our most significant hats. They need thoughtful planning as well.

I have seen my life as a working mom in the pits of overwhelming responsibility, and I have seen the difference it can make when I create a dream and vision for what I hope my life can be. My first life lesson in my *TILT*ed life demonstrates how important it is that we have our own dreams for our lives. We learn that we have to *TILT* to let go of unrealistic objectives and instead focus on what we *can* do. We *can* still have goals and dreams for ourselves personally. We *can* make great memories along the way with our family as they grow, regardless of our circumstances.

But if we do not pay attention, the years will slip by, and we will not have captured those opportunities that are gone. My personal path to achieving my mom goals is littered with broken Polly Pockets, hamsters that died, and my children's one-of-a-kind artwork that

I accidentally threw away. My path has not been perfect; it is just imperfectly mine. Yet even imperfect beginnings and messed-up middles do not have to define us into empty endings. On any given day, we can take the puzzle pieces of our lives and nudge them to positively fit together into a beautiful—if slightly misshapen—piece of art that is uniquely us. Then we build, with thoughtful dreams, from there.

Recap of Chapter 1

- √ Dreaming for yourself is a life-altering example of leadership for your children.

- √ There are simple ways to reconnect with your dreams. Start by breaking your life down into important buckets and focusing on those.

- √ Help your children dream also, by starting with age-appropriate small goals.

- √ Goal setting for ourselves, and for our children, gives us a big purpose to focus on, instead of feeling only lost and frustrated in the daily rush of life. We know that we are building toward something that is important and matters. The chaos just happens along the way.

Personal Profile in Mom Courage:
The Happy Mom

Of all the lessons I've learned over my two decades of being a mom, the most important one is this: if you aren't happy—fulfilled, growing, loving your life—your kids aren't happy. This is very hard for all moms to hear and to fully understand. We've been taught to put ourselves last, and it feels natural. I know it's especially tough for working moms. I lived it. You work hard all day, while pushing aside the societal working-mom guilt that continues to infiltrate our culture, no matter the stats and the facts. The internal soundtrack sounds something like, "If only I was a work-at-home mom, little Johnny would be happier, smarter, more popular, _____."

That's all nonsense. The most important thing for little Johnny is that his mom is happy. So, are you living the life of your dreams or at least taking steps to get there? In my first novel, *Here, Home, Hope*, the protagonist Kelly Johnson created a "Things to Change" list as a way to overcome her midlife malaise and put passion back into her life. Just like Kelly, many women wake up one morning realizing they've put everyone else's needs in front of their own and in the process have lost touch with the passion in their lives. If that sounds like you—if you've lost the spring in your step and find yourself with mist in your eyes—perhaps it's time to craft your own T2C list. Here's how:

1. Decide you'd like to change things up in your life. Realize that by putting yourself first, you're actually making life better for those you care about the most. The number-one thing kids want: a happy mom. It's true.

2. Grab some supplies. Kelly grabs a stack of Post-it notes. That could work for you, too. She puts one item to change on each note and ends up papering much of her house and car. If you're inclined to be more private, grab an empty journal or pad of paper, or simply open up a document on your computer and type "Things to Change."

3. Remember your hobbies. The special interests you had before you became busy taking care of everyone else are still important. What are your secret dreams, what activities make your heart sing? These things, people, and activities are where your passions lie. How many of them have fallen by the wayside? It's time for a change.

4. Remember the real you. Who are you, at the heart of yourself, and what do you want? When is the last time you spent time thinking only about you? This is it—your one life. If you don't care passionately about you, why should anyone else? Every experience—the good and the bad—has made you who you are today. You are unique.

5. Don't go it alone. One of the most important T2C on Kelly's list: don't forget the care and feeding of friends. What that means to her is that she had let her friendships languish while she focused on her family, especially her kids. Reach out and reconnect to the people in your life who are part of your story. Make sure friends are part of your midlife makeover. Women need connection and community. You deserve it.

Hopefully I've convinced you that it's OK to care about yourself and your happiness. It's not just OK; it's imperative. By making sure you are happy and living a full life, you are modeling the best of what the future can hold for your kids. And that will make them happy, today and in the future.

Kaira Rouda
Mother of four
Author: *Here, Home, Hope*; *All the Difference*; and
Real You Incorporated: 8 Essentials for Women Entrepreneurs
www.kairarouda.com
Twitter: @KairaRouda / FB: KairaRoudaBooks

GUILT-FREE TIPS –
Ten Ideas to Help You Make
Your Goals & Dreams a Reality

1. Believe in yourself. If you struggle with this, find someone around you who does believe in you and will support you.

2. Set one to three goals in each of the most important areas of your life: personal, health, relationships, professional, financial, and spiritual. Write them down—and be specific. They should have timeframes attached to them so you can back away from the final date to see what you need to do to be on your way *this month* to achieve that goal.

3. Read your goals every day.

4. Take one small step each day in the direction of your goal. Be comfortable being uncomfortable. Send that e-mail to someone who could help you, call that person who is smarter than you, ask for help. You will not believe how it will affect your life!

5. Write your goals on an index card that you can keep with you to reread often. Or write them in an app on your phone. Mine are starred in my task manager app for quick retrieval—I read them constantly. If you search online for "goal setting," you can also find many current goal-setting tools that may work for you.

6. Make goal setting and problem solving a family affair. Encourage your children to brainstorm with and encourage one another to define the goals they are hoping to achieve.

7. Remember to celebrate the achievement of your goals. Big or small, they are all stepping-stones to your desired result. Half the

fun of achieving the goal is the anticipation of the celebration. Plan early and enjoy the anticipation, and then the celebration.

8. Remind yourself of how many other people who rose to greatness in their own ways also experienced many failures. We are not alone!

9. Read Dan Zadra's book *5: Where Will You Be Five Years from Today?* Think about your future, and make plans in pencil (they can change!). With attention and work, the things you plan on will show up in your life in surprising ways.

10. Remember: "The future belongs to those who believe in the beauty of their dreams." (Eleanor Roosevelt)

2
Leverage or Let Go—Dirty Shorts Can Be Worn Twice Sometimes

"Time to go to bed!"
—me to Elle
"I don't want to; it must be morning time.
Listen, Mom...Cock-A-Doodle-Do!"
—Elle (age 5) at 8 p.m. bedtime

Mom Quiz #2: What Day *IS* It?

Check if anything below applies to you!

☐ You know it is Monday because the kids refuse to wake up in the morning.

☐ You know it is Tuesday because that night three of your children have soccer practice, a three-hour gymnastics practice, and track practice. Chick-fil-A will once again be serving dinner.

☐ You know it is Wednesday because the laundry baskets are overflowing already from Sunday.

☐ You know it is Thursday because the refrigerator is bare; there are no Eggos for instant breakfast, no snacks for school in the pantry, and—heaven forbid—you are out of macaroni and cheese.

☐ You know it is Friday because it is the easiest day of the week to get the kids up in the morning—it is *almost* Saturday!

☐ You know it is Saturday because your kids woke *you* up.

☐ You know it is Sunday because the kids never wake up.

☐ You know it is Mother's Day because that is the one day of the year you are supposed to be able to put your feet up.

Why Is the Grass Always Greener?

> "One of my favorite things to do at
> the beach is to get our bikes.
> It makes me so joyful!"
> —Chloe (age 10)

What is our most valuable asset that goes away regardless of what we do and never returns? No matter who we are, no matter how much money we have in the bank, no matter where we live in the world, no matter how big or small our job title is—we all have the same amount of it. What is it? Time.

My second life lesson is having an active awareness that today is really all we have. We should know this. It is too easy to forget in our off-kilter lives, and yet it is enormously important for stabilizing ourselves. Awareness of our limited time with our children, of how quickly each stage passes, and of ways to make each stage uniquely special can change our parenting experience. Even an awareness of the limited time we personally have on this earth can change our lives. An awareness of our time, and therefore a careful use of it, can change everything.

Children seem to already make the most of the time they are present in. They are happy to enjoy "the moment"—they like the grass they are currently standing on. There is fun in the rain and splashing in puddles until they are eating mud. There is joy in crayons and any furniture or wall to use them on. There is delight in eating spaghetti with their fingers and squealing as it flies off the tray all over the floor.

During so many of "those" times—as I was on the floor attempting to clean up the carnage or trying to figure out how in the world to get rid of the stinky-diaper-pail smell—I found myself wishing for the next moment. "Imagine when the kids sleep through the night...Imagine when I can go into the bathroom all by myself...Imagine when they clean out their own gooey noses...Imagine when they get themselves dressed without putting

29

their clothes on backward...Imagine when they can drive themselves where they need to go, and I am not driving the mama-van anymore...Oh! Imagine when I might be that cool and carefree again."

Well, I have not actually found the grass on the "other side" to be greener. Although I do feel quite liberated now to be able to use a public restroom stall all by myself again, there are other milestones my children reach, and then I miss those times. Crazy.

Maybe, in fact, the grass under my feet is blue and that is exactly what it should be. My life does not follow a perfectly straight line but rather has a quite haphazard, *TILT*ed pattern. While I am focused on the professional and personal objectives I want to accomplish, I seem to zig and zag to get there. Instead of being frustrated and overwhelmed with the zig and the zag, I have had to learn that it's normal. Why did they not teach us more life lessons like that in school growing up?

Better make the most of it: clean up the syrup and pancake guts left in the sink, wipe off my now-sticky notepad, and move on. Enjoy the blue grass under my feet and stop looking for greener pastures. Make the most of today, and the greener pastures will come.

Neck-Deep in Diapers

> "Guilt. The one accessory
> no mother is ever without."
> —Julie Tilsner

The first time we irrevocably change our world by adding a child to it, we experience all kinds of extreme emotions—joy and pain, laughter and sadness, extreme exhaustion and blissful happiness, and guilt.

In 2004, I was neck-deep in hundreds and hundreds of diapers; in washing baby bottles and toddler cups; and in an unending flow of spit-up-covered laundry, socks that never fit, and toys scattered everywhere. How can we find the joy in those days or think about the end of that crazy time? All I could think about was sleep, which never came.

I had a ten-year-old, an eight-year-old, a two-and-a-half-year-old, and a newborn baby. I had no idea how hard it would be just trying to get out of my car and safely into our grocery store without any of my children being run over—let alone trying to get them all in the grocery cart and have any room left for the groceries I needed to buy.

Somewhere along the way, I lost my ability to pay attention to today. I know the kids are great at finding fun in each day. But I lost it. Maybe I lost it when I had to go to the grocery store five times in one week because we kept running out of milk and bananas. Maybe I lost it due to a consistent barrage of questions—all at the same time—from four other humans. Maybe I lost it on the Christmas Eve when I stayed up until the wee hours wrapping, sorting, and setting up for Christmas Day. Maybe I lost it just trying to get through Target without the kids asking for everything in the store—repeatedly—when I originally came in for only two things: socks and underwear. I definitely lost it in 2004 when our fourth child was born.

Be Aware and Survive the Five Years of Crazy

> "Do you know what you call those who use towels and never wash them, eat meals and never do the dishes, sit in rooms they never clean, and are entertained till they drop? If you have just answered, 'A house guest,' you're wrong because I have just described my kids."
> —Erma Bombeck

0 PRECIOUS BABY IS BORN.

Prepare for take-off, even though most prep does not work or fit your baby.

1 PRECIOUS BABY IS ONE.

She is cuddly and into everything she can stick her fingers in when you look away for a second.

5 YOUR SWEET CHILD IS FIVE & ALREADY ABOUT TO START SCHOOL.

How is that possible?! Your First Five Years of Crazy are over, and you miss that sweet baby.

2 PRECIOUS TODDLER IS TWO.

She likes to put anything that will fit into her mouth and run the other way when you look away for a second.

3 PRECIOUS TODDLER IS THREE.

She likes to talk and ask you questions. About everything, over and over and over. Her cuteness is her survival.

4 PRECIOUS TODDLER IS FOUR.

She likes to play and run and play and run. She still loves to ask questions— not just to you but also to perfect strangers.

In enjoying today, it is critical to understand that our life with our children will go through a crazy phase. At least one. Maybe two or three. This will happen. Many women in our generation were raised to focus on our futures—career goals after college. For those of us who chose to add children to that life path, we created some additional hurdles.

So it's important to remember that expectations help us be prepared for what might be coming, rather than being completely blindsided by the future. Respecting that today is short-lived keeps it in perspective. We want to learn how to jump these family hurdles without knocking too many over. We have to remind ourselves that when we are up to our eyeballs in fingerprint-covered walls, overflowing broken-crayon tubs, and a seemingly impossible after-school activity schedule, five years of crazy actually go by in a blink.

It can be hard to remember the significance of our mom role when we are juggling baby wipes, runny noses, or missed meetings because we are taking a sick child to the pediatrician. While my children's quotes usually have something to teach me, sometimes I am too busy with details to pay attention. Dirty dishes, toys all over the floor, and crying kids have a way of distracting me. I try, but I cannot honestly say that I am always plugged in to hear them.

It is during these "tougher" moments of feeling guilty, frustrated, and out of balance when one of the children will notice. They intuitively know I need it, and they will hug me and tell me how much they love me. Or they will make me laugh—the four-year-old with her pudgy cheeks and big smile will giggle her little-stinker giggle while she tells me how they colored *underwear* pictures in preschool because it was "U" show-and-tell week.

Devra Renner, mom of two and coauthor of the book *Mommy Guilt*, says, "When guilt starts to take the enjoyment out of your day-to-day life with kids, that's when you know it's time to address it." We all have those moments when we feel more frustration than enjoyment.

Five Ways to Keep Perspective—and Your Sanity

I have decided perspective can depend a lot on your height. Little children do not have the same concerns we do. To help with that, here are five ways to help gain perspective during those five years of insanity:

1. Remind yourself that their young years are limited—they will be in school before you know it.
2. Focus on today—not what happened yesterday or what might happen tomorrow. We only live in today.
3. Do not waste time worrying. Much of what we worry about might not even happen. Do not try to cross a bridge unless you actually reach it.
4. Take action on what you want or need to do today. Positive action gives great satisfaction.
5. Call an older mom whose children have grown and left the house. Ask her how quickly the years pass.

Much of our early parenting challenges relate to physically caring for our children. In their young years, they cannot get up and ready on their own, get around on their own, or get food to eat, let alone use the bathroom by themselves.

The other, and possibly more difficult, parental challenges are mental. Now here I am on the other side of that physical-crazy already. Already. I made it. Now our children are twenty, eighteen, twelve, and ten. Now our children do not need us to dress them anymore (though sometimes that is a problem), and the dependency and relationship has transformed into mostly how we care for them mentally. "That girl is so mean to me—what do I do?" "How can I communicate with that teacher who doesn't like me?" "Why can't I quit my team?" "How can I get along with my friends?" "Why is my sister so different than me?" "Why isn't my coach putting me in to play right now?" We no longer have all the physical demands from them, but these developmental needs are actually harder and equally important at this stage in their lives.

We cannot wait for the perfect future—when all our to-dos are done and we have more leisure time to enjoy ourselves—to then reach out to our children. They will be gone by then. Not just physically gone, but we can lose a relationship that, if treasured, will give us far more than we ever give to it.

A Deep Appreciation for the Parenting Cycle

Whoever thought I'd look back at those early days, juggling four kids under the age of four, as a parenting picnic? Yes, you read that right—the eating, napping, bathing, diaper changing, nighttime waking, crawling-in-different-directions-at-the-same-time schedule that, in spite of the energy it took, was something I could rely on. I was in charge. End of story.

Flash forward to the raging hormones, the slamming doors, the homework assignments that would challenge Einstein, and the overall drama that signaled our loud entry into the teen years. Did I mention that I had four—all approaching, entering, or in the midteen cycle at the same time?

Suddenly, the diapering and stroller days seemed oddly quaint. Nostalgic even. It was a well-ordered time of piano lessons, after-school sports, and playdates. A period of order before the kids discovered their own voices, long before the driver's license in their wallet meant that our growing separation was no longer just an emotional reality but a physical one. Now they could drive away—in four different directions at the same time.

But we came through. I have the gray hair and the wrinkles to prove it, and you know what? It wasn't that bad. As I continue to be involved—hopefully not too involved—with my twenty-three-year-old son, my twenty-one-year-old daughter, and my eighteen-year-old twin boys at college, I like to think of the building blocks that brought us here—battling the insane math equations, the piano practices, setting limits, and their challenge to my digestive process on those hair-raising practice drives around the block.

I like to think that the good choices they will hopefully make as they head into their own futures will draw on the examples I have set. I like to think I have given them the freedom to dream, to succeed—even to fail and pick themselves up and continue. Those picnic days may be gone, but we're embarking on a whole new and exciting chapter.

And as I stand midway, with my parents ahead and my kids following, I feel a deep appreciation for the parenting cycle. I have raised them, and now, perhaps, they will raise others—hopefully with a small part of me in their past and continuing to help in their future. Just don't ask me to take their kids out for driving practice. I won't do it.

Beth Rosen
Mother of four
Creative, 4 Keys Media
www.4keysmedia.com
Twitter: @Bethrosen
Beth.4keysmedia@gmail.com

Live in Today—Don't Miss the Moments to Love and Connect

> "My theory on housework is, if the item doesn't
> multiply, smell, catch fire, or block the refrigerator door,
> let it be. No one else cares. Why should you?"
> —Erma Bombeck

We are never actually in yesterday, and we are never actually in tomorrow. We are only in today. When we are so future focused, we can miss the sweetness that is only truly found in the moment we are in.

In reflecting on my *TILT*ed life so far, I decided that focusing on *today* needed be one of my basic life rules. Focusing on today is particularly important for me to achieve what I want as a mom. When our son was growing up, he would ask me to come to the sofa to talk and hang out with him. I am sad to say that too many times I did not make it over to him. Busy with this to-do or that load of laundry, I missed too many of those moments to be close to him. We have a great relationship, but I still wish I could have some of those missed opportunities back.

Most often, children see the opportunities to find the best thing to do in the moment. At any given second, they can say: "Mom, will you come color with me?" "Mom, will you come play Monopoly with me?" "Mom, will you come read to me?" "Mom, can we ride bikes together?" As moms, we often see all the things that need to get done, the e-mails we should respond to, or the work we have to complete. While we might be able to check things off our list, we can also miss too many of those special moments. It is like a seesaw, and we have to remind ourselves to stop long enough on the top of it, at the bottom, or anywhere in between to connect with our children, with our spouse, and with ourselves. Today is all we really have—we need to remember to LIVE in the moment we are in.

Want A Different Perspective On Daily Life? Be Present In It.

Mindfulness means focusing on the present moment without judgment. Being present offers us a different perspective in daily life. It allows us to let go of future worries or past regrets that deplete us of valuable energy and head space. It may seem contradictory to say that being focused in the present moment helps us to set goals and dreams for the future, but it's quite the contrary.

Mindful awareness helps us recognize negative thought patterns and those self-sabotaging ruminations that love to creep in when we're most vulnerable. Mindfulness is a gentle way for us to observe our own thought patterns and skillfully decipher which serve us and which don't. This is vital to setting goals and staying on track. It helps us to clear away the excess clutter and maintain a clear vision of what we want.

Kristin Ervin
Mother of four
Owner and Facilitator, *Got Mindfulness?*
www.gotmindfulness.com
kristinervin@gmail.com

In searching for ways to enjoy the present, we have to find careful ways to manage our time. Time management provides our best and simplest solutions. We could say it is the American way of life to just keep squeezing more and more in. But to a large extent, time management is a choice. Each day we choose how to use the twenty-four hours we have all been given.

Those choices can be hard to make. Some choices are made for us: we have to go to work to make a living, we have to go to the grocery store to have milk in the refrigerator that is not expired, or we have to do some laundry or the kids will only have dirty underwear to wear the next day.

Superficially, those examples could look fixed—in other words, that we have no choice in whether they need to be done. If we dig deeper into each of them, however, we can find opportunities for choices in each of those adult responsibilities. Some moms choose to change or alter the cost of their lifestyle in order to not work outside the home. Some moms will plan their grocery shopping in advance, purchase carefully, and only have to go to the store once a week. Other moms will buy more underwear to get through a longer period of time without having to do the wash. Choices. Choices we all can make on different levels.

How do we guide our choices? Let's first look at some time grabbers that may tempt us to *TILT* in the wrong direction.

Time Management Tips for the Overcommitted

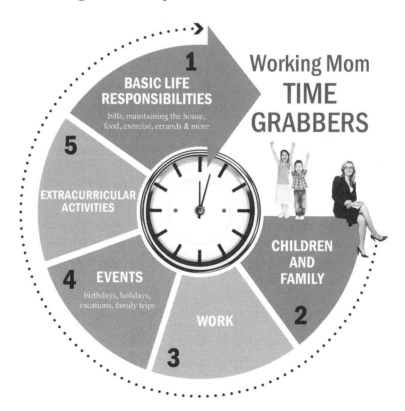

Top Time Grabbers:

1. Basic life responsibilities (bills, maintaining the house, feeding the family, errands, and more)
2. Children and family
3. Work
4. Extracurricular activities
5. Events (birthdays, holidays, vacations, family trips)

There are many, many possible responsibilities that can eat up our time. What can we do about it?

Top Time Solutions:

1. Know your values and priorities.
2. Make choices that serve those priorities.
3. Use leverage to absorb as many of the responsibilities as possible.

Instead of committing ourselves to the asylum right now, let's add to or improve some of our time-management skills. Balance is impossible; memories are better. Here are some ideas that can help us realize just that—to stop striving for the impossible and make positive choices to enjoy today.

Time Management Mom Idea No. 1: Shop Online

One of my simplest solutions to living in today is to not run errands. How is that possible if you have a bunch of children? I am always looking for simple, streamlined solutions to get more vitamins, printer ink, socks, guinea-pig cage bedding, makeup, shoes, children's clothing, and even some of my clothing without having to drive all over town.

I take care of over 80 percent of my shopping online. And I'm not alone. A recent study of five hundred online shoppers found that:

- About 73 percent do at least half of their shopping online.
- Also, 66 percent prefer to shop online versus in-store.[3]

For me, online shopping includes the additional bonus of reducing impulse purchasing. When I am online, I do not buy on a whim. When I go into a store, those clever merchandising people know just how to display their wares in such a way that I "discover" another ten things I did not know I needed, and I purchase them in moments of weakness. When I shop online, I go straight to what I want and buy just that. I rarely get distracted and purchase things I do not need.

Time Management Mom Idea No. 2: Manage Technology Time Grabbers Now

Cell Phones

Cell phones are wreaking havoc on social skills and relationships everywhere. While I love aspects of what they do for me, they are interfering with critical human interactions on an hourly basis. I control my cell phone, my texts, my e-mails, and my voice mails, or else they would control me. Here are some tips to keep constant contact in check:

1. **You do not have to answer the phone just because it rings.** When my cell phone rings during my work time, I rarely answer it—unless it is my child or the school calling. Similarly, I almost never answer my house phone. Nine times out of ten, it is a solicitor who has found a way around my do-not-call list, or it is someone who can leave a message that I can return later.

2. **No cell phones at the dinner table.** No one in our family is allowed to have a cell phone at the dinner table—at home or out in a restaurant. There is (almost) no call that needs to interrupt our family dinnertime that we all work so hard to have. That is family togethertime, discussing our day and mostly laughing about silly things—all the while bonding and building our relationships.

3. **Kids, taxi time, and phone calls—not a good combination.** I do not take calls on my cell phone when my children are in the car. If I really have to take the call because I cannot return it later, I always respectfully excuse

myself to my children. Even when they were as young as four years old, I would say, "Excuse me, but I have to take this call." Then when I get off the call—which is as soon as possible—I explain to my children why I had to take that call and what it meant to them in their life.

E-mail Flooding and Dam Building

With almost 145 billion emails being sent around the world each day (according to an e-mail stats infographic by Mashable.com on November 27, 2012), we would get nothing else done in our lives if we read and responded to every email we received when we received it. Emails have grown to such a proportion that it feels like they are taking over our world, one computer at a time. And in a way they are, as we spend over 11 hours a week reading and answering them. We *can* get them under control and protect our time. It just takes a little organization on the front end and discipline on the back end. Here's what I do:

1. I look at and respond to my e-mails and voice mails only a couple of times a day. Most workdays, I check them at the start of my day, for about fifteen minutes. Then I check them again at the end of my workday and respond as needed, in the time I allowed for it. This obviously means I cannot get to them all. So I have to choose what needs my attention the most. The rest have to wait.

2. I have several e-mail accounts with different purposes, and I look at them each only at certain times. For example, I have four different professional e-mail addresses that separate those e-mail streams. I manage and respond to them based on how those businesses run and what needs a response.

3. For each account, I create separate folders to organize the stream coming in and to work through e-mails as I can. I move e-mails into their relevant folders as quickly as possible to keep the inbox clean. And I have one urgent folder, labeled "Clear." I put e-mails that need a response within a week into that folder. I check that one regularly to sift through and clear it out.

4. I link only certain e-mail addresses to my devices. For example, my shopping e-mail account is only on my computer. I do not have it on my mobile devices. It is not that important and does not need to be monitored like my other e-mail accounts.

Regardless of your personal methods, all the streams of information that come at us now are overwhelming and definitely a time-suck. However, we can manage the flood by putting up our own dams.

Time Management Mom Idea No. 3: Learn When and How to Say No

> "Learn to say 'no' to the good, so you
> can say 'yes' to the great."
> —John Mason

Saying no. Saying yes. Either one is our choice. For some of us, saying no is hard to do. Some of us have such a heart to please others that we do not want to let anyone down, but the hard truth is that whatever answer we choose, *it is our choice*. Here are some suggestions for learning when and how to say no:

1. Volunteer for, versus chair, the committee.

We do not have to be the president of the parent-teacher organization at our child's school right now. We can instead volunteer to help a few times for big events when they really need it. We do not have to run the entire fall festival for our child's school's big fundraiser. We could instead help out by finding some donations or by helping the day of the event. We do not have to be the head coach for the soccer team. We could support her by bringing event snacks and waters.

2. Remember there is no right or wrong, but there are choices.

Some moms love to be a coach, and their children are delighted to have them manage their team. Some moms are fulfilled by running the fall fundraiser and successfully supporting the school. Some moms want to positively impact the direction of the leadership for their children's school, so they *should* run for president of the PTO. The objective is to not sacrifice ourselves or our children in the meantime.

3. Say yes to the things that matter most.

Many of our children want us to come on every field trip, to every school program, and when they are in the lower grades, to lunch every day at school. If we lived at their school, that might be possible. But when we are also working outside the home, it's not. Instead, we might be able to commit to one lunch a month, to the big field trip each year, and to their end-of-year program or party. We might not be able to go to everything, but we can find a way to do the few things that matter the most to our children.

4. Saying no to some things is still saying yes to others.

Whether you are saying no to a higher-level committee position, or no to how many school events you can attend, or no to taking on that extra project at work—these are all situations that can still have yeses in them. Our children are often more mature than we think. Sitting down and discussing the whole picture of a period of time often helps them understand a situation better. For example, when you look at a whole school year with them, you might not be able to come in and read to their class every week, but maybe you can have lunch with them at school twice in the fall and twice in the spring. That is four yeses! If you cannot be the coach of the soccer team, you can always help with treats or as an assistant. If you cannot take on the whole extra project at the office, look for a way that you can help the team. Saying no to some things might still mean some yeses that help your child or your business team.

If you give everyone around you a full-blown yes to every request, then you will end up over your head and not helping anyone. Learn how to say no.

Time Management Mom Idea No. 4: Build Leverage into Your Life

Leverage in our lives helps us create lives of value. We use technology, knowledge, and tools to build more leverage into our daily lives. A Crock-pot is such a tool: it cooks all day and has our family's dinner ready when we get home. Time-management tips are leverage. Following are some additional ways we can build leverage:

1. Buy time.

Hiring other people to help us is amazing leverage. We can buy time by hiring them to take some of the responsibilities off of us. Whether it is hiring a landscaper to mow the yard, a housekeeper to clean the house, a plumber to fix the leaking faucets, or a college student to run simple errands for us, we are buying back time for ourselves.

2. Barter or share.

When our budgets do not allow for us to hire help, we can be creative through bartering or sharing to accomplish some of our responsibilities. Maybe the housekeepers come twice a month to handle the big cleaning. Maybe your children can carpool with another working-mom friend so that one morning a week you get your grocery shopping done and another morning she does. There are options; some of them just take some creativity.

3. Grow your own help: your kids!

As our children grow, they also become part of our solution. They can help with responsibilities around the house. When my high school kids began to do their own laundry, it changed my world. I went from thirty-five-plus loads of laundry per week down to fewer than twenty. Any extra help can make an enormous difference, allowing us to be able to give our spouse, our children, and even ourselves more of our attention when we are home.

Time Management Mom Idea No. 5: Use Time-Blocking in Each Day

> "Begin doing what you want to do now. We are not living in eternity. We have only this moment, sparkling like a star in our hand—and melting like a snowflake."
> —Marie Beynon Ray

Time-blocking is one of my most effective time-saving answers for my busy life. I time-block pretty aggressively. I know how limited my time is, so I protect it. If I do not protect it, everyone else will gladly take it away from me—maybe not on purpose, but I still quickly lose the few productive hours I have. Here are some ways to make sure your time is your time:

1. Do the work that moves you forward.

I know each month what my most important professional objectives are. So when I am working, I focus on those. There are plenty of insignificant activities around my work that I could fill my time with, but they would not move me toward accomplishing my goals. So I don't let them distract me. If you are not sure how to figure out what those activities are for you, or if you have too much to do and don't know what direction to take, ask! Be clear about which work matters—then focus on that. Gary Keller and Jay Papasan's *New York Times* bestseller, *The One Thing*, simplifies this the most eloquently: "What is the One Thing I can do, such that by doing it, everything else will be easier or unnecessary?" (the1thing.com). This actually applies to *all* of our buckets (which I discussed earlier) for which we set goals. This clarity of focus and effort will change your life.

2. Play with your kids.

Your work on your business could easily go twenty-four hours a day, seven days a week. I am an entrepreneur, so containing work to regular hours can be that much more challenging. But too much work will overtake your family life. I block time for my family so that when I am with my children, they have my attention. Even if that time with them is when I am playing taxi-driver all over town, we connect and talk about what is going on in their lives as I rack up the miles on the mama-van.

3. Don't run errands every day.

There is only so much we can buy online. For the rest of what we need, I shop all at once, not over several afternoons. I plan about one day a week to run the errands I cannot manage online. Keep ongoing lists in your phone or on notepads so your family members can let you know when they opened the last box of trash bags or coffee filters. Write it down so you remember when you do go to the store.

4. Exercise to clear your mind.

My attitude, my energy, and my health all require exercise. So I make time for this. I explained to my children that for me to live a long, healthy life, I have to fit exercise in. Since I am teaching them self-sufficiency as well, I can help them get started on their homework, then exercise while they do it. Then, while I am making dinner (on the nights we are home), I can review with them to be sure they are set for the next day. I am a better mom with exercise.

5. Take some red-wine time.

I am a better wife when my husband and I make time for our relationship as well. We like to relax, catch up, and talk about the day over a glass of wine. It has been our Friday-night tradition for years, in between football, soccer, track, gymnastics practices, and more. Sometimes we just have to sit down together a little later on Friday night—but we almost always do.

6. Stop wearing a watch.

Need some unrestricting relief? For a mental break from serious scheduling, I stopped wearing a watch. Unfortunately, that did not stop time—but at least I am not feverishly checking the time on my wrist anymore. I use my iPhone clock to manage the time. I use its alerts feature for upcoming appointments (personal and professional), and I use its reminder app to remind me of anything else I need to pay attention to.

Time Management Mom Idea No. 6: Plan Over Time

Plan the biggest priorities into your year (biggest goals first)

Then plan your month (to help accomplish the big goals)

Finally plan your week (to move towards the big goals)

Plan your year.

Plan your month.

Plan your week.

I wish that in our early parenting years, I had understood the true flexibility in our schedule for vacations. I did not look ahead to realize that as our son progressed through football and wrestling, or as our daughter progressed with her gymnastics team, those activities would dictate when our family could go out of town. The pace of life moves quickly, and I was not paying attention to this. All of a sudden one spring, when we wanted to plan a summer trip, the football schedule only gave us two open weeks to take the trip. When we wanted to plan our family Christmas break, our son only had a couple of days off from wrestling over the entire holiday; we could not go anywhere. Planning further ahead would have helped me see that these times were coming.

I have found that spending time planning ahead keeps me focused as the year moves along. Focus makes it possible for me to live with intention to accomplish my goals, as well as enjoy my family time along the way. Planned or not, time does not stop for us. So I have chosen to plan with purpose—for the year, the month, and the week ahead.

1. Plan your year.

It's important to start with a bigger picture of what you hope to accomplish professionally and personally. This is a yearlong picture of your life—your annual objectives. These include having a major goal in each of my buckets that I wrote about in Chapter 1 (Relationships, Spiritual, Health, Personal, Financial and Professional). Without this picture, we will just haphazardly fall through the year without really going anywhere. With this annual plan of objectives, we take action to move us in the direction we want to head. I do major annual planning in September and October. I make the time for it and step out of my day-to-day (or weekend) routine to lay it out.

2. Plan your month.

What do you have to do this month to get closer to your annual goals? Break down the bigger objectives for the year to understand what you have to do this month to make the annual goals possible. What is important for you to accomplish with your work and your family in the next thirty days? For each month, I have a highlight list of my three to five most important focuses, and I read that list a few times each week. I update it toward the end of the month for the next month.

3. Plan your week.

Break down the month's objectives into four weeks. Write checkpoint goals on each of the four Sundays of the month, and just focus on those action items. Some little things will have to be left undone; some of the laundry, some of the shopping, some of the projects at work will have to wait. The little stuff has to wait so the big stuff can be accomplished. I look at each week's checkpoint goals on my task manager app daily at the end of the day to be sure I am clear on my objectives for the next day.

We are busy, and it can be a challenge to find time to do anything beyond what we are currently juggling. However, if we do not slow down long enough to put some plans and organization in place, then life will just keep us on its hamster wheel, running round and round and not really getting anywhere. You might think I have established a lot of rules around our life. Maybe too many for yours. I do not want to overwhelm you with this idea. But I take my life and my life with my family seriously. As far as I know, this is my one shot at it. I have a strong desire to live my best life professionally and personally and to build memories and special family relationships that last a lifetime. Being *TILT*ed allows me to make momoirs. It inspires and guides me to have structure in my life so I can live the life I hope to live. Planning is my biggest secret to making the most of each day.

Less Stress by Avoiding Miscommunications

As a busy working mother of three active sons (ages eleven, sixteen, and seventeen), I've learned that communication and schedule clarity are key as soon as kids start to take part in activities. Parents still like to participate in activities, too, so my husband and I have come up with a fun message center to keep track of everyone's appointments and important dates, and we positioned it on an easel in the kitchen (we put it away in our bedroom office when we have company). We went out and purchased a three-foot dry-erase board and have taped in five-inch squares to form a calendar. With dry-erase pens, we add everyone's schedule in identifiable colors. I try to update it weekly or whenever I add something to my iPhone when I'm not home. It keeps track of everyone's locations and keeps carpooling schedules within a quick glance on busy mornings while walking out the door. I'll ask my son, "What time is your basketball practice over tonight?" and he'll reply, "Let me look on the board." So many miscommunications have been avoided thanks to our board. As my children get older and have families of their own, I hope to share this and many other working-mother tips with them so they too can experience less stress and enjoy the family more.

Beth Aldrich
Mother of three
Culinary Nutrition Trainer and Health Coach, Restoring Essence
Nutrition
www.BethAldrich.com
Twitter: @RealMomsLuv2Eat
BethAldrich16@gmail.com

Connecting with Your Kids Today—Making Time for Things That Matter

> "My mommy just loves to kiss my cheeks.
> She just loves me so much!"
> —Elle (age 6) talking to a friend

While I plan a lot around my life professionally, my time management with my family is even more important to me. Connecting with my children is one of my definitions for successfully living in today. I try to think about where they are in their lives, who they are, and what is important to them. I look for ideas on how to connect with them easily and in a meaningful way. I know what makes each of them feel special, and I try to build in pieces of that as often as possible. The funny thing is, I get as much or more out of making them feel good as they do receiving the attention.

From having their favorite pair of shorts clean for school the next day, to making a late-night sandwich for them, to playing a quick card game, to being sure we read and cuddle at bedtime—this list varies as much as our children do. Connecting with them is not always fancy, but usually just a fancy way to do ordinary things.

Little-Kid Connections: Making the Ordinary Extraordinary

Here are some ways I've tried to make my connections with my younger children extraordinary:

1. Ice cream a-la-fabulous

A couple of my children really like ice cream. So we do not just have ice cream in our house; we do it up. We have special ice cream bowls and a couple of flavors at the same time, topped with "extra creamy" Cool Whip, chocolate syrup, and, of course, rainbow sprinkles. They are works of ice cream art!

2. Mom's Café

Sometimes on the weekend when I am helping the little ones get lunch, I will pretend they are coming to "Mom's Café." I drape the kitchen towel over my arm, grab a pencil and paper, and "take their orders." Of course, like any mom of four, I can serve up a mean plate of mac and cheese—just give it a little extra love and hotdogs, put it on a pretty plate, use fancy decorated napkins, and light a little candle. You get the picture.

3. Finding fun in the simplest of things

When my children are happy and excited, I ask them for their top-ten list of favorite things to do. Not only will I have that list when they tell me they are bored, I also have that list when we are ready to play! Just as in any friendship, I look for the little things that *they* like to do— then just play with them. Of course, the Internet is always a great fall-back for ideas when your creative mind is running a bit slow.

Regardless of how you decide to spend time with your kids, the important thing is just to connect—and connect consistently. I typically go for the simple approach and do little things for our children repeat-edly. My connection ideas are pretty basic—short on complication but big on thoughtfulness—which I've found my children appreciate.

Teaching Our Children To Connect With Each Other

I think it is important to teach my children how to really care and connect with each other. I let them know when one of them is having a hard time. For example, I tell the others if one didn't do so well on a test, or missed a catch on the baseball field, or they didn't win the class election, or the boy they liked asked a different girl to the prom. Our kids need to pick each other up and talk to each other.

Our kids learn to communicate, love, and relate to their family first and to empathize with others. They want to know the other one cares and that they can help each other. They want to know not only that their parents have their back, but that their sibling also does. Celebrating the good times comes easily, but we also really need each other in the ups and downs along the way.

Whenever possible, take everyone to the other's baseball, football, and volleyball games; horse shows; debates; plays, etc. Cheer loudly for them or carry their water bottle after the game. It means the most to them that everyone came. The bonus is the boost talk after the game, which is a skill that lasts a lifetime for everyone. It helps the children from becoming wrapped up in their own lives, by paying attention to what is happening in their sibling's life. Connecting and communicating with their siblings helps each child develop skills to think and care for others.

Diedra Lockhart Sorohan
Mother of three
Managing Partner, O'Kelley and Sorohan, Attorneys at Law, LLC
www.OkelleyandSorohan.com
dsorohan@oslawllc.com

Big-Kid Connections

It can be harder to connect with the big kids. We have to go about it in different ways. The teenagers are beyond playing Polly Pocket, Uno, and kicking the soccer ball around in the backyard. We sometimes have to be more creative than we are when making obvious fun for the younger ones. Yet there are still so many things we can do with them to connect on a regular basis. Here are some ways to connect with older children:

1. Share acts of service.

Sometimes our connections with our older children still come through helping them (acts of service). Whether it's taking them to buy the cleats for cross-country, finding that special dress for graduation, or throwing a fun get-together for friends, look for your chances to still give them special attention.

2. Listen.

As Judi Brownwell writes in her book *The Skills of Listening-Centered Communication*, the only way we can develop meaningful relationships within our families and communities and across continents is through effective listening. The secret to connecting with any older child or person in our life is this simple: focus on them.

This is the time it is more important than ever to ask questions and listen. We need to listen without judgment if we want our teens to share openly with us. They may talk about the movie they just saw and loved, a project they are working on in their chemistry class, or maybe a new routine they are learning for their gymnastics competition. They may talk about online games they like to play or friend issues they are trying to work through. Watch their faces light up and their energy jump when you ask about and listen to whatever they talk about or care about.

As Michael P. Nichols writes in *The Lost Art of Listening*, the essence of good listening is empathy, which can be achieved only by suspending our preoccupation with ourselves and entering into the experience of the other person. Part intuition and part effort, it's the stuff of human connection.

3. Focus on their interests.

Support them by supporting their interests. Search on YouTube to help them find an inspirational video for the class project they are putting together. Take them to a Military Academy Day in the area if they might be interested in a military career. If they love music, learn how to use iTunes so you can talk their language. Gift them a song from an artist you know they love. If they love to read, get them to the library often so they can check out more books.

4. Make it a date.

One of my favorite ways to connect with my teenagers is to take them on a "big kid only" date. We'll eat at a local fondue restaurant, followed by a movie they want to see. There are many dates that big kids still like to go on: bowling, video arcades, hikes, even playing laser tag. Build these into your family calendar. Making time together is a big part of staying connected with your older children.

5. Speak their language—welcome technology.

We have what I consider a great opportunity to connect with our older children that the generations before us did not have: technology. While technology can be an intimidating challenge to learn and integrate into our lives, I have always found it worth the effort. Here are a few points of contact to get you started:

a. E-mailing: the keyboard connection

E-mailing can be a good way to communicate and connect with our teens. Even if it's simply sending them a funny video or an inspiring story when they're down, we can bring a smile to their day and let them know we're thinking of them.

b. Texting: letting your thumbs do the talking

Texting is something most teens spend far too much time doing to begin with, so we know it's an immediate and definite way to communicate. It's a chance for us to let our teens know we are thinking about them, whether it's to wish them good luck on a math test or encourage them before the big game.

c. See you online: social media

In 2011, the total number of social-networking accounts world-wide was nearly 2.4 billion. This number is expected to grow to nearly 3.9 billion by the end of 2015.[4] Facebook, Twitter, and other social media venues today are like our "hangouts" were when we were growing up. The difference? It all happens in a public forum. Make sure to help them understand this. You can keep a quiet, low profile to monitor their usage, but if your teen is managing his or her online persona well, let it be his or her hangout. Just be a respectful friend to them there.

In our *TILT*ed life, we are striving to make memories that matter over time. The key to enjoying today or these years with them is to pay attention to each period of time. The years pass so much faster than we realize. Before we know it, they will be off to the next phases of their lives, and we will be missing the simple chances we had to share our love with them. Enjoy making those little memories with them; you will share them for the rest of your lives.

Why Wouldn't I Take Time for That?!

As a working mom of three children, too often before now, I would say, "Not now, honey," "Maybe later, honey," "I'm sorry, honey, Mommy is busy right now," "I just have to finish this first."

It took me several years to realize that those words should not be in my vocabulary. Don't get me wrong: there are moments that require us to delay some time with our children; but the dishes, my phone call, my e-mail, the laundry, the grocery shopping, and the "urgent" client can all wait.

Just last week, I was getting ready for my daily run, and my sweet seven-year-old daughter, Anna, wanted to run with me. My first thought was to sigh and tell her that we couldn't run together right now because I was ready to do my run and she couldn't keep up with me—I'd only have to turn around! I barely have enough time to squeeze in a run as it is! I quickly suppressed that thought and created a new one. There is no reason I can't take an extra ten minutes to have a run with my daughter and then take the time I need for my "real run"! I said, "Sure, Anna. Let's do it!"

I asked her how far she wanted to run. She asked me what I thought was a good distance. I said, "Let's go for a mile." She looked up at me and said, "That's pretty far, Mama!" I told her to give it her best shot. She reached up to hold my hand and said, "Never give up when you are trying something new. Right, Mama?"

Holding my proud mother tears back, I said, "That's absolutely right, Anna." I never would have had this moment with my daughter had I chosen not to take the extra ten minutes. Ten minutes is all she needed to have special time with me, to try something new that stretched her abilities, to set a goal, and to have a conscious thought about setting her mind around trying something new and being encouraged by it.

It was one of my proudest moments as a mother. For my seven-year-old daughter to make a conscious decision to take on a challenge and be willing to try and face the result either way makes me realize she is exactly the type of person I want influencing me in my life. Why wouldn't I take time for that?!

Jennifer Mest
Mother of three
Realtor, J. Mest Group, Keller Williams Realty Atlanta Partners
Real Estate Trainer / Owner, ProBasics
jennifermest.com
Linkedin.com/in/jennifermest
Facebook.com/jennifer.mest
Twitter: @jennifermest

Don't Waste Time Feeling Guilty—Take Action Instead

> "When Grammie is here, maybe you two
> could organize the playroom."
> —me
> "No thanks. We will be too busy playing!"
> —Elle (age 6)

In my early parenting years when my friends would ask me what I was up to, I would usually tell them I was just hanging around with nothing to do: "Oh, I am sitting on the sofa, eating bonbons, and watching Oprah." This has never actually happened. The sofa and I are more like long-lost relatives: we could be friendly if we ever got to hang out together. I am pretty sure my friends know that.

Finding the time and attention to actually focus on the moment we are in and enjoy our time with our children can be a real challenge. And allowing guilt to get in the way only makes matters worse. When I am working, I feel guilty that I should be doing more for my children. Then when I am with the children, I feel guilty that I could be doing more for our business and my work. Yes, I am fully aware of the mental loop—and I have struggled with it for a while. But this is not a business problem; this is a matter of the heart.

Lucky for me, I found a simple solution that put me more in control. When I feel guilty, overwhelmed, or time challenged, there is a small, temporary fix to overcome the feeling: I just *take action* in the moment. Any negative emotions I am feeling are minimized by positive action. Even a baby step helps.

When you feel guilty, choose one small thing to do to move you forward. You might not be moving mountains, but every positive action requires that first step. Interestingly enough, positive action begets more action. Positive little steps start to sway the pendulum back into moving us forward. We take one small step, and it energizes us to take the next one.

Small action steps coupled with a bigger plan for our lives give us the momentum to move forward in the right direction. We want a target to aim for to rebuild our confidence that what we are doing matters. We are powerful. We are not "just moms" or just running-all-around-town taxi drivers. Each of our lives has a purpose. Significance is a serious issue.

The role of the mother in our homes and communities is critical and at the foundation of the health of both. Women are contributors, supporters, buyers, decision makers, confidence builders, and much, much more. The world would not turn without them. So, instead of allowing the weight of our responsibilities to overshadow our self-confidence, we need to learn to stand taller with it. Because we can. Because we are strong. Because we are needed and we matter. Because our children need us to model the people we want them to become.

So, I'll say it again: balance is an unattainable goal. We come to realize this as we stretch and strain to be good moms and to accomplish professional goals. As much as we try, we cannot achieve balance. However, turning our focus to the important stuff in the present helps us pull through the sticky, overwhelming times. We can choose to focus on the sweet moments in each day. We can look down on our lives with a broader view and understand that our periods of crazy are just that—only periods of time. Not forever. We can look for our chances to connect with our children and bring the fun of our life with them to the forefront of our days.

So live in today. Really live it. Really enjoy it.

I look at my twenty-year-old son today (who is quite a bit bigger than me), and it seems like just yesterday I was playing on the driveway with him on his Big Wheels. He actually played through three of them. Now he drives his car to and from all his activities. When he was little, he wanted to hang out and play with me; now I chase him down for a hug before he leaves. I am very aware that he will graduate from college in a few short years.

We each have stories with our children—moments when we felt we did the best and times when we know we could have done better. Let go of all of that; these moments are in the past, which we know we cannot change. Even the future is just a thought and a possibility. In my second life lesson in my *TILTed* life, it is clear to me how vital it is that we focus on today: it is all that we can truly impact.

We have to keep reminding ourselves that each season we have with our kids has its own uniqueness—and it does not last forever. The sweet skin of a baby that is so yummy to hug and kiss, the beauty of a sleeping toddler with the face of an angel, the unconditional love of a child telling us that we are "the best mama in the whole wowld," the sound of children's laughter filling our home, a hug from a teenager— we can get through the hardest moments knowing that these amazing moments will come, too.

Children find happiness in their days. Even with all that we juggle, we can, too.

Recap of Chapter 2

- ✓ Keep a clear perspective. Be aware that the challenging moments of parenting come and go—they are not here forever.

- ✓ Live in today—be present in the present and don't miss the moments to connect.

- ✓ There are many simple solutions to managing your time. Choose one to put in place this month, then add another one next month.

- ✓ Make time to plan—your year, your month, your week. Planning ensures you take the actions you need to take to live your life with your priorities at the forefront, rather than lost in the shuffle.

✓ Connect with your children now. If you wait, it may be too late. Choose something simple and put it on the calendar this month.

✓ Don't waste precious time feeling guilty. Just take one step forward today.

Personal Profile in Mom Courage: Reconnect with Your Kids Every Day

Just yesterday, it seems, they were babies who fit in my lap. Now, two of the five are out in the world having their own adventures. It happened much too quickly, and I want to hold on to each remaining moment I have. So every day, I start the day with cuddles. My mind may already be trying to churn ahead to what I need to get done, but I put it aside to focus on being in the moment with my children.

When they wake up in the morning, rather than jumping right into the routine, we have morning cuddles. It's a good start. At the end of each day, I spend ten to fifteen minutes with each child to tuck them into bed. This is a ritual for us, and something the kids count on as much as I do. I climb in bed with my kids, and we talk about our favorite parts of the day. We share unplugged, totally devoted, totally engaged time with each other—no outside interference of TVs, phones, or other digital devices intruding. We connect, we laugh, we talk. We cuddle. We say, "I love you." It ends every day—no matter how hectic or stressful, no matter how demanding, no matter how guilt ridden from what we didn't do together—on an intimate and loving note, with the kids confident that they are loved, heard, and appreciated.

Our lives get busy, and we often get caught up in the momentary minutiae of the day that seem so important...only to look back and realize that we missed what really mattered. No matter how pressured you are feeling to get it all done, remind yourself that the dusting and laundry can wait. The response to the e-mail can wait. The project you are working on can wait. Your next tweet, Facebook status update, or text message can wait. Turn it off, unplug, and devote time every day to truly engaging with your kids.

Shadra Bruce
MomsGetReal.com
www.facebook.com/MomsGetReal
Twitter: @momsgetreal
Because motherhood is messy business!

GUILT-FREE TIPS –
Nine Ways to Find
Happiness in Today

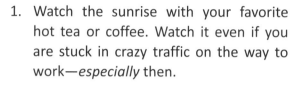

1. Watch the sunrise with your favorite hot tea or coffee. Watch it even if you are stuck in crazy traffic on the way to work—*especially* then.

2. Do something today for someone who cannot thank you or who will not know you did it. You will be amazed at what that does for your mental attitude.

3. Sign up for Amazon.com Prime membership (currently a $79 annual fee). Enjoy two-day free shipping for a year, along with other goodies. "Amazon Mom" is also included in that membership, or you can try it for free for three months. There is nothing like having something you would otherwise need to drive around for two hours to find instead delivered to your doorstep two days later. Ten minutes on the Internet in exchange for an hour and a half freed up for playing with the kiddos (or for reading this book).

4. Exercise. It is known to not only improve your physical health but your mental health as well. You do not have to run a marathon tomorrow for this to have a positive impact on you. Not sure how to get started? For easy convenience, buy workout DVDs like I do, or consider checking out BodyRock.tv for short workouts online that you can do in the privacy of your own home. As Nike says, "Just do it!"

5. When your grocery-shopping cart is overflowing, let the person behind you in the line check out before you do! Then enjoy their smile and gratitude.

6. Wear a bracelet that reminds you, "The joy is actually in the journey, not just in the destination." I have one. Every time I notice it, it reminds me to keep my focus clear.

7. Have a glass of red wine or relaxing hot tea.

8. Don't worry about yesterday or tomorrow—neither of which you will ever be in. Be present in today. It is a gift—that is why it is called the "present." Read *The Present: The Gift that Makes You Happier and More Successful at Work and in Life, Today!* by Spencer Johnson.

9. Keep a gratitude journal. Have one on your nightstand. Write down each night before you go to sleep at least five things that made you smile or that you are thankful for. The one on my nightstand right now is *Gratitude: A Journal*, by Catherine Price. It is beautiful and full of cool thoughts along the way. Makes me want to pick it up, write, and be thankful.

3

Expired in the Pantry and Other Tales of an Imperfect Motherhood

"Mom, the expiration date on this ranch dressing
in the pantry was three years ago."
—Parker (age 16)

Mom Quiz #3: Do You Think You Should...?

Check if anything below applies to you!

☐ I think I should know it all before my first child is born. After all, I read all the books.

☐ I think I should never lose my cool. Well, maybe I will once. Well, it could happen every few days. Well, maybe more than I can count. OK, fine—I will probably lose it at least once a day!

☐ I think I should know it all once the baby has been home for a month. After all, I have been a parent then for thirty days.

☐ I think I should never have to miss an important business meeting because my child inconveniently was sick and throwing up all night long—and then gave the lovely illness to the next sibling, who then gave it to the next sibling, and we all went to the pediatrician's office instead.

☐ I think I should be able to fix all of my child's personality issues. I personally have none.

☐ I think I should always be right there so my child never falls down and eats dirt.

☐ I think I should know everything there is to know about parenting the day my child graduates and goes to college. After all, my child will be completely independent of me at that point—right?

☐ I think I am pretty sure I will never know it all.

A Lot of Imperfect

> "Mama, I was the only child in my class who did not have
> an Easter basket for our Easter egg hunt. You forgot—
> you were supposed to give me one to bring in today...
> I was so sad."
> —Elle (age 3)

I am the definition of the imperfect parent. Last night alone I had laundry sitting in both the washer and dryer—both unattended to. I burned the meatballs and almost left the seeds in the spaghetti squash as I cooked it. We finally ate at about 8:30 p.m., but by then the burnt meatballs were cold. There is more, but there's no need to completely embarrass myself. I am bouncing, fumbling, and bumbling along my parenting path. I *TILT* my seesaw up, then ride it right back down again. Some of it is by accident; some of it is actually by choice.

Motherhood's accidental imperfections are going to happen no matter what we do. Our first child grows up and introduces us to all we are supposed to know—like the fact that now they have *church-school* graduation ceremonies, *preschool* graduation ceremonies, *fifth-grade* graduation ceremonies, *eighth-grade* graduation ceremonies, *high school* graduation ceremonies, and *college* graduation ceremonies. Some of the mistakes we make are because we have not been through this before—like when I was so proud that I made it to my child's school for the class Valentine's Day party, only to find out I showed up on the wrong day.

As the children grow up, so do we.

Then there are the intentional imperfections. These are the ones we choose to let slide. Out of necessity. Out of curiosity. Out of sanity. These are the critical choices we make in relation to what is most important to our family. Store-bought versus home-baked cookies for snack day? A business meeting or my child's class party? Some of my parenting imperfections are choices I have to make.

My third life lesson from my *TILT*ed life came from learning that I could not do everything, that I would make a fair amount of mistakes, that I would have to make some hard choices, and that when I woke up the next day, it would all be OK. Life is imperfect, and so are we. So is the "perfect mom" neighbor. Really! She has milk expired in her refrigerator, too. Her potted flowers die from lack of water—she just hides the pot on the back porch better. I know because she told me.

Realizing that we will not have it all together all of the time is hard for some of us. A lot of imperfect is still liking ourselves when our simple-looking Martha Stewart Christmas tree project took three weeks to hot glue, instead of three hours. It is choosing to not being too embarrassed when the roller-skate birthday cake we tried to make for our daughter's ninth birthday party started sliding off the tray, so we took the pictures really fast before it actually fell. I have the pictures to prove it.

Just When I Thought I Had It Figured Out: A Timeline

> "You know that you cannot dodge your shadow.
> I tried, but it always follows me around!"
> —Elle (age 8)

I thought I was pretty smart when I was a teenager. I told myself, "Of course that (ridiculous) hat looks great with my outfit!" When my sophomore-year boyfriend did not treat me very well, in my immature confidence I told my friend, "I do not care what you think about my boyfriend; he is really a great guy! Plus, he has big muscles and a cool car." At junior-year homecoming, I thought, "Yes, I do love that dark gray eye shadow *all over* my eyelids." When my hair was "flat," I told myself, "I need another perm. The bigger my hair is, the more beautiful it is!" Oh, all that I was convinced I knew when I was a teenager!

Then I thought I was pretty smart coming out of college. "That will be a great job with a big title: sales manager." (I was actually just a glorified stock clerk who had to work all the holidays.) When we were purchasing our second car, I told my husband, "Let's buy the white car. I am sure there are no problems with it, even though it's marked down to nothing." When we were hiring people to work with us, I was sure I could overlook details. "Let's hire that guy to work on our business team. Just ignore it on the first day when he comes to work with his shirt open to his belly button, wearing a long, gold-chain necklace, and then falls asleep on his desk."

As we progress through our lives, we learn that we are not as smart as we once thought we were. Motherhood also seems to highlight this issue. In hindsight, it is easy to see how much we had yet to understand when we were younger and how much we still have to learn in almost all aspects of our lives looking forward.

When this realization that we do not really know it all hits, it can be daunting and even depressing. In my early parenting years, I thought I was the only mom making mistakes, missing details, and not dressing my children in clothes that perfectly fit them. As some years passed, I learned that I was not alone. Once I began to understand that I was actually normal, I realized how much of my parenting happiness would come from the choices that I made. I had to come to grips with my personal disappointments in my mothering that I allowed to cause me such guilt, and then I had to learn how to take positive action through careful choices. Careful choices for myself, for my mothering, and for my children. So I became imperfect on purpose.

Staying Humble, Saying We're Sorry, and Forgiving Ourselves

> "Mom was pretty when she married Dad."
> —Courtney (age 6)
> "But you never saw the wedding pictures!
> Her hair was so big you'd be really creeped out!"
> —Parker's response (age 8)

Parenting is quite a humbling experience. I have learned that I cannot rest too long on a "win"—whether it's that I think my child is potty trained (and then she pees on the rug in a store display), or I think my children will not use a bad word again (and then they do, in public, LOUDLY), or I think they will not tell everyone that their mom likes wine (and then they always announce to their friends that our living room is our "wine room"). My first effort to come to grips with the parenting missteps I was making, along with the franticness and guilt I felt, was to be humble and to choose to forgive myself.

A *Psychology Today* article describes the combination of humility and parenting as follows: "Parenthood can be a very humbling experience. Children have a way of enabling us to see our limits and weaknesses regarding patience, compassion, or courage."[5] The minute we get too comfortable or too confident, something will happen to pull us back to reality. Humility is a wonderful personality trait for a parent. If we think quite a bit of ourselves, just keep high school photos nearby—where the children can see them. They will bring us right back down to earth.

What do I mean by humility for parents? It is not just about how we might feel about our missteps, it is also about paying attention to our parenting skills. We need to think about where our children are in their lives, to be thoughtful about what they might be going through, and to be certain that we are doing our best to address their environment and needs at the different stages of their childhood. As soon as we get too confident in our abilities, we stop watching. Below, I share some thoughts on choosing humility.

Four Lessons in the Power of Humble Parenting

1. Be humble by listening first.

Talk later. Try hard not to talk about yourself too much. Get your children to talk (and, for that matter, your friends). We are not learning when we are talking. An important part of humility and building lifelong relationships comes from being a better listener than talker.

2. Be humble by giving others credit.

This is especially important for our children, and especially in front of others. Recognize their accomplishments. We have to spend a fair amount of time on their issues anyway—grades that are not good, poor friendship decisions, eating too many Oreos, and so on. Look for chances to appreciate what they have done right or done well. When we give our children credit for a job well done, especially in front of their siblings and family, we have given them a double self-confidence boost.

3. Be humble by being the bigger person and being willing to say you're sorry.

We make mistakes—and some weeks we can make quite a few. It is easy to try to push them under a rug so our children don't observe them. That, however, is doing a great disservice to us and to them. What is the definition of insanity? Repeating the same mistake over and over. Unless we think about our mistakes to learn from them, we will keep repeating them. So will our children. When we make a mistake, especially one that affects our children, we need to say we're sorry. And we need to say it right away. Do not wait; the sadness around your mistake only ferments and grows. Say you're sorry now.

4. Be humble by forgiving ourselves.

As parents, we have to know that this gig is a tough one. Understand that we will mess it up and probably mess it up often. We are human. We cannot expect to be perfect. We need to forgive ourselves when we make our inevitable mistakes. Reflect on them. Learn from them. Then move on.

Why Don't Kids Come With A Manual?!

The day I became a mom, I felt like I was literally touched by God. It was the greatest gift I thought I could ever have. I am now a mom of three wonderful children and couldn't imagine my life any different.

I try my best, but still I make mistakes. My goal is to leave my children with a good moral foundation. I teach them love and respect. I hope and pray every day that I am doing a good job so that they will have the ability to make the choices they will have to make in life. I hope they each live a good, successful life, helping others along their way. I am trying, but I often wonder if I am doing enough.

It would not really matter if there was a manual that came with children. Because NO ONE would read it! It would be too long, and after reading it, no one would think they could do it.

We have to be a mother, a father, a friend, a coach, a teacher, a nurse, a doctor, a dentist, a seamstress, a chef, a baker, a mechanic, a storyteller, a judge, a cop, a taxi driver, an artist, an actress, a singer, a banker, a designer, a painter, a gardener, a builder, a rock star, a dreamer, and more.

Every day is a new lesson to be learned about parenting, and every day is a gift. Is it hard? Oh yes it is hard, but is it worth it? Most definitely.

Janice Baldwin
Mother of three
Realtor, Keller Williams Realty Atlanta Partners
www.janicebaldwin.com
Facebook: www.facebook.com/waltoncountyrealtor
Twitter: @janicebaldwinkw
Linked In: http://www.linkedin.com/pub/janice-baldwin/6/68a/765
janicebaldwinkw@gmail.com

I go to bed many nights feeling as if I should have done so much better. I should have tried harder to keep my calm. I should have explained myself better so they could understand. I should have found the time to play that game or read that book, or I should have had a better answer to their grown-up questions. But dwelling on our mistakes too long only tears us down. The reality of life is that we will make many mistakes along the way.

An all-too-true *Parents* magazine article hit home when it said, "We all know who that perfect parent is supposed to be: The person who's always loving and always around when kids need help with homework or need to be tucked into bed at night, who never loses his or her temper, never desperately craves time to be alone, and never misses assemblies...No such parents exist, of course. And if they come close, it's sometimes at great cost to themselves and their families. Mothers and fathers who strive for perfection often, ironically, do their children more harm than good."[6]

It is often too easy in the chaos of our mom lives to be too hard on ourselves. When we do that, we lose our ability to move forward positively. We lose it for ourselves, and we lose it for our children. No one wins. We need to choose to forgive ourselves every day. We are human and will mess up.

You must be a pretty good mom if you are reading this book. Not only do you have *great taste in books,* but you must also care about your life, how you are parenting, and how you are leading your children in their lives. Do not give up on who you are and who you can be. Your children will not. Neither should you.

> "Mom, I love you even though you have gray hair.
> Besides, Parker and Courtney were the ones who made it turn gray."
> —Elle (age 5)

Choosing Carefully—Understanding Our 20 Percent

> As I am saying the last, last good night at the
> bedroom door, one of the little ones will ask:
> "Mama, one more thing..."
> at which point I am too tired and just reply,
> "This is the last question! What do you want now?!"
> Her little answer in her quiet voice comes back:
> "I just wanted to tell you—I wuv you fowever, Mama."
> "Oh sweetie, I love you, too."

Once I understood that I was not alone in my imperfections, and I found strength in humble parenting, then I looked for the biggest answer I could find to solve my parenting challenges. I found it in my decision process and the choices that I made.

We are tired at the end of the day. Our days are full from beginning to end with what to have in the kitchen for breakfast, what to accomplish at work, what activities to get our children to, what errands to squeeze in on the way home, what clothes need to be washed that night, what stories to read, what messes to pick up, what work to do for the next day, and at some point long after the sun sets, what time to finally put our head down on that pillow to sleep. Yet there are choices in what we do with the time we have and the responsibilities we shoulder. Many choices.

In truth, we do not have to do everything—in fact, we lose our effectiveness when we try to. It's called the Pareto principle (the law of the vital few and the trivial many), and it can help us plow through the overwhelming abundance of choices we need to make every day. It states that roughly 20 percent of something is always responsible for 80 percent of the results. "Eighty percent of the results come from twenty percent of the causes. A few things are important; most are not," writes Richard Koch in *The 80/20 Principle.*[7]

We do not have to have our homes guest-ready clean, with no papers on the countertop and no dishes in the sink, all the time. We can do our best, have our children help, and instead sit and chat with our family in that saved time. We do not have to plant a master gardener's garden. We can plant two pots and still enjoy flowers. We do not have to put every decoration we own on our Christmas tree every year to make it beautiful. We could actually rotate half of them, and the tree would still sparkle on the ceiling when we lie on the floor below with our children to admire it.

We also cannot please everyone. When we try to make everyone else happy, we sacrifice ourselves. Part of choosing our 20 percent thoughtfully is knowing that when we try to please everyone, no one wins—certainly not us.

With our professional lives, we make choices. If we pick the most important activities for our work and business, we will make the professional impact we aspire to. What 20 percent of activities will move us most effectively toward our goals? Whatever our goals are, this focus on what matters most gets us there quicker and with a more fine-tuned effort.

"Being a mother and a professional doesn't always mean getting the best of both worlds...Being a working mom means making hard choices," said a working mom nominated by the University of Pennsylvania president for an award recognizing her dual role as a hard-working professional and parent.[8]

Choosing What Work Options Are Best For You

When my kids were 3 and 4 years old, I started to get antsy. Although I loved being a stay at home mom, I could never help but feel awkward every time I went to a party and someone asked me what I did. So when my son Gus started kindergarten, I went into business for myself.

Initially I was looking for a job that would allow me the flexibility to care for my children, be a wife to a busy executive and still run the house. However, my business quickly grew and now just four years later, I have five staff members.

The best part about it? I love it. I love my job, I love being a business owner, and I love all the messiness that comes from our big life.

Did I need to make some choices about what was important to me? Yes. Absolutely. Would I change a thing and go back to being a stay at home mom? No. I tell my mom friends - you need to do whatever you need to do so that you can be the best mom that you can be. And for me, that meant becoming a business professional.

Wendy Papasan
Mother of two
Realtor, Keller Williams Realty Austin, Texas
www.AustinBestHomeSearch.com
Facebook: www.facebook.com/wpapasan

Applying the Pareto principle to parenting, we can have the important impact we want on our children by choosing to focus on only those few, most important aspects of their lives. When we focus on the most important mom activities thoughtfully (the 20 percent for our children), we make the biggest impact on our families.

We can apply the 80/20 rule to our household as well. Could our kitchen counter be cleaned off all the time, the corners of the children's rooms kept clear of school projects no longer needed, and the basement clutter thrown away? Yes, yes, and yes. But children do not notice those details as much as they notice when we do not give them time or attention. So yes, we could go through the markers every month to be sure none are dried out. We could spend time organizing and wiping out our pantry shelves more. We could do a better job cleaning out their sock drawers and giving away the ones that do not fit.

Instead, while they are still interested, maybe we should swing with our kids at the playground.

We probably have let go of some standards that are important to us but, in truth, can wait. We might find that many of the little housekeeping details are unimportant in the long run. But the memories we build with our children are forever. Building our children's belief in our love for them should be an overlying factor in the choices we make. Many wiser moms will counsel us on the critical role love plays in the development of a child; this role and how we demonstrate it needs our careful attention.

Remember, we do not have to take over the world; we just need to pick and choose carefully the significant few—the 20 percent of activities—that matter to us and our family. If we focus on those vital few, we can be the moms we want to be as we live our lives.

> "Mom, if you were food, you would be ice cream because I love it SO MUCH!"
> —Elle (age 7)

Parenting to Their Weaknesses—or to Their Strengths?

> "Mom, did you know that I know almost everything? When I'm twenty, that's when I will know everything."
> —Chloe (age 6)

Once we choose what we will focus on in our motherhood, how do we then choose the most important aspect to focus on to help our children develop? There can be many answers to that question. Believing that my role as a mother is to help each of our children become the best version of themselves, I chose to focus on building up who they each inherently are.

Before we have our children, we believe that our home environment will dramatically shape them into who they become. We believe that our children will end up fairly similar in their behaviors—after all, they will all be raised in the same household.

Then we have them. Then we learn how wrong we were.

We have our first child, and as we get to know him, we see his behaviors and interests begin to emerge almost before he begins to walk. Then baby number two comes along, and just when we thought we knew all the parenting tricks, none of them work on this child. Baby number two is different—she comes with her own desires, her own strengths, her own weaknesses, and her own interests.

This early exploration of our children's personalities poses challenges for us. Can they run quickly in a race, or are they the last to stumble over the finish line? Can they easily learn how to read music to play the piano, or do they continue to bang at it, terribly loud with a harsh tone? Can they throw a football without it wobbling through the air, or are they better at tackling the guy with the ball? Or maybe they should not play football at all. What classes are they doing well in at school? Where do they struggle? Do they like gymnastics but cannot balance on the beam to save their life? Do they write stories for language arts with ease and humor, or do they spend hours struggling at the kitchen table to come up with the first sentence?

As we progress along this haphazard parenting road, we spend a fair amount of time trying to understand our kids' positives and negatives, their strengths and weaknesses. Parents naturally want to "fix" the weaknesses. But do we align our parenting efforts with "fixing" their weaknesses? Or building their strengths?

Helping them is not necessarily easy, especially since we have our own strengths and weaknesses. It is tough to be a good parent in an area in which we do not feel we are strong. Identifying our children's personality styles and what they excel in can take years. And we may have to search for help from others to support our children's strength development. Regardless, we need to keep an open mind, unencumbered by our experiences and prejudices toward different personalities. Whatever their interests and personalities, that is who they are.

It is easy to worry about issues we think our children will have. I asked Courtney at age six why she could not wake up happy and smiling in the morning. She said, "I just wasn't born that way." Now at age eighteen she is downstairs and ready to go to school every day on time (yes, I said eighteen) and usually with a smile on her face—or at least a grimace with the ends of her mouth turned up. But it is a long way from where we started when she was younger.

We need to keep our worries under control; the majority of what we worry about never happens anyway.

So How Do We Parent if We Cannot "Fix" Them?

Once our children start talking and sharing what they are thinking, we begin to see their personalities. Some are naturally good at friendships, at using their imaginations, or at learning to read. Some are well coordinated and learn to ride a bike quickly. Others do not get along well with siblings, are better at throwing toys than playing with them, and could not do a cartwheel if their lives depended on it.

> "Art is my favorite subject.
> Reading is hard for my head."
> —Courtney (age 7)

As first-time parents, it is easy to be a bit neurotic when it comes to achievements or milestones we think our kids should pass by a certain age. If we have more children, then we realize they are mostly on their own timetables—and that is OK. With intense focus and spare time, we can make some things happen faster (reading, math, playing an instrument, etc.). However, if we do not have a lot of spare time, we should definitely not overthink our children's development or waste time worrying about it. Choices on where to focus begin with us in parenting our children.

I did the best I could to help and support my children reach those little-kid milestones. But I stopped worrying too much once I realized that, with regular love and attention, they would reach them regardless. With the first child, I worried when his baby teeth did not fall out by the expected age. By the fourth child, I did not worry and was not even surprised when she lost four baby teeth in the first two weeks of second grade. She really raked it in that week from the tooth fairy!

Our children might start out with a "weakness" we really worry about. Maybe they're too nice, and all the other children on playdates take away their toys. Fast-forward sixteen years, and those same children are playing football and pancaking the other team's football players all over the field, or they're wrestling their opponents until they grimace in pain struggling to get out of a cradle position, and they win the match.

In Ann Smith's article "The Perils of Perfectionism in Motherhood," Smith admits that, from conversations she's had over the years with her mother, sisters, and friends about raising their respective children, they tended to have the same thing in common: they all worried too much about the wrong things.[9]

We all try to choose where to focus to help our children become the best they can be. What we may consider an issue today could very well be outgrown tomorrow. In the funny ironies of life, we might even find it later becomes a strength.

Focus on Their Strengths and Build Them

> "Mom I did good on my English quiz today—
> I used my whole head!"
> —Courtney (age 11)

Helping our children do well in their lives can be a large source of angst for parents. We understand that where they find a place to excel, whether it is in writing, art, dancing, robotics, student council, band, baseball—is not as important as the simple fact that they found it. If we cannot help our children identify a place in which to excel, they can go astray. Once we have helped them find a strength, we can focus there, help them find success there. That is the choice. When children have success at a young age, they will take those experiences with them for the rest of their lives. They will make plenty of mistakes along the way and experience failures, even when they are aligned with their core strengths.

In the last ten years, more has been written about focusing on our strengths than trying to fix our weaknesses. This applies to people of all ages. Several authors discuss angles on the effective impact of focusing on strengths, including these:

- John Maxwell, "Finding Your Strength Zone" in *Leadership Gold*

- Marcus Buckingham, *Now Discover Your Strengths,* and *Standout: The Groundbreaking New Strengths Assessment from the Leader of the Strengths Revolution*

- Stefan Swanepoel, *Surviving Your Serengeti*

- Gary Keller and Jay Papasan, *The ONE Thing*

- Tom Rath, *Strengths Finder* and *Strengths Based Leadership*

For our children and for ourselves, we need to build our own strengths to become the best we can be. If we are natural communicators and socializers, then we are more apt to enjoy and do well at the sales part of the business. If our strengths are in crunching numbers and the analytical, organizational side of running an operation, then we are probably happier and more successful in the finance or accounting part of a business. Any operation needs both kinds of people. So there is no right or wrong regarding who we are or where our strengths lie. But for our children and ourselves, we are much better off focusing on our strengths and growing in the areas in which we naturally excel. When we do this, not only will we be happiest in our careers and lives, we will also more naturally find success.

Whether parenting our children or learning ourselves, there is no right or wrong strength to possess. What's important is the process of discovering our strengths and passions and then choosing to focus on developing them to reach our potential.

Making Mistakes: Losing Your Cool—It Can Happen

> "I don't need an eraser; I don't make mistakes."
> —Parker to his first-grade teacher

Making mistakes might seem to be a recurring theme here, and it is for me. I have struggled with the guilt I have felt around not mothering the way I wish I could all the time. So I have had to work on solutions to downplay the guilt and choose to have a bigger focus.

I remember one time our school gave me the concession-stand schedule for the football season, and I almost lost my cool. They expected me to work the concessions on a school night to help sell pizzas and popcorn. The date they needed me was a night when my husband was out of town, my two big kids needed to be driven to and from their activities, and I had a six-year-old and a four-year-old I had to take care of and get to bed. When they would not let me pay for a substitute, I lost my cool.

The poor other football mom who got my call (she and I laughed about it three years later) was, thank heavens, also a mom of many (four kids), so she understood my juggles and listened politely before finally begging to get off the call. In calling her, I threw out a request for a lifeline; I felt like I was drowning in the responsibilities of so many little lives.

We need to be sure to reach out when we need a lifeline; we might be surprised how many people around us are willing and interested in helping us through a tough time. Human nature usually wants to help a mom—especially one who is asking for help.

I have lost my cool on many other occasions, unfortunately—like when I was desperately trying to get through the grocery store to get home at the end of the day and all my kids wanted to jump on the grocery cart for a ride. Do they not know how much a grocery cart weighs when it is full of groceries to feed six people, plus Capri Suns for the whole soccer team and the birthday sheet cake for Saturday's party for twenty of their "best friends"? The other adults around me knew how much it weighed—too much!

Recently, the football mom I lost it with earlier found me standing alone at halftime in front of the same concession stand she and I had spoken of, eating a slice of pizza. All alone. She asked me where my little ones were. I told her they were in the girls' room; they were already growing up and could do that safely with me just around the corner. We smiled at each other.

Wow. Only a few short years later, what made me lose my cool was already resolving itself: they were all growing up. My son was on the football field, my oldest daughter was sixteen and able to take care of herself at a game, and I could eat a slice of pizza all by myself while the little ones ran to the restroom. Three short years earlier, I had been frantic over juggling more kids than I could handle.

What is making life crazy now may be only a few short years from resolving itself. It happens. Much faster than we realize when we are in the middle of it. Now, I try to maintain more calm instead, in the middle of the whirlwind that I call my life. I can lose my cool over mistakes I make, I can feel overwhelmed when the kids are not perfectly towing the line and more. But ultimately I have learned that when I choose to remain calm in the chaos, the kids respond better, and the chaos can disappear. Choices.

Making Mistakes and Always Learning—Even In The Summer

> "Sorry I didn't hear you; I don't do learning in the summer."
> —Courtney (age 11)

Another critical choice I have made as a mother is not only to personally learn from the myriad of mistakes that I myself make, but also to teach our children to do the same. Learning from our mistakes is a critical parenting element for us to pass on. Of course if we choose to try to become the best we can be, then we are in fact learning every season of the year, every year of our life.

Like our children, we are on a journey to understand our weaknesses and pursue our strengths. I think it is OK for our children to see that there are some things we are not so great at. Laugh about them together—we are all human. For example, I am not my best at 6:30 a.m. when I am trying to get a bunch of children out of the house for school with all of their snacks, school papers, important books, ice-cream money, and so on. Ask my children; they will tell you my patience at that time of day is slim to none.

There are certain things I am good at and several areas where I am not the one to ask for help. I used to think I needed to be able to answer every question our children came up with because I was "the Mom." However, I do not have all the answers and don't think I should act like I do. I know I am not a brilliant economist; nor should my children ask me for help on their science homework. If they ask me to help them with an English paper or how to put a project together creatively and effectively, then I can excel.

The point is, we are not great at everything, and we are all going to make mistakes, but learning from these mistakes is where the choice lies. When something goes wrong like a bad test grade, a lie that breaks down trust, or an argument among the kids, the problem or mistake has to be dealt with, not ignored. When mistakes are brushed away, not attended to or not discussed, then no learning takes place. Those mistakes will continue to show up in our lives and in the lives of our children until they are addressed.

The learning happens in the conversation around resolving the mistake. Whether our child has to go talk with her teacher about her poor algebra grade to find out how she needs to study differently, or our child has to learn to be honest in order to keep our trust, or siblings have to sit down and talk about an argument they had—this is where they grow.

Unattended problems will reoccur, developing into a failing grade, a troubled child a parent cannot trust, or a broken relationship in the family.

So when any of us makes mistakes, what results is either an individual conversation or a group process of working through it. What could we do differently next time? How did your teacher tell you you could improve? How will you treat your sibling with more respect in order to foster a lifelong relationship? We can choose to ignore mistakes, and then just wait for them to reappear in our lives until we learn that lesson. Or we can choose to listen and learn right away, improving ourselves and our children all along the way.

Ultimately The Choices We Make, Make Us

"It is hard to out-smart your own brain!"
—Chloe (age 9)

Choosing to purposefully allow imperfection in my life has completely changed my parenting perspective. Then deciding what matters the most to my motherhood and our family, and acting on that, has created an environment in which we are all thriving. Our children are each becoming exactly who they should be—delightfully and uniquely themselves.

Instead of being frustrated about all that I do not know, I understand now that I will always be learning. New experiences with our different kids do not have to be frustrating either; they can be stimulating. Life does get easier over time as we learn how to manage it and as our children grow.

We will never have it all figured out. The reality is that we are imperfect, and so are our children. As we work through juggling our motherhood, our professional objectives, and our personal hopes, we will drop the ball along the way more than once. We will be *TILTed* way beyond the out-of-balance point. Instead of losing our sanity in the process, we need to understand our life objectives, make thoughtful choices, and put our efforts into the most important responsibilities.

In my third life lesson, I realized that in our *TILTed* lives, ultimately the choices that we make on every level *will make us*. Small decisions will lead us down a small path. Big-picture decisions on what matters the most to us (our 20 percent), will create a much happier parenthood.

What we can do is cut ourselves some slack, consciously choose what is most important to us and our family, then focus on making those few things happen. We can keep trying to be better, but let the unimportant imperfections slide by. While we are all born with certain characteristics and have each had different life experiences, we can also rise above them based on how we choose to take on life.

Recap of Chapter 3

  √ No one is perfect. We need to do our best and also forgive ourselves.

✓ An important part of happy parenting comes from choosing what matters the most to us, what has the biggest impact on our family (the 20 percent), and then focusing on only those things that matter.

✓ Choosing to parent to our children's strengths (rather than their weaknesses) actually helps to build stronger, more confident children.

✓ Learning from our mistakes, rather than ignoring them, is a critical choice for us and an important lesson to teach our children.

Personal Profile in Mom Courage:
I Am Doing GREAT Work!

My phone just pinged with a new notification. It must be urgent, right? Someone needs my attention stat. What if it's someone asking me to bring something to the kids' school tomorrow? If only I could get the kids settled. They keep asking me to go play with them outside, but I feel like I have a million things to do inside.

This reminds me of an ancient story about a man named Nehemiah. Nehemiah led a small group of workers to rebuild the wall of Jerusalem. The wall had been destroyed by insurgents. This was the city of Nehemiah's ancestors, his family, so it was personal. With the king's permission, Nehemiah and the people worked day and night to rebuild.

But the enemies encircled them, looking to distract Nehemiah and destroy the progress on the wall. One day, they sent a message to Nehemiah to come outside and meet them. Nehemiah replied, "I am doing a great work, and I cannot come down." Four times the enemy sent their message, and all four times Nehemiah gave them the same response. He stayed focused on the task he believed God gave him, and the wall was built in a record fifty-two days.

Might the same be said about parenting? That it too is a great work? One of my favorite communicators and his wife, Andy and Sandra Stanley, talk about guardrails around our time as parents. There will always be distractions like phone calls and e-mails and bosses who want us to work late. Facebook statuses to be updated and a million other things to "catch up on." We must be brave enough to say no to the good in order to make room for the great. We must remind ourselves over and over again that, "I am doing a great work, and I cannot come down."

Off to play outside with my kiddos for a while. The rest of the world can wait.

Danielle Schneller
Mother of three
@momwithaminivan
http://momwithaminivan.com/

GUILT-FREE TIPS –
Eleven Ways to Overcome
Mistakes and Live with Imperfection

1. Blame the kids (just kidding).

2. Admit it. Own it. Get over it. Mistakes happen; life happens. You have to pick yourself up, learn from the experience, communicate with those involved to say you're sorry, and then go on. Dwelling on a mistake only takes your strength away from moving positively forward. Model the behavior you want your kids to follow.

3. Attend at least two seminars a year on your business, on living a great life, on something you want to learn about, or on something totally different. If you stop learning, you stop growing. As I tell my children, "You don't want a dumb mommy, do you?"

4. Remember that challenging yourself can and should be fun. What you do doesn't have to be expensive or exotic—it should just challenge your status quo. Go zip lining. Take a cupcake-decorating class. Train for a 5K or half marathon. Take tennis lessons. Be a kid again—go roller-skating. Do something different!

5. Read about all of Abraham Lincoln's failures. Then consider all that he accomplished and know there is hope for us! We can all overcome the challenges in our way with the right determination and perseverance.

6. Learn a new language. Take an online class so it is at your convenience—Rosetta Stone is supposed to be very good for this.

7. Laugh. Growth occurs when you are open to it. Watch funny YouTube videos, read funny books, and find the humor in your

daily life. Laughter opens your heart and mind to the possibilities around you. Open minds are the only ones that can grow.

8. Do something that you said was "unnecessary" or maybe "too hard." What new technology have you avoided up until now? Look at Dropbox or Skitch or Evernote. How could they help you? Experiment with one and give it a try!

9. After completing your next business project, or event, or job, ask the leader of it to evaluate you. Ask them for their good feedback and for your "opportunities to grow." Listen carefully to what they say, then determine how you could do better next time. Feedback is the breakfast of champions, after all!

10. Sign your kids up for an art class or lessons. Sign yourself up, too!

11. Read *The Best Advice I Ever Got* by Katie Couric and *Failing Forward* by John Maxwell.

4

Too Tired To Be Inspired

"Never underestimate the power of encouragement."
—Parker (age 8)

Mom Quiz #4: We Are *Always* Inspired, *Aren't* We?

Check if anything below applies to you!

☐ I am inspired when the toilet-paper roll runs out and there is still another roll in the bathroom cabinet.

☐ I am inspired when I make it on time to my business meeting with all my needed paperwork, rather than my child's schoolwork.

☐ I am inspired when the baby pukes but it does not land on me.

☐ I am inspired when I grab the loaf of bread to make a grilled cheese sandwich for my daughter and the bread is not green.

☐ I am secretly inspired when it is raining outside so soccer practice is canceled.

☐ I am inspired sitting all alone in a quiet mama-van in the carpool line (which I'm doing even as I write these).

☐ I am inspired when I show up for my business presentation wearing one blue sock and one black sock—and no one notices.

Hitting the Reset Button—Wow, I Needed That

> "Oh, the pain and agony of being in the kitchen!
> Us girls are doomed to it forever!"
> —Courtney (age 13)

I often wish I could function more like a dependable computer than an imperfect human. My children need me, and my husband and business associates need me, but sometimes I just malfunction. Well, computers do that, too. It is really more probable that "dependable computer" is an oxymoron. Sometimes my Internet connection is bad, my software needs to be reinstalled, and my attitude is like a computer virus.

My fourth life lesson in my *TILT*ed life comes from a deep realization that I need to keep positive ideas and thoughts in front of me. My viewpoint can easily get out of whack and drop me quickly to the bottom of the seesaw. But the world keeps moving regardless.

As busy working moms, we can often feel frustrated, overwhelmed, and underappreciated. We start our days early—assuming we slept through the night with no interruptions—trying to get our children up, fed, and out of the house to school with all their homework for that day and having *actually* brushed their teeth. Of course, we also threw in a load of laundry and frantically glanced through the refrigerator, hoping something was in it for dinner, before we raced out of the house. By 8:30 a.m. at the office, we already feel like we should be halfway through the day, yet the action has only just begun.

We need to reset, or reboot, pretty often. Zig Ziglar said that inspiration is like bathing: we need it daily to stay fresh. I believe him. The challenges of our professional lives and goals, along with mothering children, can be daunting on a daily basis.

Not only can positive inspiration help us today, but also its effects can last, improving our quality of life for an extended period. In a 2010 study on inspiration, seventy-nine participants were exposed to Michael Jordan's "extraordinary competence" through watching videos of his performance skill, mastery, and grace. The study found that the participants' exposure to inspiration enhanced their well-being. Further, it was not just short-term well-being that was impacted. It was found that "inspiration had an enduring impact on positive well-being" up to three months later.[10]

The pace of life does not slow down, even when we want it to. Life moves, the children grow, new businesses are formed, brilliant ideas are hatched, and millions and millions of videos are viewed each day on YouTube, all in a whirlwind around us. Every day.

We have to find different resources and ways to keep our attitude in the right place, our focus high-minded, and our efforts on track with our objectives—or at least be sure we can smile with genuine warmth across the dinner table at our family. This attitude struggle is very personal, involving the people we love the most and our complex desires to live a good life.

So now I have personally admitted it out in the open: I need to recharge my battery and attitude regularly. OK, usually daily. Anyone who tells me they are always happy and have a perfect attitude can only be one of the original Disney princesses. Therein lies the issue: as much as some would like them to be, Disney princesses are not actually *real*. We, however, are. To stay inspired, we need to *seek it*. Inspiration does not just show up on our doorstep. We have to search for it. But, wow, when we do, we will find it all around us.

Sources of Inspiring Strength

There are countless moments when we need strength on our mom journey: when we did not sleep through the night to take care of a sick child yet still need to work the next day; when we are finally out running errands and realize we just used the last diaper and last bottle to feed our starving baby who ate thirty minutes ago; when we are facing serious life issues in our family and have to keep it together for our children.

> "This morning I got lost in my shirt."
> —Courtney (having a hard time getting dressed, age 9)

Inspiring strength is actually everywhere. That said, it will not just show up for us; we have to seek it out. When we do, we can realign ourselves with our biggest purposes. As Jeffery Dollinger, president of InventNow, explained in a recent *Fast Company* article about facing difficulties, "To succeed you don't need to be a rocket scientist; you have to have persistence, willpower."[11] So here are some tips on where to find the inspiration every working mom needs:

1. Internet: Google it—over a billion results!

Today with the Internet, it is easier than ever to find inspiring ideas, and it's at our fingertips. Honestly, I found over 97.5 million links on this one idea. I just searched it in Google, and over a billion inspiring results instantly appeared. Here are a few of my favorites:

- happiness-project.com
- HappyNews.com
- Goodnewsnetwork.org
- Gimundo.com
- 1000awesomethings.com
- Givesmehope.com
- And there are many, many more!

2. Positive self-talk:

Inspiration can come from how we actually talk to ourselves. Positive thinking often starts with self-talk—the endless stream of unspoken thoughts that run through your head every day. Our self-talk is very powerful. University of Minnesota Professor Dr. Eric Klinger in his research paper, "Modes of Normal Conscious Flow," a person has around 4,000 thoughts in a day. At that rate, what we say to ourselves matters.

Staying inspired starts right in your own head. Positive thinking doesn't mean you keep your head in the sand and ignore life's less pleasant situations. Positive thinking just means you approach the unpleasantness in a more positive and productive way. Turn negative thinking into positive thinking in these ways:[12]

- Identify areas of your life that you think negatively about. Start small by focusing on one area to approach in a more positive way.

- Stop and evaluate what you're thinking over the course of the day.

- Give yourself permission to smile or laugh, especially during difficult times.

- Surround yourself with positive, supportive people who can give you helpful advice and feedback.

- Follow this rule: don't say anything to yourself that you wouldn't say to anyone else. Practice positive self-talk.

3. E-mail subscriptions for quotes and RSS feeds:

Once you have located a few inspiring websites that are in alignment with your thinking and your objectives, you can dig deeper. Look for stories, videos, or quotes on the subjects you are interested in; often you can subscribe to receive these inspirations via e-mail on a regular basis. You can also sign up for RSS feeds (Really Simple Syndication) on many websites now. When you sign up for one, the site will send you brief updates on a regular basis on the articles they are publishing. Through subscriptions or

RSS feeds, simple quotes and inspiring stories coming to you on a regular basis can give you just what you need to hear, when you need to hear it.

4. Reading:

I uncover so many great ideas and inspirations in my reading. Sure, I can pick up a great fiction book for entertainment, but being tight on time, I usually search out books on my main goal topics: family and relationships, spirituality, health, personal, financial, and professional growth. Here are a few tips to help you focus on inspiration in each bucket of your life, along with some of my favorite authors in those areas:

- **Family and relationships:** Give and receive. Love and be loved. Hug and be hugged back. All of our relationships will grow and inspire us to the extent that we give to *them*. When I need more inspiration in my family relationships, I reach out to the individual members to give to them in some way that reminds them how much they are loved or how special I think they are. I find inspiration comes back to me through those interactions, in the spirit and gift of the giving, in the care they give me in return, and in the words of love and appreciation that inevitably follow. We cannot give expecting a return, but it usually comes anyway. Healthy and happy relationships are a two-way street. Start by being the giver. Some good authors in this area include Maya Angelou, Stephen Covey, Dan Zadra, John Gray, Mitch Albom, and Barbara DeAngelo.

- **Spirituality:** Many people find daily inspiration already inside themselves. Meditation and prayer are worth their weight in untold wisdom-gold. Particularly enlightened people seem to make time for meditation and prayer. When we are in our most trying moments, this can be incredibly uplifting. Making time for our spirituality more often will calm our mom-frayed nerves and help us remember why we are here in the first place. Some of my favorite authors in this area include Marianne Williamson, Andy Stanley, Robin Sharma, Andy Andrews, and Eckhart Tolle.

- **Health:** Taking care of ourselves physically is a critical piece of our happiness. Too often we let this piece slide in our fast-food-as-we run-all-around-town meal solutions. Some of that is OK, but too much is always too much. Exercising helps us mentally and physically. We want to be around a long time to enjoy the family we are working so hard to raise, and being consciously active will give us more energy in the present and future. In the area of health, some of my favorite authors include Loren Cordain, Jillian Michaels, Dr. Mehmet Oz, the editors of *Prevention Magazine*, and Ron Betta.

- **Personal:** Often personal inspiration is found through personal growth and development. Some self-focus can be healthy for your soul. Reading books that help you develop yourself, your skills, and your hobbies can feed your personal passions and fuel your fire. If you need to find more inner peace, try reading some of Deepak Chopra or Dr. Wayne Dyer's work. If you want to improve your technology skills, read about all that you could do if you learned how to code. If you want to climb a tall mountain, read about someone who climbed Mount Everest.

- **Financial:** Peace and happiness in our financial lives most often comes from living below our means and from being sure we give something to those less fortunate. Financial responsibility is just that—our responsibility. We need to seek those who have done this well for ideas and inspiration on how to manage it in our own lives. There are many people experienced in financial success who teach money responsibility, such as Dave Ramsey, Clark Howard, Robert Kiyosaki, Suze Orman, George Clason, Thomas Stanley, and Jim Cramer.

- **Professional growth:** The inspiration available to us in this category is overwhelming—and awesome. We just need to search for the ideas that can help us get to the next level in our professional growth. With guidance, we each need to choose the best idea to put in place in our lives in the next sixty days. We cannot take over the world in a few months, but we can be inspired to go to the next level with focus and concentrated effort on a goal that will lead us toward professional success. Every small step inspires us to make the next, needed one. Some of my favorite authors in this area include John Maxwell, Jack Canfield, Gary Keller and Jay Papasan, Stephen Covey, Ken Blanchard, Tom Peters, Meg Whitman, Anthony Robbins, and Guy Kawasaki.

There are thousands and thousands of books that help us think and live better. When we cannot make the time to get to every seminar, books can travel by our side and patiently await our attention. Written words of wisdom resonate, redirect us to a higher level of thinking, and push us to grow.

Great Books To Help Us Stay On Track

It is so easy to get wrapped up in work or the kids. Keeping each child on their own plan and still having time for each individual plan can really take up most of our time. We get pulled in so many directions that keeping a balance can be harder than ever. Here are some of my very favorite reads to keep me on track:

- *Wonderful Ways to Love a Teen* by Judy Ford
- *Wonderful Ways to Love a Child* by Judy Ford
- *Raising Cain* by D. Kindlon and M. Thompson
- *Teen Proofing* by John Rosemond
- *Things I want my Daughter to Know* by A. Stoddard

Diedra Lockhart Sorohan
Mother of three
Managing Partner, O'Kelley and Sorohan, Attorneys at Law, LLC
www.OkelleyandSorohan.com
dsorohan@oslawllc.com

5. Friends and family:

Our friends, family, and coworkers can offer great shoulders to lean on, and they are an obvious resource for ideas, answers, and support along our journeys. Choosing our friends carefully is a must. Having negative people around us who spend most of their time complaining, or who take more than they ever give, bring us down. We have to be thoughtful of who we surround ourselves with. If we urge our children to pick good friends, friends who support them, friends who are positive, friends who like them for who they are, *shouldn't we do the same for ourselves*?

There are friends who will share our values and life priorities, offer us advice that is realistic for us to use, and support us in our goals for our lives. Then there are others who will make choices that are unacceptable to us, tell us regularly that the sky is falling, or only tell us the reasons why our ideas are unrealistic and unattainable; it is our choice to not be friends with people like this. Choose the friends who will take the bus with you or lift your wings when you forget how to fly.

6. Social media:

Social media has been gathering steam quickly as millions of people find new ways to connect through it. Facebook, founded in 2004, has over one billion users connecting with people from afar and sharing not only family photos, but also words of wisdom and links to inspiration. Twitter has become a place for mompreneurs to share tips, information, and inspiring stories. There are many other social media sites, including Pinterest, Instagram, and Vine, and more are being created every day. By building a social network of working moms through the social media we like best, we can help each other be better versions of ourselves.

Here are a few of my Twitter favorites to follow for inspiration:

If you want inspiration on life:

@Tinybuddha
@Charityideas
@Johncmaxwell
@Juliedefina
@Spreadingjoy
@Inspirebookclub
@Foodforthesoul
@lisamccourtbook
@drwaynedyer

If you want inspiration on life as a woman:

@amazingwomen
@Womenofhistory
@Besteveryou
@Greenskydeb
@lindasasser
@alignwithlove

If you want inspiration on life as a working woman with children:

@Elisatalk
@30secondmom *
@annieburnside
@melissaonline
@Bethrosen
@DrCHibbert
@ahildrichdavis
@momsgetreal
@kairarouda
@inspiringmoms
@seeds4parents

@momager1
@Socialmoms
@Todaysmoms
@heather31mom
@momwithaminivan
@atxtrish
@Butterflymoms
@marcifair [OK, I had to add mine :)]

*All of the 30Second Moms are really great women who want to share and inspire!

My Number-One Resource for Inspiration

Everyone needs inspiration in their lives, especially moms. We are so busy taking care of others that we often neglect ourselves. This may lead to feeling discouraged, and can definitely be overwhelming! The first thing I try to remember when I feel this way is that I'm certainly not alone. Chances are I have a mom friend who's feeling the same way. I pick up the phone and call a friend, and we usually both vent and feel better. Somehow, knowing someone else is right there with you really helps ease the pain.

Another option: I take a walk with my dog. No matter the weather, getting out and pounding the pavement always, always makes me feel better, and my dog is a wonderful companion. Added bonus: you're burning calories and strengthening muscles at the same time. I also take yoga breaks. Quick mat stretches reframe my thinking and ease aching muscles.

If I need inspiration to go back to being the best mom I can be, my number-one resource is my social network. Why? Because, quite literally, they are always there, and they are among the most inspiring people I know. In particular, the crew at 30Second Mom always has a kind or helpful word, and there isn't a subject that one of them doesn't know something about. I'm so grateful for them—it's like having a team of moms at your beck and call! They're also among the ones I turn to when I have to make big decisions or need guidance about parenting. Not sure what I would do without them!!

Elisa All
Mother of three
Founder / CEO, 30 Second Mobile
http://www.30secondmom.com
@30secondmom
elisa@30secondmom.com

7. E-zines:

Too often for me, news is sensationalized and tragic, neither of which serves my purposes as a woman, a mom, or a professional. Through e-magazine apps (like Zite for the iPad), we have the ability to control our "news feeds." We can look for good news, solid news, news that matters and helps us grow and be aware of the world we need to operate in. We can choose to read stories about moms, kids, real estate, gardening, world news, parenting, wine, financial news, business—anything we can imagine. So with our limited time, e-zines allow us to control and filter our news feeds to be the most productive for us individually.

8. Quiet moments:

Quiet is inspiring. We need more of it in our lives. It is easy to turn on the radio, to look at a news app, to focus our minds on the problems in our lives. That is all easy. And distracting. And discouraging. In the few pockets of quiet time we might have in a day, let's remember this simple rule: garbage in, garbage out. Quiet is hard to find, but not impossible. It is certainly not quiet at my dinner table. It is not in my home at six-thirty in the morning when I am trying to get all the kids out the door on time. It is not found at bedtime as we all run around to finish the last of what has to be done for the next day.

Other than being alone when we go to the bathroom—a major mom milestone—when else might we find quiet moments to ourselves? Here are a few ideas:

- In the doctor's office as we wait—seemingly endlessly—for our appointment.

- In the very early hours of the morning or late at night when everyone else is asleep.

- In the mama-van when no one else is in it except a stuffed-animal collection and a few crunched Goldfish crackers.

- In the shower. We can do a fair amount of thinking in there.

- When we are folding the laundry. Not much thinking to do about the folding.

- At lunch, when we eat alone.

We do have pockets of time in our day; we just have to be intentional with them. How we choose to use them can define us.

9. Momoirs:

> "Mom, I know why you wear a belt: so your pants don't fall down and everyone sees your underwear."
> —Chloe (age 4)

The biggest surprise source of inspiration for me is my actual momoirs: making memories with my children and the quotes I hear from my life with them. Fulfilling my family and mom goals fills my heart and motivates me to keep pressing on. Meeting my little girls at school for lunch once a month is just one of those mom goals. When I make time to share with them, I fill all of our hearts. Part of my inspiration comes from loving and inspiring them.

Our children's quotes can be the most touching inspiration for many moms, if we are paying attention to hear them. As soon as our children start talking, their funny perspective on life can make us laugh—and make us cry. My journal, overstuffed with their quotes scribbled on the backs of envelopes, on Post-its, on any scrap of paper nearby, is a treasure trove of inspiration. And today, with smartphones and other devices, it is easy to quickly type-capture them to reflect on later.

> "Life is not measured by the number of breaths that we take...
> But by the number of moments that take our breath away."
> —Greeting quote used on our 2005 Christmas card

10. Gratitude:

> "Mom, I don't tell my teaches because I
> don't want to hurt their feewings.
> But I miss you all day and wish I was with you."
> —Elle (age 6)

Be grateful. It is so easy to forget to think with a grateful heart, and it is so powerful when we do remember.

It is too easy to be pulled into a downward mental spiral of complaining, worrying, or feeling sorry for ourselves. Gratitude is an amazing attitude adjuster and pick-me-up—especially in the business of getting inspired. It has a powerful ability to bring laser-sharp focus in our hearts for all that we are truly blessed with, and to push aside the things that really do not matter. Gratitude changes our attitude.

Keeping a gratitude journal on your nightstand is a simple way to keep gratitude in front of you. Every night before you turn off the light—especially after a hard day—write down five to ten things you are grateful for. Usually that exercise will help you find perspective on your struggles so you can fall asleep more peacefully and wake up in a better state of mind. At the least, you will see the journal as your hands pass over it to turn the light off just before you fall asleep. Sweet, grateful dreams.

11. Giving back:

Reach out and help someone else in need. This is one of the fastest ways to get out of your own rut and be inspired. In our communities are organizations that help those less fortunate—battered women's shelters, food pantries, domestic abuse and violence shelters, as well as nursing homes and other care centers. These organizations always need volunteers to support them.

When I was twenty-one, I had a goal to create a foundation that would serve children in need in our communities. It took me thirteen years to start it, but I did, in 2005: Kares 4 Kids. Due to the generosity and giving hearts of many people, Kares 4 Kids has now served over fifteen thousand children and counting. It will be one of the greatest things I will do in my lifetime.

The most fascinating discovery for those who choose to give is often what they receive back. It can make a world of difference in your and your children's lives. Volunteering is good for the recipient and equally good for our souls.

How Do We Keep Our Inspirations in Front of Us?

"I forgot to scream on the waterslide; I got lost in the fun-ness!"
—Chloe (age 7)

We can keep track of the quotes that impact us by putting them in places where we will see them regularly: tape them to the bathroom mirror to be sure we start off our days thinking right. Put them on notecards and prop them up on the dresser. Put photos and quotes on the refrigerator or laundry-room walls. I put them in my mama-van console so I see them every time it is open. Think about what you actually look at on a regular basis, and *put the things that inspire you there* so you see them often.

Collect great quote books; they do not cost too much money and are priceless in their impact. Mine are scattered all around me—on my nightstand, all around my office, in my laundry-room drawer, on my dresser. Scatter them around the house for others to find—for example, on a coffee table or a side table. We never know when we need a little mental pickup or when our children may need one—it is more often than we might think.

I have had an electronic organizer since they started making them, in an attempt to keep my life in order and not miss anything important. I started with the Palm Pilot, then had a BlackBerry, then fell in love with the iPhone. On each device, I found a way to record inspirational thoughts. Usually using a task manager, I put collections of quotes under different to-dos. Then I put different due dates on them. When that date arrives, the inspirational thought pops up and reminds me to keep my focus. I change their order in the to-do list so that different quotes come to the top. I store some away to pull out again later. I change my inspirations often and add new ones all the time. It keeps them fresh and keeps my interest.

Find a system that works for you. You'll be surprised at the brightness these daily reminders bring into your life.

Our Children's Chalkboard

The wisdom of inspirational quotes has guided me, taught me, and helped me stay focused on what really matters in many areas of my life. If quotes have made such a difference for me, I thought maybe they would also for my kids.

Inspirational quotes can come across as too corny—certainly to pre-teens and teenagers. I wanted to find an easy, not-in-your-face, non-dorky way to share them with my children. So several years ago when my oldest was eight, I created our "Children's Chalkboard" at the top of the stairs in the house. About every week or so, I put up an inspirational or time-appropriate quote for the children.

I really wasn't sure when I first started this if the Children's Chalkboard quotes were having any impact, but I liked the idea and stuck with it. A couple of months later, my husband was driving my son home from a football game and said to him, "You had some great plays in the game, and I noticed that you were doing a great job out there encouraging and leading your team in between plays."

Parker, all of age eight, looked at him and said, "Dad, never under-estimate the power of encouragement."

I was so happy to hear he'd said that—it was the quote on the Children's Chalkboard that week. The kids were paying attention. They were actually reading the quotes and thinking about them.

Another week I was in between quotes—I leave the board blank for a few days after I erase a quote to be sure the kids notice that I changed it—when one of my son's teenage friends came over. They were hang-ing out in Parker's room, and his friend asked him when I was going to put up another "coaching idea" again. Wow! Even our children's friends were paying attention. Needless to say, I had another quote on the chalkboard before his friend left the house that afternoon.

Sometimes the Children's Chalkboard is whimsical: a countdown to a family vacation, welcoming a friend for a sleepover, wishing someone happy birthday. One of my friends put one up in her home and writes very simple things on it, such as, "Are you smiling today?" Simple is smart.

Below are several quotes I have used to get you started on your own chalkboard:

- "Learn from the mistakes of others. You can't live long enough to make them all yourself." —Eleanor Roosevelt

- "Winning is not everything, but the effort to win is." —Zig Ziglar

- "We are not what we know, but what we are willing to learn." —Mary Catherine Bateson

- "First we make our habits, then our habits make us." —Denis Waitley

- "The secret of getting ahead is getting started." —Sally Berger

- "The highest reward for your work is not what you get for it, but what you become by it." —John Maxwell

- "Don't think outside the box. Think like there is no box." @ Womenofhistory

- "We only learn our limits by going beyond them." —Unknown

- "Nothing worthwhile will ever come to you without a price." —Mario Andretti

- "There are two ways of meeting difficulties. You alter the difficulties or you alter yourself." —Phyllis Bottome

- "It is not the mountain we conquer, but ourselves." —Sir Edmund Hillary

- "Although the world is full of suffering, it is also full of the overcoming of it." —Helen Keller

- "People don't care how much you know, until they know how much you care." —Mike McNight

- "We ask ourselves, who am I to be brilliant, gorgeous, talented, fabulous? Actually, who are you not to be?" —Marianne Williamson

- "Failure is a big part of life, but it's how we react to failing that will determine our destiny. If we learn from it and move on, it can help to make us all we can be. If you fear it to the extent that you never take risks, you'll never grow." —Mac Anderson

- "Do not let what you cannot do interfere with what you can do." —John Wooden

- "It's important to give it all you have while you have the chance." —Shania Twain

- "There are no real failures—just experiences and your reactions to them." —Tom Krause

- "By being yourself, you put something wonderful in the world that was not there before." —Edwin Elliot

- "Only as high as I reach can I grow,

  Only as far as I seek can I go,

  Only as deep as I look can I see,

  Only as much as I dream can I be." —Karen Ravn

When one of our children was having some friend issues, I wrote, "To find good friends, you must first be one."

And to keep the quotes at the top of their minds, we occasionally discuss them. Sometimes at dinner, I ask the kids if they understand the new quote I just put up. That always makes for interesting dinner conversation.

When We Change Our Focus, We Change Our Life

Shawn Achor explains so well the impact of one's attitude in his book, *The Happiness Advantage*: "The key then is not to completely shut out all of the bad, all the time, but to have a reasonable, realistic, healthy sense of optimism. The ideal mindset isn't heedless of risk, but it does give priority to the good. Not just because that makes us happier, but also because that is precisely what creates more good. Given the choice between seeing the world through rose-tinted glasses or always walking around under a rain cloud, the contest isn't even close. In business and in life, the reasonable optimist wins every time."

In speaking with so many friends who are businesswomen as well as moms, I hear the same struggles. I hear the same challenges of loving their children but wanting to make the most of their lives and gifts. So many of us, wrapped up in the responsibilities of taking care of our own families, forget to reach out, or stop reaching out, to others for our own inspiration and care of ourselves. We each struggle in our own journeys, with their ups and downs, to make our own momoirs happy ones. What one person faces and finds to be a great challenge may be so simple for the next person. So I try not to judge myself; instead, I just try to improve myself.

Inspirational ideas keep us focused; they spur us to be better people. They challenge us to take the high road. They question what activities we are filling our time with. They remind us constantly to be sure that we are, in fact, living in our 20 percent and focusing on what really matters. The lack of inspiration to refocus our chaos-challenged minds can result in feeling discouraged, frustrated, overwhelmed, or even depressed. No one wins when we are in those mental states. Surrounding ourselves with thoughts and ideas from people who share life's wisdom can help us take our glass from half empty to half full.

An article in *O, The Oprah Magazine*, "Three Smart New Ways to Kick Pessimism to the Curb," reminds us how important it is to refocus our brains from negative thoughts to positive thoughts. One expert, Rick Hanson, PhD, a neuropsychologist, founder of the Wellspring Institute for Neuroscience and Contemplative Wisdom, and author, explains it this way: "There's an expression in neuroscience: Neurons that fire together wire together. This means that new patterns of thought can actually change the physiology of our brains. So while we can't ignore bad news, we can train our brains to become more alert to good information. When you notice a positive detail in yourself or someone else, or in your environment, try savoring it for at least ten seconds. Most of these observations will be as simple as 'the sun is shining' or 'this coffee tastes good,' but do this a handful of times each day and you'll feel an emotional shift."[13]

My fourth life lesson from my *TILT*ed world came from a strong recognition that I needed constant shots in the arm of positive thoughts and ideas. By keeping inspirational articles or quotes or books in front of me, I keep my attitude and priorities straight to stay focused on what matters.

As we each pass through our years with our children, we have a choice to make: We can see the dust collecting on the lamp shades, find all the personality "faults" that our children have, focus on the lack of time we have to curl up on the sofa and watch a movie, dislike and complain about the work we do, or be disappointed in ourselves on a regular basis that the Super-Mom cape just does not fit us. Or we can decide that we do not need to wear that Super-Mom cape after all. Instead, we can appreciate the season we are in, and as we love and inspire our family, we can do the same for ourselves.

Recap of Chapter 4

- ✓ The reality of all that we juggle can be overwhelming and discouraging. Know that more often than not, we need to inspire and uplift ourselves.

- ✓ There are many sources of inspiration—some surprising—all around us that can help us keep a positive perspective.

✓ Keeping inspirational books, quotes, and stories, and good friends close by makes a difference.

✓ We can also inspire and help our children grow by sharing words of wisdom with them. Through a simple, not-in-your-face idea, all of my children have read inspirational quotes since they were very young. They have put them on their bedroom walls, on their social-media sites, on their cell phone's wallpaper, and more. Most importantly, when life gives them a challenge, they have them in their hearts and minds to help them keep perspective and move forward.

Personal Profile in Mom Courage:
A Lifelong Beginner

I have three sons, and I have been practicing this whole mother thing for almost seven years now—going on eight if you count those months of pregnant anticipation with the first.

I still feel like a beginner. Sometimes people—new mothers, first-time expectant moms—ask me for advice or want to know the best way to do something. How to find the perfect nanny, how to soothe a teething baby, how to change a diaper in an airplane bathroom. Or they ask how many naps a toddler should take. When is it OK to give kids hot dogs? Is it ever OK to give them hot dogs?

Sometimes I give advice, and sometimes I don't. It depends on the mood, or the day, or how hard I am being on myself. The truth is, some days I'm really good at this mothering gig. Some days I make it all look and feel so easy. Some days I know my kids are going to be all right.

Other days, I might be going through the routine, getting kids out the door in the morning, breezing into the office, and commanding client meetings. But on the inside I am curled up in a fetal position begging for mercy.

I have tried every combination of the mother-and-kid equation. I have worked part time from home, stayed home, worked part time out of the home, and worked full time out of the home. And for me, each one holds its own appeal, and each one offers benefits and has downsides. (If you have found the perfect job, please let me know because I want in.)

Yes, that's exactly what I'm saying: mothering is a job. It's a wonderfully rewarding, incredibly trying, all-consuming, never-ending job. And it's an important one. But it's not perfect.

When the peas hit the fan and there is a floater in the bathtub, I question how I'm going to get through one more day. And then a little hand reaches out for mine, or three little voices yell out "Mommy!" in gleeful unison when I walk through the door. And there is suddenly a clean slate—a fresh start to try again. And this time, to get it right.

Katie Ross
Mother of three
@BoysandCurls

GUILT-FREE TIPS – Eleven Intriguing Ideas for Inspiration

1. Search YouTube videos for stories about heroes. Try typing in "inspiration," "inspirational kids," "inspirational speeches," or "inspirational hero." Watch Kyle Maynard (author of *No Excuses*) if you think you have issues to overcome. He will humble you—and inspire you.

2. Save e-mails from friends and loved ones that make your heart smile. Make a folder in your e-mail account for "Inspiring Thoughts." When you need it, go there and reread. Make your heart smile again.

3. Hire a life, business, or personal coach. The right coach in your life can help you identify what you need to do, keep the right focus, and inspire you to be a better version of you.

4. Watch TED "Ideas Worth Spreading" videos. The website hosts "riveting talks by remarkable people, free to the world." From Malcolm Gladwell (*Blink*) to Caroline Casey (*Looking Past Limits*) to Jill Salzman @foundingmom (a Twitter friend), who presented on "Actions Speak Louder: Why Moms Make the Best Entrepreneurs!," you will find presentations that fascinate and inspire you.

5. Sign up for e-mail newsletters from leadership companies. They will e-mail you regularly with inspiring quotes, stories, or books to read. WalkTheTalk.com is a good one. So is Success.com.

6. Meditate. Pray. Connect to your spiritual self. Find peace and quiet somewhere, even if it is in the car after you have dropped off the kids at school. If you want to study peace, meditation, or simple ideas more, read *The Path of Mindfulness Meditation* by Peter Strong, PhD; study Deepak Chopra; or for a lighter read,

check out *Tiny Buddha: Simple Wisdom for Life's Hard Questions* by Lori Deschene.

7. Be a hero yourself. What deeply touches your heart? Children in foster care? Victims of domestic violence? Lonely people in nursing homes? Special-needs children? Whatever it is that resonates with you, volunteer for a while with an organization in your community that serves those people.

8. Don't underestimate how much you can learn by subscribing to podcasts for monthly or weekly inspiration and leadership training. I personally tune in monthly to John Maxwell's Maximum Club for his teachings on life and leadership. Moms are some of the most important leaders in the world and we need to keep honing these skills!

9. Find a "Mom Blog" or two that you can relate to and commiserate with and make a point to read it regularly. The blogosphere can be a great source of information to make you laugh and remember that you're not in it alone in the crazy world of parenting. You might like Jes's Delight blog (http://jesdelights.blogspot.com), or Life Imperfected (http://lifeimperfected.blogspot.com), or Mastering Mommy Brain (http://lifeimperfected.blogspot.com).

10. Read *Tuesdays with Morrie: An Old Man, a Young Man, and Life's Greatest Lesson* by Mitch Albom, or *The Last Lecture* by Randy Pausch and Jeffrey Zaslow.

11. Write down your children's silly sayings. Read, reread, and reread again.

PART III
Memories Are Better

5

Loving Your Family and Loving Yourself

"I love your cooking, Mom.
You know, your Chinese and your pizza."
—Courtney (age 6)

Mom Quiz #5: You Feel Loved When...

Check if anything below applies to you!

☐ You feel loved when your child turns his or her dirty socks the *right side out* for you to wash them.

☐ You feel loved when your teenage daughter actually responds to your text.

☐ You feel loved when you walk in and the kitchen counter is clean. Then you realize that it's only because someone was *paid* to do it.

☐ You feel loved when you actually sneak a few minutes for yourself and sit down on a comfortable chair you have not visited for quite a while. Five minutes later you are worried and feeling antsy. Why has no one interrupted you? You know that either a kid has fallen into a toilet or they are trying to decorate your walls with abstract Crayola art. You jump up in search of the potential problems.

☐ You feel loved when your teenage son takes out the trash without being asked one hundred times. You only had to ask him ten times.

☐ You feel loved when your sweetest little daughter colors a rainbow for you, writes you a love note, and leaves it to surprise you on your bathroom counter—to remind you that it is all worth it.

A Love Deeper Than I Ever Imagined

> "Mom, I love you all the way to the end of the universe and back.
> That is very far, because there is no end to the universe."
> —Elle (age 5)

What was the first thing that came to your mind when you saw your newborn baby for the first time? It could have been that she seemed to be missing a lot of hair—or maybe that she seemed to have quite a bit of it. It could have been relief that the delivery was over. Maybe you wished so many people were not in the room with you. It could have been awe over the miracle that just occurred. It could have been that you felt an overwhelming, unimaginable joy—a happiness like you had never felt before. Whatever your first thoughts might have been, you birthed a person with whom you will forever have a very special relationship. You created a love like no other.

My fifth life lesson is about the importance of protecting, respecting, and cherishing this love. The love of our children, throughout their lives, will guide our behavior as moms. Building and caring about our relationships with our children and our spouse over time will be one of our greatest legacies. Love gives us strength, courage, and hope. Lack of it can deny us any or all of that.

In the rush of our *TILT*ed lives, love can too easily slip through our fingertips. It is easy to forget to focus on this critical facet of our relationships. There is work to be done, groceries to buy, business presentations to make, and a household to try to keep together. We shoulder a lot of responsibility, and it can be difficult to keep all the important balls we juggle in the air at the same time. Since we have to choose what we give our attention to, we have to understand what weighs the heaviest in value. What should we be sure we give time and thought to in order to manage the *TILT* in our lives?

Love needs to be one of those things we do not neglect. Of all that we can focus on, love can hold the greatest satisfaction we experience in our lives. Unattended relationships do not last—either with spouses or with children. And as we seek to fulfill all our roles and responsibilities, we can even start to lose another critical love in our life: the love of ourselves.

Bronnie Ware's book *The Five Top Regrets of the Dying: A Life Transformed by the Dearly Departed* describes this in detail. After twenty-plus years of caring for those who were dying, Ware wrote that the single commonality between them was their final conversations around the *love* in their life—or the lack of it.

One of my most important life goals is that my family never lacks for love from me. Of all the facets of life that I focus on, this is one of the most important.

Same Parents...Different Kids?!

> "I don't want to have any boys when I am a mom—they are trouble.
> I like girls better."
> —Elle (age 6)

It was hard to believe whenever someone else told me that all of my children would be different. Come to find out, they are. You'd think the overlying influence on a child's personality would be their environment. Surprise! It's not.

We quickly discover that our children come to us preprogrammed in more ways than one. Some are more curious than others—they do anything to get into the kitchen cabinets and eat the toilet cleaner. Some are quiet and just sit alone in silence, chewing on a toy. Some are always active, and wherever they go they are running—whether or not they are watching where they are going.

And regardless, we can't really change them; our role is more to simply guide them.

With my first two children, I was actually surprised when I found that their interests differed from mine. I liked dancing and Barbies when I was little—wouldn't any girl of mine like them, too? Of course, I have *so* many children, one or more was bound to be different from me, just by numerical odds. It has become a source of humor in my family that some of us like karate or Barbies or band, and others do not. Funny enough, the only activity they all had in common was one I never played growing up: soccer.

My children are truly four unique individuals, each with his or her own personality and interests. From whether they want to read the whole book for the class project or just the CliffsNotes, to how they interact socially and personally with people, to what activities they want to participate in, even to whether they want ketchup with their chicken nuggets—they are all different.

Thank heavens the world needs so many types of people—nurses, entrepreneurs, librarians, engineers, teachers, computer techies, and so on—since all of our children will probably grow up to have very different careers. It makes it interesting, learning how to parent so many personalities.

As our families grow, not only do we have learn to appreciate and find the humor in how unique we all are, but we also need to learn to respect *how important* we each are in our own ways. It can be challenging to help our children appreciate those differences. As moms, we try to help them love and respect the human beings they are each becoming in order to foster long-term relationships among them. Sometimes they need our help to find the good in each other.

- "Mom, she is making weird noises with her mouth!"

- "Mom, how can she like pink?! I hate pink!"

- "Mom, will you tell her to please stop singing! It is driving me crazy!"

- "Mom, why won't he play with me? He does not like me!"

- "Mom, does he have to play baseball?! It is sooo boring!"

- "Mom, do *not* make me to see a *Princess* movie!"

- "Mom, I *would love* to see a Princess movie!"

Several people have written books on this subject, such as Gary Chapman's book, *The Five Love Languages of Children*, which gives us suggestions for better understanding this parenting issue. Each child likes to be shown love in different ways. Some like to be shown love through "acts of service." Some prefer gifts—is there a child who doesn't? Some children like hugs and cuddling. Others just want to be reminded often how much we love them. Chapman has even created a mobile-device app to help us understand this better when we are out and about.

Being aware of loving our children for who they are is a cornerstone of our parenting. Separating them from their behaviors and focusing on correcting their behaviors is critical. When something has gone wrong for them, if we reprimand them as a person, we undermine our relationship with them. Rather than clamping down on them, we help them more by separating their actions from who they are as a person. Who they are as a person will not necessarily change; how they act can be changed. Reprimand the inappropriate behaviors. Compliment the good behaviors we want them to develop.

Dr. Ira J. Chasnoff, president of the Children's Research Triangle and a professor of clinical pediatrics at the University of Illinois College of Medicine in Chicago, is considered an expert on children. In his recent *Psychology Today* article about discipline, he writes that he always tells parents to "catch 'em being good!" He explains that negative reinforcement or any kind of punishment simply does *not* work to change a child's long-term behavior. The only thing that works is positive reinforcement.[14]

Don't Be Too Attached to the Outcome

I wish that I had been less attached to the outcome with my boys. I would have embraced their imperfections and not spent precious, irreplaceable moments attempting to "fix" them. I would have realized that "fire fruck" and "Fristmas free" were not going to follow them into adulthood and that these were baby talk, not an indication of a speech impediment. I would not have felt compelled to correct the imperfections, knowing that when they were gone, I would miss them.

I would have also let them fail more. I would have refrained from trying to save them from what I believed was a sure catastrophe and allowed them to make the mistakes that would lead to growth and self-discovery. In a nutshell, I would have relaxed more with them, had more confidence in their strengths and talents, and moved out of their way a little more. Instead of spending time waiting to exhale, I would have breathed with them, in confidence and faith for their unique abilities.

Paige Powers
Mother of two
Grandmother of three
Team Leader, Keller Williams Realty Atlanta Partners
paigepowers@kw.com

Our children each walk down their own life paths, at their own paces, to the beat of their own drummers. Part of our plan in loving them is to give them confidence to follow that unique path, with its zigs and zags, and to be sure they know we love them for who they are along the way. Our world needs each of us for different reasons.

For many children, we are the most important person in their world—or one of two, along with their other parent. If they know they are loved for who they are, they can grow up with the confidence to take on the ups and downs of their journey. Without that love—loving *each one for who he or she is*—we can limit their future and their future relationships. Ultimately, we cannot change them. Our role is to guide them.

> "Yaya is talking weird."
> —Chloe (age 6) to me about Elle (nicknamed Yaya)
> "I not talking weird; I talking Yaya."
> —Elle (age 4) overheard

As Our Children Change through the Seasons of Life, so Must We

> "If I wrote down a list of all of the reasons why I love you,
> I would need a lot of pages!"
> —Chloe (age 9)

A couple of months before Courtney was due, I thought it would be smart to wean my almost-two-year-old son, Parker, out of his crib. In my mind, he would then be used to a "big boy" twin bed well before his new sibling was born and sleeping in his crib. Little did I know that my husband and I would then be taking turns sleeping at the top of the stairs outside his room every night for the next few months as he adjusted.

We took turns so at least one of us could sleep each night because every night, Parker woke up in fear, took all his clothes off their hangers in his closet and threw them on his floor, and then ran to us for reassurance. Every night.

We were at our wits' end trying to come up with another way to handle this transition for him. We tried different ways to help him through it but did not want to put him back in the crib and have to go through it all again later. Finally, we realized that the bumper pad and enclosed space of his crib had given him a lot of comfort and safety, so we set up his twin bed with things around him to recreate that for him. When our last child, Elle, was on the way, I can tell you we bought Chloe, age two, a toddler bed for that transition. We do, thankfully, get a little smarter as we go along.

We learn that when our children cannot run away from us, we have so many ways to shower love on our children: We hug them and hold them constantly. We feed them and give them baths. We kiss their sweet little cheeks as much as we want. They get more physical attention from us then than at any other time in their lives.

As they begin to grow into the next seasons of their lives, we demonstrate our affection for them differently. Even though they are not as physically dependent on us as they used to be, that doesn't mean they don't need our love and attention just as much. It only means that the ways they are *receptive* to our affection and love changes.

For any newer moms reading this, please know that at a certain point, we *do* begin to sleep through the night again and get our wits back about us. However, just when we begin to sleep through the night, our children start driving. Then the real sleepless nights begin.

We need to remind ourselves that as our children grow through the years, they still always need our love. Even when they get into those stages where they feel the need to act cool or act like they do not need us, they still do. We know that. They might have just forgotten temporarily. We have to look for opportunities to love them anyway and love them every day.

Say "I Love You" a Thousand Times a Day

Looking back on my life with my young children, I would have put the tea towel down and taken more walks with my children, smelled more flowers, pushed more swings, read more books, laughed more, tickled more, snuggled more, and said "I love you" one thousand times a day.

Mo Anderson
Mother of two
Grandmother of three
Vice Chairman of the Board, Keller Williams Realty International
www.kw.com
facebook.com/moanderson
mo@kw.com

Three Phases of Love

1. Elementary school:

In this phase, our love becomes more than just wiping the leftover food goo off their little faces. We teach them how to ride a bike, we play games together, we come to their annual school-program performance, and we still read books with them at bedtime and tell them we love them as we tuck them in. Our teaching them and playing with them is showing them our love, which has thankfully begun to evolve to more than just the endless flow of baby wipes in babyhood.

2. Middle school:

In middle school, our affection becomes mental love. We try to keep our brains and mental faculties intact while attempting to get them to use theirs. We still hug them, wrestle with them, and kiss them whenever we can catch them off guard. But many times, showing our love at this stage means helping their heads think better. It also changes into being sure we get them to their after-school practices on time. It can be taking them on special one-on-one dates to dinner and a movie. It might be helping them get the right percussion sticks for their band class. It definitely needs to include teaching them to use deodorant. It still always needs to be telling them how much we love them—daily.

3. High school:

During the high school phase, showing them our love becomes not calling their name out loud across the school quad to yell good-bye. Or not sending that big valentine card to our son at school—those are only supposed to come from girlfriends at this point. We can show them our love by not pushing them into extracurricular activities that only we want them to do, but by supporting them in the activities they are interested in. We show them love by giving them a little respectful space as they get ready to leave our nest. We can give them boundaries but also begin to give them freedoms. However, showing our love still always needs to include telling them how much we love them—daily. It is also about expecting them to say it back, no matter how many of their teenage friends are around them—we deserve it.

Regardless of which phase your kids are in, always actively take part in each stage as they progress. Do not wait. Be present. Every older mom will tell us how quickly the time with our kids goes. Before we know it, that little boy who needed us so desperately in the middle of the night is now a seriously accomplished athlete—a four-year letterman in two varsity sports who is going off to play football in college. It seems like just a few months ago he was asking me to play Legos with him.

Love them now.

The Hardest Moments Are the Most Important Ones

> "You are driving me crazy!"
> —me to Courtney (age 4)
> "What does driving you crazy mean?"
> —Courtney (age 4), after a pause

Parenting is not for the faint of heart. On a daily basis, children will test us and our patience time and time again. We try to focus on making the most of the days we have with our children and look for our chances for sweet memories. At the same time, we also experience some of the hardest times with our children. We experience their growing up.

The problems we encounter as parents are also incredibly inconvenient and become even more so as our children grow older. We are not at liberty to choose our battles—we can't just skip a problem because it sounds too difficult right now and we have dinner to get on the table and a business presentation tomorrow.

No, problems have an annoying persistence about them. They just show up when they want to—usually late at night—and give us whatever grief they choose to. It would be easier and less time-consuming to back down than to deal with them. However, that is when our kids need us the most—when it is hard and inconvenient. That is what parenting is really all about.

Our most important parenting moments are actually when we most want to pull our hair out and yell in frustration. They are when we most need our patience, skills, and focus to help resolve the problem. Throwing our hands around in the air and raising our voices and yelling is easier, but it gets us nowhere. While we might let go of some steam, we learn the hard way that our yelling is pretty ineffective. When we raise our voices, our children shut down. They get caught up thinking about how upset we are with them or possibly how upset they are with themselves. We actually lose them, and their attention for fixing the problem.

Not only is parenting in the toughest moments important, but remembering to parent in the good times as well. Sometimes if all is going well, we forget to appreciate how our children are doing. Looking for chances to give them positive reinforcement is important in building their confidence in themselves.

According to a recent article from Purdue University's School of Consumer and Family Sciences, it's important to take time to notice when our children are behaving well. This positive reinforcement helps our children learn what they can do well. Not only do children appreciate this attention, it makes them want to repeat the positive behavior. The article suggests that we be very specific; tell the child exactly what behavior, actions, and words we liked. We also need to try to find ways to use rewards and praise regularly.[15]

A few deep breaths, a level voice, and maybe a glass of wine—for us, not the kids—actually work much better than raising our voice. There are times of extreme frustration, when even walking away to discuss an issue later is the best option. Sometimes it is better to walk away than to say something we regret that can never be taken back. Later we can talk about what happened and what could be done differently next time. Later should not mean a week later, but waiting a few hours or until the next day can sometimes give us the perspective to help us be sure we are thinking like an adult, not just an extremely frustrated parent.

Setting Boundaries Early: Out and About with Kids

> "When I was wittle, I was a twoublemakew!"
> —Elle (age 5)

We have so many mom-challenging moments with our kids, and setting boundaries starts early—think even the day they take their first step. Let the boundaries begin!

We can lock up every cabinet door, cover every electrical outlet, and put a gate at the top and bottom of every set of stairs, but little toddlers are like water searching for a place to seep into: if there is a hole, they will find it.

We have to steel ourselves for the toddler years and know that the boundaries we begin to set here will help us—or hurt us—for years to come. Children are smarter than we give them credit for. It is easy to discount them because they are so much shorter than us and not very intimidating, but we cannot let those adorable little faces fool us.

One of the early boundaries we set is around behavior when we are out and about with them. While it would be easier to kid-proof the house and keep them inside, that is not reality. How about those grocery-store trips with a bunch of kids in tow? Always interesting. When we witness another mom juggling her kids and shopping, we get a glimpse of what we look like when we are carting along our crew. It's not always pretty.

> "When piwates burp, they don't have to say excuse me."
> —Elle (age 4)

However, when we are willing to go through the pain and public embarrassment early on of continually requiring our kids to behave well, eventually they will toe the line. As Carolyn Williams writes in her article "The Importance of Giving Children Boundaries," "Setting boundaries is critical to forming a respectful, well-adjusted child. In addition, basic boundaries enforce safety for your child. An older child needs specific boundaries around getting homework done on time and being respectful. An adolescent needs specific boundaries that clarify your family's values. All of these boundaries share the common goal of keeping your child safe given outside influences. With clear boundaries, your child knows precisely what is expected."[16]

Set a standard and then demand that they stand by it. They do not realize it, but boundaries are a form of love. We care enough to teach them how to act responsibly in different situations. "No, do not touch the glass on the shelves in the store." "No, do not take the toy and play with it on the floor." "No, do not run around and terrorize the other people shopping here."

We have to work through plenty of embarrassing public moments with crying or screaming children—a baby on our hip, a toddler holding our hand, and two more lurking in the shadows—as we determinedly explain to our children how they have to behave.

For my husband and I, we did not stay seated in the restaurant enjoying our dinner while our whining toddler annoyed all the other restaurant guests, we did not leisurely stroll through the store while our child created havoc, and we did not leave the fast-food restaurant until our kids had cleaned up every last straw paper they blew across the table. But we survived it, and so did our children. And so can each of us. Many store owners have even gone so far as to come up to me and thank me for how well behaved my children are. My children are not mice or statues; people know they are there. But they follow the standards we have set for how they must behave and they respect the people and businesses we frequent.

Setting Boundaries beyond "Black and White": Elementary and Middle School

> "I don't eat fast to get to go play on the computer.
> I always eat at my normal speed limit."
> —Elle (age 7)

Many say that the character and value groundwork we lay with our children is pretty much set by the time they are around age ten. If that is true, then the love we give them and the boundaries we build around them in these years are *critical*.

We can and need to love our children unconditionally—and with standards and without ulterior motives for them. In their elementary and middle school years, my husband and I teach our children to be good, kind, and respectful. We expect them to be coachable and learning based. We are raising them to give everything they do their best effort and to try hard. We expect them to give to those less fortunate.

When our children are young, everything is black and white: yes, you can do this, or no, you cannot. Plain and simple. Yes or no. As we lay this values groundwork with our children and they grow older, they begin passing beyond these "black-and-white years."

In their preteen years, our children begin to realize that the world really is not black and white. It is gray. There is not always a yes or no answer. Sometimes there are many answers to a problem, which complicates the solution process—which answer is the right one? Their problems evolve into:

- "What do I do when Tommy is cheating and copying my math work at our table?"

- "My teacher is making us *all* walk at recess for getting in trouble, but I did not do anything wrong!"

- "Why did Sarah invite all the other girls in our class to her birthday party except me?"

- "My teacher hates me! She always gives good grades to my friends but not to me!"

From the parenting side, our issues with our children also evolve. They become:

- Our child's teacher e-mails us to tell us that our child is failing his class—and we did not know about it.

- Our daughter tells us she finished all her homework so she could play, but then we find her with her light on late after bedtime trying to finish it in bed.

- We tell them they cannot be on any electronics after 9:00 p.m., but then we find them late at night sneaking to play on the Xbox.

These are small problems compared with what we will face later, but correcting small issues in these years lays a solid foundation to build on. When we find our children disrespecting or disobeying rules now, we have to adjust the privileges they currently enjoy, or we will all pay the price in the upcoming years.

An even bigger developing issue can arise when children disrespect the rules in relation to themselves. At this point in their development, we can begin to explain to them that it is *their life, their future, and their opportunities* that are in jeopardy—not ours. In their late-elementary and middle school years, our kids start to understand that they are separate from us. This process can be fostered, not fought. It is an awesome opportunity to empower them by helping them walk through their own problem solving. When they believe in their abilities to take care of themselves and their lives, they begin to believe in themselves and build needed self-confidence.

In these years, we want to stay plugged in closely with our children: ask them regularly about what is going on in their lives, and listen carefully to their answers; give them guidance to find the solutions that work for them in the environments they are in. We discuss with them their problem-solving evolution from black-and-white solutions to gray ones.

As parents, we are in the problem-solving business. As people and as adults, we are in the problem-solving business. Our children are in the problem-solving business, too. While their issues may seem to pale in comparison with our adult responsibilities, it is all relative. Their issues are big to them. Our job is to help them learn how to seek and find the answers they need as they work toward solutions.

> "Wow, it is a beautiful day outside!"
> —me
>
> "Oh no. I don't like the sound of that."
> —Courtney (age 11)
>
> "Why?"
> —me
>
> "Beacause you are going to make us go play outside."
> —Courtney (age 11)

Surviving the Teenage Years: When They Need Us the Most

> "I heard you, Mom. I just wasn't paying any attention to you."
> —Courtney (age 15)

Well, we know that we survived our own teenage years, so surely we can survive them with our kids. Right? In my family, our approach to getting ready for those years might be a bit different from most people's. My husband and I start talking with our children around fourth or fifth grade—age nine or ten—about the years that are coming up around the corner. We want to prepare them, to set some ideas out ahead of time so they better know what to expect. Our life experience so far supports that when people know what to expect, they can handle difficult situations better. If we treat our children like they are older than their ages, most often we find that their behavior rises to the level of our belief in them.

Parenting makes us vulnerable—we love our family deeply, and we take on their pain or disappointments. When one of our children is hurting or dealing with a failure, it hurts us just as much or more. It would be easier on us to solve their problems and be done with it. Unfortunately, that teaches them nothing. That is a short-term solution that becomes a long-term handicap.

According to a 2011 BBC article, "Boundary setting is not about controlling our kids, it's about helping them learn how to stay within certain limits and not stray outside for their own safety. Following the crowd is not always the right option and hopefully through firm, loving parenting we can help our children make positive choices for themselves."[17]

At this point, we also help our children get a bigger-picture view of their lives than they might have. Middle school and high school are a bubble in the early years of life—only seven short years, and they are gone forever. Yes, college might come after that, but college can be a very different experience, with greater flexibility to have more friends and to move around. In middle and high school, kids are in a microcosm with usually one cafeteria, one "popular" crowd, and one homecoming queen. When teens are stuck in the middle of that, day in and day out, it is easy for their views to become distorted and out of sync with their perception of the rest of their lives. When they go on to college and beyond, whether or not they were the homecoming queen will fade into the background. What will matter is their self-confidence in who they can become.

Ways to Guide Young Adults

There are so many ways to help our children through these few formative years and to sustain and build their self-confidence. Here are six ways:

1. Give them an honest, real, hormone-infused understanding of these years.

Everyone is growing and going through puberty. Their friends and peers are going to start going through some physical and chemical changes in their bodies that can heavily impact the way they act. Kids' emotions are a roller-coaster ride of highs and lows, which absolutely impacts how they behave. Often the behavior can be negative or hurtful. Guide them early to choose good friends. A few good friends who will really like them for who they are and stand by their side no matter what are worth more than a hundred "popular" acquaintances.

2. Be their friend when their school friends are not.

We are a backup for our children, someone they can fall back on when other people are not there for them. Sometimes their friends do not support them, or make choices our children do not want to make. We can be there as a shoulder to lean on, someone to go have an ice cream with or go to the movies with. Not only is this a responsibility, it is also a great opportunity to build our relationships with our children. Plus, it is fun! Our kids are pretty fun to hang out with.

3. Keep them involved in extracurricular activities that are good for their physical and mental health.

Support them in these activities for all the learning opportunities outside of the classroom: lessons around teamwork, sacrifice, discipline, failure, integrity, goal setting, and success.

4. Help them see how solid grades can impact their future.

Take them to visit a college they really want to attend. Take them to meet an admissions counselor there to find out what it takes to be admitted to that college. Give them a real vision of what it would be like to go to school there. It makes striving for a good grade in chemistry more meaningful.

5. Have family dinners every week.

Have as many family dinners a week as you can manage, and connect everyone together. Whoever the family is comprised of—single mom, grandparents at home, stepparents, and so on—that *is* the child's family. Having that group around them in these years creates a safe zone for them.

6. Have the hard conversations.

I have had to have many tough conversations and arguments with my kids. It's difficult and often heart wrenching for me to argue with them or to speak sternly and firmly to get a point across. But teenage years are not for the meek. Teens may fight back, but they are also testing us. They are testing us to see if we care enough to push back. Because in the unspoken parent-to-kid language, pushing back and setting boundaries shows them that we do really care. That they are important enough to us that we will fight *for* them. That we will fight for who we think they can *become,* for their future, for their possibilities. Because young-adult children know that if their mom— and dad—love them and believe in who they are, then they must be pretty special. They will carry that in their hearts for the rest of their life.

Embrace Your Own Beauty and Be Who You Are

The world can be tough and it is our job as parents to prepare our children to handle life with all its joy and challenges. Teach them love and respect, consideration and compassion, discipline and tenacity. Teach them that it's OK to fail and how to learn from their failures to grow and improve. Teach them that they don't have to be friends with people that mistreat them and that it is so important to just "Be Who You Are." Embrace your own beauty and your differences and learn to love unconditionally. What a beautiful gift my mom gave to me when she taught me that.

As moms we need to stick together. We are all so desperately trying to be the best moms that we can be. We all want beautiful, happy, healthy children. No judgment...only love and support.

Kim Estes

Mother of two

Team Leader and Managing Broker, Keller Williams Realty Atlanta Partners

kimestes@kw.com

Communicate, Communicate, Communicate...and Communicate Again

"We have presents for you, but I'm not supposed
to tell you because it is a secret!"
—Courtney (age 3) to Parker (age 5)

Teaching our children how to be good communicators is one of the most important life and love skills we can help them with. We might imagine that loving our families is mostly about sweet hugs and shared laughter. Often the reality is that loving our families is a fair amount of working through problems and teaching our children how to do the same. So many problems in both our personal and our professional lives come from poor communication.

Our relationships with people are one of the critical components of our happiness in life. No matter what our age is, good communication skills are the glue that holds our relationships together. Communication skills help our children navigate through the challenges they will undoubtedly face. Teaching our children how to communicate with different types of people, in good times and in bad, will give them a skill set they will use every day of their lives.

What Are Good Communication Skills?

1. Listening

Really listening to the other person to understand what they are trying to share includes listening without any distractions. Put away the cell phone and look the other person in the eyes. It is focus and attention.

2. Body language and tonality

We can completely change the message we are relaying through our body language or the tone we speak in. All moms of teenagers know what it feels like when, as we speak to them, they stand with their arms crossed and roll their eyes—very aggravating. We also know that words spoken in a harsh, versus an empathetic, tone can easily be misunderstood.

3. Repeating back what you think you heard for clarification

Sometimes it helps to repeat back what you think you heard. This conveys to the other party your sincerity in understanding their message. It also helps you be sure that *you* are clear on what *they* want you to hear.

4. Empathizing with the other person's perspective

Often in communication, the other person just wants to be understood. It may be that you both disagree on something, but if the other person knows that you at least respect his or her perspective, that often settles the situation. If you cannot come to an agreement on an issue, sometimes politely agreeing to disagree can be a way to still protect the relationship.

Helping our children learn how to be strong communicators is a huge gift to them. We have to learn how to talk with each other when feelings are hurt or issues arise. Do not give up on this important parenting piece. We are also building the foundation for our future relationships with our children. We do not want our relationships with them to end when they are no longer under our roof. We are building relationships to last a lifetime.

More Communication Tips for Problem Solving

1. Two-way conversations find better solutions.

So how do we work through problems with our children to come up with solutions? More often than not, if we are doing all the talking, they are doing all the daydreaming. A two-way conversation is more effective, with both parties respectfully listening to understand the issue. Then we can guide our children to come up with a solution. How? Ask them a lot of questions. When they come up with the solution, then it is brilliant. If we come up with it, then we are just talking to ourselves—which is often not very effective.

2. Discuss the better solutions so they know the best options for next time.

Once we get to the solution on the other side of an issue, we can make a point of talking with our kids about what happened. We need to walk through what went wrong and how they could handle it better next time, to take the few extra minutes to teach them as they go, or they will have to repeat these mistakes and lessons over and over. Someone called that the definition of insanity. Being a mom pushes us close to that edge, but we do not *have to* jump over it.

3. It is more work later if you do not walk through it today.

Some parents choose to just say no instead of going through this process. It can be arduous to walk children through a mistake, through their decision process, through all the ways they might have handled it, then finally to the place of remembering the lesson for next time. My husband and I decided long ago that we would not be just "no because we said no" parents. There are some things that are not discussed— they are just the rules. Other issues we know our stand on, but we will try to let the kids navigate toward our answer so they learn the process. Taking the time to teach them these decision processes now will help us all in the upcoming years. Our children learn from their mistakes and how to work through them to better understand how to make good decisions later. We will not avoid problems later, but we will walk down a smoother road with them.

4. Our guidance is their lifeline.

As frustrating as our children's issues can be in the preteen years, the high school issues that follow can be harder. We need to make sure our children know going into those years that we are all on the same team. As challenging as parenting can be in these years, our efforts are the most worthwhile: we are demonstrating to our children that when life is tough, we will be there for them. They will define "tough" differently at every stage. What needs to be consistent is our guidance and help in their problem solving. Guiding them to work through these challenges now builds a relationship strong enough to get us through some of the major life decisions they will face in the upcoming years.

As our children grow, the going definitely gets tough. And when the going gets tough, we cannot back down or back away. Although our children might push all of our buttons, we cannot give up on them. In the moments we share with them, especially in the hardest moments, our parenting relationship really matters. We matter...we are the world to them.

It might sound strange, but memories are made here as well. They are not the flowery, life-is-great moments, but these gritty how-to-handle-tough-times moments make an impression on our older children. Not only are we teaching them a skill that will help our life long relationship with them, the ability to communicate well will also help them build every relationship they have along their own journey.

Loving Our Family: Easy, Creative, Thoughtful Traditions That Connect Us

> "Mimi, be sure you keep the toilet lids
> closed so Yaya does not fall in."
> —me, talking to the four-year-old about the two-year-old
> "Yeah, no Yaya bye-bye."
> —Mimi (age 4)

The teenage years might be challenging at times, but they can also be full of great fun and memories. We can enjoy our children as young adults, sharing with them, laughing with them, and learning with or from them. It's so much easier to understand iTunes when we have a teenager in the house! *When* we have a teenager in the house. That only lasts for a few short years. In this limited time with our children under our roof, we can make so many memories with fun and creative traditions that connect us. The key is to be simple, silly, and consistent.

Life is hectic. Our efforts for our children do not need to be done at the Martha Stewart level to be memorable or make an impact. Some moms have the time and inclination to take their thoughtful ideas to that level, and that is great. If, however, your choice is either to do something simple or nothing at all, go for simple.

Remember KISS: Keep it Simple, Silly. We can all complicate life—that is easy. We need to keep our efforts simple but high on the impact scale. So do not be deceived by the ease of the ideas I will share below; they are easy on purpose.

Since the day-to-day care of our children is expected, it does not have the impact that these ideas have. Day-to-day care is like having a roof over your head: necessary but not exciting. Laundry is necessary, unfortunately, but not fun or exciting. Being sure the milk has not expired in the refrigerator is necessary but not fun or exciting.

On the other hand, little surprise treats or notes in a snack bag—that makes children smile. Surprising them with a date to have a frozen yogurt *is* fun and exciting. Any opportunity we take to make them feel special and loved builds to a lifetime of payouts. So here are some ideas. Use these or create your own and put them on the calendar for this year.

Lunchbox and Locker Surprises

> "Mom, why haven't you put any notes in my lunch box yet?"
> —Elle (age 7) second day of school

For the little ones, put a small surprise in their lunch box or snack bag four or five times each school year. Nothing crazy—just enough that they know they are never far from your thoughts. It can be a note on their napkin, a small special yummy, or a goofy card from the store. Look for little-kid cards with special sayings to encourage them on a school project, remind them to be a good friend, or support their good decisions—anything to remind them you are thinking about them.

Once the kids are in middle school, we have six years of locker fun and thousands of options—dollar-store treasures, a bag of homemade brownies, a funny magnet they can use to hold up notes, their favorite cookies, a magnetic photo frame with a fun picture in it, silly decorations, or a couple of dollars for a treat that afternoon. Decorate the outside of their locker for their birthdays. The key is always doing it early, around a week before their real birthday. Tape some fun wrapping paper to the outside and put bows on it. Then put their favorite treat(s) and a card on the inside—inexpensive, easy to do, and a great reminder of how special they are to you.

Different and unusual little surprises a couple times a year are a great reminder to older children that they are loved. My favorites for teenagers are random: silly squishy skeletons at Halloween, Peeps marshmallows for every holiday, and Darth Vader bobbleheads.

Birthdays: Simple, Consistent, and Secret

This one is very important. This is the day each year that we celebrate our children's birth; we celebrate that they are in our lives. Thankfully, the Internet has so much information online about celebrating amazing, themed, over-the-top parties that I will keep this discussion simple.

My secret? It is so obvious, but it was learned the hard way: schedule the celebration before the actual birthday so they don't think you've forgotten and may even be surprised.

Also, have an easy celebration on the actual birthday: make them their favorite dinner and their favorite cake just for the family. We also have a cake for the party guests, but this cake is just for us. Somehow their birthdays seem to last a week or longer as we go from decorating around the house, to their "early" parties, to school cookies or ice cream with their friends, and finally to their actual family birthday dinners. They *must be* loved—we celebrate them each year with over a week of little events!

Somewhere around age sixteen, typically the planned, themed birthday parties stop. So know that we only really have about twelve to fifteen birthdays we can put together for them. That's it. When we are in the middle of it, it feels overwhelming. Then we look up, and fifteen years have passed and we're planning one of their last kid parties. No more birthday goody bags, no more silly invitations or Power Ranger decorations.

Enjoy each one.

Creative Connections: Making Traditions Special

We have most of the usual celebrating around holidays. What our kids will remember are the silly traditions we started for several of the lesser holidays. They are our silly twists on the usual traditions. One of my favorite little mom books I found early on was *Little Things Long Remembered—Making Your Children Feel Special Every Day*, by Susan Newman. Some of the following unique ideas have come from it.

Valentine's Day: Favorite Treat Trails

On Valentine's Day, we do the usual valentine exchanges for school. At home, I add "treat trails" for our family. The kids wait together in one of their rooms, with the little ones giggling and the big ones kind of agreeably going along with it. My husband and I make four separate trails—one for each child—using four differently wrapped candies and picking a "favorite" one for each child. Each candy trail weaves a haphazard path from the bedroom door, across the hallways, over "obstacles," down the stairs, around the corner, and up to the child's seat at the kitchen table. Waiting for them there is a small goody bag filled with small Valentine's Day "treasures." Their forever-playful dad likes to eat some of the candies along the trail, leaving just the crumpled wrappers. They all come out of the room in a rush, scooping up the candies and chasing down Dad so he does not eat them all. They end up with a bag full of their favorite candy by the time they get to the kitchen and then look to see what treasures are in their goody bags on the table.

Saint Patrick's Day: Our Family's Leprechaun

> "You know what you would find in your pot
> at the end of your rainbow, Mom?
> A pot of me!"
> —Elle (age 8)

For Saint Patrick's Day, we go green! I put out silly decorations. We celebrate with green food all day long. We have Lucky Charms cereal and green pancakes for breakfast. I put something green in their lunch or snack bag: green snacks, green Peeps, green grapes!

We also have a family "leprechaun" who visits the house in the middle of the night on March 16 to cause some trouble. He leaves gold coins around their rooms so they know he was there. He visits their bathrooms to use their potties and turns the water green. They wake up and run into the bathroom to check their toilets.

After they have checked out their bathrooms for evidence on Saint Patrick's Day morning, they have a "pot of gold at the end of the rainbow" waiting at the kitchen table. It is filled with green trinkets: green sticky hands, green light-up necklaces, green Tic Tacs, green buttons, green light-up rings, green Irish soap bars for the teenagers, green Saint Pat's Day pencils—you name it; if it is green, it works.

Then we have a completely green dinner: salad, broccoli, green beans, green Gatorade, peas, green Jell-O, spinach noodles with parmesan cheese, et cetera. I have considered adding some of our "green" bread rolls—green because they have expired—but I have not done that one yet.

Easter Egg Hunts in Their Rooms

Easter is another big holiday for us, with all the usual events and fun. Our twist on this is an Easter egg hunt—in their rooms. When they were little, we went to all the Easter events and big egg hunts and also had our own egg hunt in the backyard. They wanted to hide the eggs and search for them—over and over and over. As the big kids grew up and started to get tired of that, we changed it up. Now we fill a dozen plastic eggs for each of them with goodies that each child really likes, ranging from candy to little toys to dollar bills for the teenagers. My husband and I hide their eggs—only in their rooms. We hide them with varying degrees of difficulty based on the child's age.

Believe it or not, even our oldest has a couple of eggs in his room that he has not yet found. Often the big kids find one or two of their plastic eggs the following season, maybe in a pocket of their favorite sweatshirt, which they hadn't worn since the winter before. I think we might find more humor in this tradition than our son does—we know of one egg that he probably will not discover until the candy in it is petrified and he moves out after college. Or maybe after that.

Fourth of July Toes

This one is pretty easy, since this holiday offers so many options to celebrate the country. We decorate with our flags and banners, we eat yummy food, and we bake a Fourth of July cake with strawberries and blueberries in the shape of a flag on top. Our special twist is our "Fourth of July toes." The week before the holiday, the girls and I all go get our toenails painted in Fourth of July colors. Everyone chooses their own mix of red, white, and blue. They paint flags, stars and stripes, or fireworks. Then, I take a photo of all forty (!) of our toes. We wear light-up necklaces and bracelets to brighten up the night as the sun sets and the fireworks begin.

Halloween: Pictures and Pumpkins Everywhere

You know how hard it is to remember all the kids' costumes from year to year? So I have their Halloween night photos—all the kids together—from our first child's first Halloween and every Halloween after that. I have all the black-framed photos out on the kitchen counters only during October. I love showing off the teenagers' cute little baby costumes to their friends when they come to visit.

There is nothing simple about our Halloween traditions. We decorate all over the house with light-up pumpkins, small ceramic ghosts, fiber-optic pumpkins, noise-making rocks that say "stay away," and skeletons that dance to the music. Outside we put up orange lights in the trees, big spiderwebs, and more funny pumpkin decor.

Right before Halloween, we add light-up bats, huge spiderwebs, silly Halloween decorations hanging from the trees, and even a cauldron by the front door that we put dry ice in on Halloween night. We play creepy Halloween music so our guests hear it as they approach to get their candy treats. Our Halloween fun is *BOOtiful* and definitely memorable.

Christmas

> "Mama, you need to call Santa Claus.
> He forgot to give me my little green Power Ranger."
> —Parker (age 4)

It goes without saying that Christmas is a very special time in our home. Our Christmas holidays have the comfort of repeating our traditions year after year. For us, it is about family time and reconnecting after a hectic fall. We spread our holiday activities across the month of December so it is not all crammed into a short period of time. We enjoy playing games, especially our family favorite, Risk.

We have been making gingerbread houses every holiday for years now. I used to actually bake the walls of the house myself. Crazy. Those days are long gone, and thankfully we can buy the gingerbread house kits everywhere now. In all the years of making them, the one that the kids remember the most is the gingerbread house that fell over literally five minutes after we finished it.

We make our favorite sugar cookies each year, which actually are made in three steps over a weekend. The dough has to chill for a while, then we bake dozens of the cookies. The next day it takes us a few hours to set up, make all our icings, beautify our cookies, and then clean up the huge mess. It does not take so long because we decorate them perfectly; rather, it takes time because we are very creative in our decorating. Our cookies are deliciously worth it.

Our only tradition that might be different from most is that we eat Christmas dinner on Christmas Eve. Since cooking is not my favorite thing, I moved the big dinner to the day before. That way, instead of spending my Christmas day in the kitchen, I get to spend it in the family room with everyone enjoying their gifts and the time together. We eat a special "overnight French toast" on Christmas morning, then snack on our delicious leftovers the rest of the day. It makes Christmas day so much more fun and relaxing for me.

We have a new Christmas Eve tradition: we do a white elephant gift exchange. Each person brings a wrapped gift that has to be ten dollars or less in value. The stranger the gift, the better. Last year one of the gifts was a frog hat. It was so popular that we ordered one for everyone in the family, then wore them on roller-coaster rides at Disney this year. Crazy, silly, and never-to-be-forgotten memories.

Loving Our Spouse

While this book is focused on motherhood and ideas about parenting children, our relationship with our spouse or significant other is a factor that impacts us all on many levels. So, in the choices we make, giving attention to maintaining and building our relationship with that person has to be at the top of the list, or the relationship will not last. It is not easy to find the time to focus on so many things, but this is one of the most important.

No Matter What We Are Serving, Our Table Is Always "Beautifully" Set

When my Grandma Seibel lived on the farm in the middle of Hillsboro, Kansas, it was not unusual for friends and family to just drop in for a "visit." When they did, it was expected that there would be some type of refreshment. Yet there would be times when she had nothing to serve.

The first thing she would always do was set the table with her prettiest dishes. No matter what food she had to share, she would set the table as if something wonderful was being served! One time all she had to serve was bread. So she toasted it, buttered it, and served it with tea. Her guests raved about the treat and about her beautifully set table.

This has become a treasured tradition for our family. Over the years, each and every night I set the table—sometimes with our children's favorite character plates, sometimes with just regular dishes, or on birthdays with special party plates. No matter what I am serving, the table is always set. This creates a wonderful anticipation in our home for dinnertime, sitting around the table and sharing our meal, be it macaroni and cheese with chicken nuggets, a casserole, or the occasional steak! This beloved family tradition has created a welcoming environment in which we bond with our children, hear about what is going on in their lives, and stay close as a family.

Nikki Bonds
Mother of three
Realtor, Keller Williams Realty Atlanta Partners
www.teambonds.com
nikkibonds@kw.com

One of the ways I give my husband attentive focus is to imagine that we are still dating. I am not always good at it, but I try to be. We all act so differently during the dating phase of a relationship. We talk to each other differently, take care of ourselves differently, and think about each other differently. My husband and I go out on regular dates; we spend time together almost every Friday night at home; and at least once a month, we go out to dinner alone. Some couples do more than that.

What is critical to building this love relationship? Communicate, communicate, communicate. Give each other attention. Listen. Turn the cell phone off for a few hours and just focus on each other. Unless you are an emergency doctor, you do not need to take that phone call during your hanging-out or date time. Talk with each other. Do not let molehills become mountains. So much is going on in our lives that it is often easier to try to push aside differences or anger over situations. But those feelings do not go away; they just simmer under the surface until one day they explode.

With over 70 percent of mothers working (according to the US Bureau of Labor Statistics, 2011), your relationship with your spouse can be more than just a significant support. In a parenting partnership, both spouses can contribute to managing the household and helping get the kids where they need to be. They can pack a lunch box or help with the dishes or attend that school program when we just cannot be there due to work responsibilities. Ask them to help you. Unlike some of the generations that preceded us, the modern dad is helping the family outside of work with the household and the children. Our family is like a team—when we all pitch in, we all can win.

Carefully sewn, it is with the big moments and the little moments, the tiny threads of togetherness and thoughtfulness, that we can weave a strong blanket around the relationship that will keep us both warm, comforted, and confident.

How Do We Love and Take Care of Ourselves?

As moms, we do so many things for others: special care and yummy soup when kids are sick, a birthday carefully planned out, a T-shirt washed to be sure it's ready the next day for school, home-baked brownies, special dates to the movies, and more. We fill and fill and fill and fill. It is easy in the middle of that to lose ourselves. It can be disheartening and discouraging if we spend all of our time filling the buckets of others.

The Importance of Modeling Self-Love

Loving ourselves is one of the most important things we can do as mothers, for it's the way our children learn to love themselves, too. Though it's important for parents to *teach* self-love, research shows it's *modeling* self-love that really counts. As working mothers, we can tend to be extra hard on ourselves, trying to achieve perfection in our careers and with our family.

Many of us never feel like we can take a "break" or let down our guard, always trying to prove (to ourselves) that we're good enough. Well, let me just help us cut to the chase: We *are* good enough. We are worthy of love, and not just from our children, spouse, partner, or friends. We are worthy of love from *ourselves*. If we can stop seeking to do *everything* and start asking, "What is the loving thing to do for myself and my family?" we will find the answer shining bright and clear. The loving thing for *everyone* is to love ourselves.

Christina G. Hibbert, PsyD
Mother of six
Clinical Psychologist
www.drchristinahibbert.com
@DrCHibbert / facebook.com/drchibbert
Christina@drchristinahibbert.com

To do a good job helping others, we must also be conscious of helping ourselves. This might go against our mothering inclinations, but when we are completely spent ourselves, we have nothing left to give. When we feel good about ourselves, when we feel appreciated for what we do, when we feel loved for our efforts and care, it fills our lives with happiness, satisfaction, and joy. We are energized and ready to tackle whatever comes our way.

Sometimes with little ones, we have to actually seek that love from them. We have to teach them to show their love to us. When we tell them we love them, we remind them to tell us back—if they do not. When they are coloring, it is OK to ask them to make us a special note. When Mother's Day is coming, it is good to remind them that we like flowers. We do not have to be martyrs in the mom role. When everyone in the family feels loved and appreciated, then the world falls into place. That is our foundation that we each build upon as well. Love our family, and soak in the love that comes back to us.

We can also rejuvenate by choosing a few, simple things to do to love ourselves along the way. We cannot wait for others to do it for us; we can and need to do it for ourselves. There are many inexpensive, quick fixes that will repair our broken systems, whether they be morning meditations, lunches with friends, Bunko nights with other working moms, or a gratitude journal.

What are you building into your week, your month, your year that energizes you and helps you feel your best?

Loving Yourself...

There are many ways you might love yourself:

- Have an early-morning coffee with a friend right after you drop the kids off at school and before you go to work.

- Indulge in a cupcake from a special bakery.

- Work out to work off that yummy cupcake.

- Get a manicure or pedicure, or both!

- Sit outside on a beautiful day, alone, to hear the birds and enjoy a book or magazine.

- Write in a journal about what made you happy today.

- Call a dear friend to lean on her and ask her to tell you why you are special.

- Plant some brightly colored flowers.

- Go for a hike.

- As you tuck in your sweet little child, ask her to tell you why she loves you so much.

- Have an "early-to-bed Wednesday." It might be hard to get enough sleep every night, but maybe you plan on going to bed early every Wednesday night. It is in the middle of the week and can get you through until you get more sleep again on the weekends.

- Take that art class you have wanted to take.

- Enjoy a ladies' night out with some good friends.

- Watch a glorious, pink-filled-sky sunset at the beach.

- Rent a movie and enjoy your favorite treat with it.

- Cool off with your favorite iced tea on the front porch.

- Do something for another mom who is struggling. Filling her bucket can fill yours, too.

- Read a book about why moms are so wonderful and so important.

Be Kind to Yourself!

Be kind to yourself—it's important to leave your judgments at the door. Developing deeper self-awareness will help you recognize when you are being overly critical of yourself. Harsh criticism only causes more stress. If you feel like you are disappointed, frustrated, or upset with yourself, take time to be still and view it as an opportunity to reflect and make any necessary changes. It could be something as small as getting more rest or trying not to please everyone.

When we are mindful of our thoughts, emotions, and feelings, we can learn a great deal, especially from the "negative" ones. Instead of pushing them away, invite them in and be curious about what it is they're trying to show us. In order to get where we want to be tomorrow, we first have to keep in touch with ourselves, today, in this moment.

Kristin Ervin
Mother of four
Owner and Facilitator, *Got Mindfulness?*
www.gotmindfulness.com
kristinervin@gmail.com

We must take responsibility for filling our own buckets, too. Loving our family is obvious. Loving ourselves might not come to the forefront of our heads, but it should. We cannot feel guilty about taking care of ourselves as well—we need it. Our children need to be loved, and so do we. When we are in alignment, then we are the best at everything we do. Then we are the best woman, friend, businessperson/employee, wife/partner, volunteer, and mom that we can be.

Three Ways to Overcome Frustration with Time

It is too easy to lose ourselves in our efforts to help our children find themselves. How can we find time for ourselves?

1. Remember, there are different periods with children.

At different peaks of our motherhood responsibilities, it takes more to mother them. When they are young and need our help physically or when they are teenagers and possibly need us more mentally, we need to be more present. If we are pushing ourselves more during those times, maybe taking on a large project at work during those years, or building a new company, somewhere something will have to give. If we hope to learn how to play tennis by taking lessons a few times a week during that time, we will probably have to let go of something else.

2. There are only twenty-four hours in a day.

No matter who we are or how we slice it, time is of the essence. We can take better care of ourselves by recognizing the shifts in our children's need for us and accommodating for that in what we expect to be able to do in our lives. We *can* build a new business, we *can* take weekly art lessons, and we *can* be the project manager when helping our company secure a large new client. But we will have to let go of something else during that period. Or we will have to hire help to take care of other parts of our lives so we can manage and succeed with our professional or personal goals.

3. Have a realistic, long-term view of your life with your children at home.

Within that realistic view, plan what you want to accomplish accordingly. Part of the stress of life and motherhood is expecting more out of our twenty-four hours than is physically possible to complete. So much stress is self-inflicted. What can you let go of, especially during those peak years, to also care for yourself?

These are very personal choices. For me, on the work side of life, we had babysitters, day care, preschool, then part-time nannies (when we had four children) so that I could still work and juggle the kids around it.

Every year the mix changed a bit as I let go of some of my professional objectives so I could be more present in the peak before-school years. We worked harder (and smarter) to be able to afford extra part-time help. Once the children were all in school (when the youngest started kindergarten), then we backed down to occasional babysitters. Some moms will choose to not work at all outside of the home during those before-school years. Both answers are right—we just each have to choose.

In her book *Mommy Guilt*, Devra Renner writes, "Indeed the temperament of a household is strongly influenced by the emotions and attitude of the mother. When a mother is happy, the whole family is happier." So by focusing some love on ourselves and recharging our batteries, we can feel better and be better moms and people.

Understand that we can each make the choices in order to find more peace along our mom journey. More peace with our life equals much better care of ourselves. Stress from an overpacked schedule hurts everyone in the family. Children do not have to be in five activities at once to have a fulfilled childhood. Fight for simple so you can still find the time to enjoy the sweet moments in life to cuddle with a child, go for a walk, sit and talk with your spouse, exercise, call a sick friend, and love yourself so you can also love others.

Loving Our Family—and Being Loved in Return

> "My tummy says to go potty in your car.
> But don't worry, I wuv you, so I won't."
> —Elle (age 3)

Our little children have an attachment to us that makes superglue seem like water. No one in the world wants to be with us or play with us more than our young children do. In their minds, we are simply THE BEST. EVER. The adoration they can bestow on us can melt our hearts and empty our wallets.

At the other end of the spectrum, they also have their very serious moments. Sometimes they go from adoring to argumentative in a matter of minutes. Like the day one of my daughters went to the bathroom on the floor where she was hiding in the cabinet shop and refused to tell me the truth about where the puddle came from. I apologized to the shop owner as I marched my daughter out of the building.

"Me Time" Appointments

As a busy mom, one thing I cherish is my health! I make "me time" appointments almost every day to make sure I stay healthy and fit! I know this will help me be a fun grandmother in the future! Taking the time to care for myself allows me to share the importance of health, fitness, and most of all, self-care with my family! Whether they grow up to be mothers or fathers, seeing their own parents care for themselves instills this as a must for them in the future as well! It feels pretty great when my teens ask me to go to the gym with them! Don't wait for extra time in your schedule; make YOU a priority too!

Heather Travitz
Mother of five
Owner, Get Your FIT On with Heather Travitz
www.heathertravitz.com
@Heather31Mom / facebook.com/htravitzbiz
info@heathertravitz.com

Life gives us both ends of the spectrum. Without the rain, there is no rainbow. But do not doubt that the rainbow will come. We juggle, we struggle, we learn, and we are loved. With children, it can come back to us in more satisfying gratitude and love than we ever imagined possible.

Every child is different, but when we set the example of giving and caring, it comes back to us in unexpected ways, at unexpected times. With children, it can come back to us in more satisfying gratitude and love than we ever imagined possible.

Sometimes we need to do a better job paying attention. It is possible that affection is coming our way but we are too tired or not focused enough to notice it. It could be coming to us, but our eyes are not really open to see it. Or our heart is not open to receive it. Just as our children have their own "love languages," so do we. It could be that our little ones are loving us in their own way but with a different love language that we are not seeing. Or it could be that their love language is just not matching up with ours. They cannot yet bring us flower bouquets, give us foot massages, or let us sit quietly and read a book. But one day they will be able to.

In our children's baby and toddler years, we cannot always tell if they are hugging us out of exhaustion, hunger, or fear. Holding them and hugging them as much as we do then, we receive a lot of physical love. In those prelanguage days, the neck-gripping throat hugs are love that only a mom appreciates.

In their early language days, our children learn to draw and will often begin to express their love through art and notes. They might draw a (somewhat scary) picture of us, presenting it to us as a prized Picasso. Or they might write us a note, complete with words so misspelled that we need a translator. Keep all of these in a special mom treasure box. Later in life, when their words are perfectly spelled and their sentences perfectly structured, our hearts will smile at the sweetly imperfect love notes from their younger days.

They bring us "treasures" to show their love: flowers they pulled from the neighbor's yard, various turtles or birds they "rescued" for us to nurse back to health, little plastic balls that they no longer want to play with, a two-dollar necklace that breaks the same day they got it, broken seashells they carefully selected for us on the beach. While their treasures may not be shiny or useful or something we could do a lot with, they represent a pure love that we cannot find anywhere else.

Reciprocal love, in which we can enjoy a two-way conversation, starts to show up when they begin to speak. In their precious voices, they start to share what is going on in their little heads: all sorts of interesting kid thoughts, including how much they love us. They tell us how much they like our hair or our smile or how we tuck them in just right at night.

My youngest told me the other night as I tucked her in that she loved me so much she would die for me. Even after I asked her to never, ever say that again, I knew in my heart that I felt the same. Beyond a shadow of a doubt.

They will write stories about us in school for Mother's Day. Sometimes we hope that the teacher will not repeat to anyone what our child chose to write about us. Years later, their affection can come in the form of texts thanking us or telling us they love us too. One of the highest forms of love from teenagers is telling us that they love us—in front of all of their friends.

Keep those sweet children's love notes close by as a reminder of how much you are loved. The notes come in every shape and size, written on Post-its to napkins to notepads to coloring menus from restaurants. Use your smartphone to take a photo of a sweet note, then display it as your phone's wallpaper. Enjoy your children's art and love notes just as you would enjoy a photo.

Another easy standard to set: always hug and say "I love you" when saying good-bye. Every time. At the morning bus stop, before they run over to a friend's house, when you say good-bye on the cell phone, at any moment when you grab them as they pass by you in the house, always at bedtime—you need their love, too.

While life with our children can make us laugh one moment, then lose our cool out of frustration in the next, their love can overwhelm us and choke us up in a minute. It never fails: it seems like the minute I feel really pulled, Elle will come up to me with her pudgy cheeks and say, "You are my favowite mama in the whole wide wowld!"

Our children's love comes to us in many kid ways. We need to pay attention to interpret those ways and to absorb them and fill our buckets for the challenging days. In all the challenges, all the ups and downs of life, their love is there. Sometimes when we do not hear it enough from them, we have to initiate it. Then the love will come, individually from each of them, in each one's own way. Our job is to pay attention to see it.

On one particularly difficult day, I was having a tough time trying to juggle everything. Chloe, age two, walked into the room and saw I was upset. She did not have the words to use; she just toddled over to me and hugged me as I cried. Her hug was so precious and so needed. It is good to be receptive to that love from our children. We need it as much as they do. So many times my children have been the ones to pick me up unexpectedly when I struggled with something.

To love our families takes time, thought, and energy. But the love we get back from that foundation can so exceed what we put into it. When our children know they are loved, and when we personally feel loved back, guilt is diminished.

My fifth life lesson is about loving my family, and maybe not so obviously, learning to love myself. Loving ourselves is not a luxury; it is a necessity for a well-lived life. We are at our strongest, we live on the level of our highest purpose, and we live with our most generous happiness when we take care of ourselves as well.

Mother Teresa said, "We have been created to love and be loved." This is an important learning lesson from momoirs: that ultimately the opportunity to love our children *and be loved by them* is one of the greatest gifts of life.

> "Mom, I love you to infinity and beyond.
> I love you more than ice cream with chocolate
> syrup and rainbow sprinkles.
> Mom, are you ready for this? I love you more than corn dogs!"
> —Elle (age 7)

Recap of Chapter 5

✓ When you have two or more children, you learn something surprising: they are all different from each other! Getting to know each of their unique personalities helps us parent them.

✓ Our relationships with our children strengthen when we change our parenting style as they grow and mature.

✓ Loving our children in the hardest moments is the most important time to love them.

✓ Setting age-appropriate boundaries for our children is love.

✓ Do not think that because our children might not need us physically in their teenage years, we are not needed. They need us mentally more than ever in those years.

✓ Teaching our children how to be good communicators is one of the most important life skills we can help them develop. They will need these skills their entire life in every relationship.

✓ Demonstrating our love for our family can be fun and unique to each family, with serious and silly traditions year after year.

✓ Remember it's important to love our spouse/partner as well as our children.

✓ We can feel like we are losing ourselves in the parenting process. It's important to find simple ways to love ourselves as well.

Personal Profile in Mom Courage:
Loving...and Being Loved

One of the greatest gifts I have given my girls is self-love: being able to accept and embrace yourself right where you are. I have shown them that beauty really does come from within and that confidence is beautiful.

When battling breast cancer, I will never forget the moment each of my girls saw me bald for the first time. My hair had come out in handfuls that morning in the shower while they were at school. My husband and I finished the job with clippers, and when they came home, their reactions were priceless. They saw me independently of each other yet had the same reaction: "Mom, you can totally rock that look. You look awesome. You don't need to wear a wig." I didn't. Not once.

They completely validated me that day, and I held my head high, never crying or worrying about my looks, never hiding the truth under a wig. I was courageously battling cancer, and that's what it looks like. And it's OK.

My girls were thirteen and sixteen at the time—a time when most girls are consumed not only with their own looks but also with every detail of their families and what their friends will think. School soon started, and my youngest was entering seventh grade. As we pulled in the school one morning for me to go inside with her, I was shocked to realize that I had no hat to throw on! I worried that Haley would be mortified for her friends to see me bald and asked her what to do. I knew I had done something right when her response was simply, "I don't care, Mom. You look great, and whoever doesn't like it is the one with the problem!"

As moms we don't always have moments of validation, moments when that little voice says to us, "Hey, you are doing a good job." This was one of my finest moments!

Stacy DeRogatis
Mother of two
Realtor, Keller Williams Realty Atlanta Partners
StacyGetsResults@KW.com
www.HomesinNorthGwinnett.com

GUILT-FREE TIPS –
Ten Ways to Love Your
Family and Yourself

1. Several times a year, leave your children surprise love notes in unexpected places (such as in their sock drawer, under their pillow, in the teenager's tennis shoes).

2. Ask them what their current favorite dinner or dessert is. Tell them when you will make it for them (at least a few days away so they can enjoy the anticipation). Then do it!

3. Make your family members feel special by going on individual dates with each of them at least once or twice a year. If you need fun ideas, check out TripAdvisor for local and unexpected things to do.

4. Tell your child you're sorry when you are wrong.

5. Read *The Five Love Languages of Children* by Gary D. Chapman and Ross Campbell, MD. Learn what language makes your child feel loved—then use that on a regular basis.

6. Tell your children how much you care no matter how old they are. Send an e-mail, text, or leave a voicemail when they wouldn't expect it. Just because they are older does not mean that your love and concern for them is not important to them!

7. Give them "coupons" for things they love: getting an ice cream with you, taking a trip to the library, or going on a dinner-and-movie date. Make the ordinary extraordinary.

8. Do at least one special thing for yourself each month: buy some flowers for your bathroom counter, sit down for an

uninterrupted hour and do whatever you want, have a manicure, go to lunch with a special friend, have a massage, get up early on Saturday and enjoy the sunrise and coffee in the quiet hours before everyone is awake. Go on a date with your husband or significant other. What makes you feel loved? Do that!

9. Write down your positive qualities. Write down why you like you. Ask your children, family, or a close friend why they like you. Keep those notes in a journal you pull out at night to remind yourself how special you are. You *are* special and uniquely you, but it is easy to forget that in the busyness of daily life.

10. Hug a lot. The beautiful secret about giving hugs is that you are hugged in return. Hug often.

6

Letting Them Grow Up and Giving Us Both Wings

"Honey, go clean up your mess."
—me to Courtney
"What mess happened?"
—Courtney (age 5)

Mom Quiz #6: Are We Flying Yet?

Check if anything below applies to you!

☐ You drove to the store at 11:00 p.m. to buy poster board for your child who forgot she needed it for her project due tomorrow.

☐ Even though it was going to make you late for your business meeting, you went back home to retrieve the physical education clothes your child forgot to take them to her at school so she would not get a mark against her grade.

☐ You finished your child's math homework for her during her band concert. Poor thing—she was just too busy. How else could she have completed it in time?!

☐ You completed your child's chores because you had asked him over and over but he still had not done them.

☐ You called your child's middle school teacher because you did not think she fairly graded your child's test.

☐ You did not sleep much last night. Your child's incomplete science project was due the next day. So you stayed up until 2:00 a.m. to help him get it done well and on time.

☐ You let your child go to the movies with her friend, even though she had not put away her clean clothes like she was supposed to; it was just easier to put them away yourself.

Roots and Wings

My perspective on my motherhood changed forever when I read Hodding Carter Jr.'s quote, "There are only two lasting bequests we can give our children: one is roots, the other is wings." I have leaned on these words in many *TILT*ed moments of indecision and heartfelt struggles. When I was not sure of the right thing to do, this thought gave me the courage to make the right decision. My sixth life lesson focuses on creating the foundation on which our children will build the rest of their lives—in other words, giving them roots and wings.

Our First Gift: Roots

Our first gift to our children is that we are their roots. Creating roots for our children is more than surviving the chaos; it is the standards we choose to live by, a framework of core values that guide our decisions. We all have this framework, but not everyone is aware of theirs, nor are they consciously guiding their life by their core values. Core values can include:

- Growth
- Accomplishment
- Integrity
- Kindness
- Intelligence
- Resourcefulness
- Faith
- Legacy
- Love
- Perseverance
- Adventure
- Dedication
- And so many more

Roots, the foundation of our children's lives, are tied to the standards we choose to live by. Roots are not found in "the perfect family" or "the perfect life," since no such thing exists. Sometimes a sadness or heartache is part of our root system. Often the strongest roots are found in sharing the challenges life presents to each of us as we help each other grow through the experience.

Roots are in our family's traditions—serious and silly. They are in making memories from the fun and joy our children's years with us can offer. Roots are grown in the hard choices we make as moms in how much do we do for our children or how much we teach them to do for themselves. They come from the sweet moments of love we share. They are in our shared laughter—and in the memories we create together.

Throughout our children's lives, we help them with their own self-discovery and development. We nurture and water their roots to hopefully help them grow and flourish. Along the way, I want to urge moms to do the same for yourselves. These same foundational years for our children overlap a big part of our own adult lives. We need to remember that part of building their roots is setting the example to nurture our own personal life goals as well. All of our family's roots, well fed together, can grow an incredibly beautiful tree in which our family can flourish and enrich each other.

Our Second Gift: Wings

> "Mom, I don't know what I would do without you."
> —Chloe (age 9)

Parenting is one of the hardest jobs out there—it is so close to our hearts. Yet embedded in this big responsibility is one of life's greatest opportunities—lifting up another. While being a mom begins with more diapers than we can count and an unkempt household that may wait more years than we like for order to return, it quickly moves into a very significant responsibility: guiding the development of a human being. Being a mom is not only giving our children roots, it is also about giving them wings.

Appreciating the Values My Small-Town Roots Instilled in Me

Age gives you gratitude and appreciation for that which you took for granted in your youth. There are so many things I overlooked and did not realize the value of in my youth, like the appreciation for growing up in a small town. Now, I have so much gratitude for that place, my roots, and the values it instilled in me. It gives me joy that my children have had the chance to experience it and I have helped them to appreciate it already!

Rosemarie Pelatti
Mother of two
CEO, New Line Enterprises
Operating Principal, Keller Williams Hudson Valley Realty
Twitter @rpelatti
newline23@gmail.com

Parenting is about encouraging our children to grow into young adults with character and integrity, to learn who they are and what they might become, and to begin to take responsibility for their lives, as well as about being a shoulder they can lean on during the process. Yes, it is about trying to keep them dressed in clothes that fit, missing an important meeting when the school calls to tell us they are sick, and teaching them how to brush their teeth at least twice a day. But beyond their physical needs, our mom responsibilities are quite significant, and it is easy to forget that in the middle of the chaos.

Wings are the skills our children will need throughout their lives: how to communicate, how to have and reach for their goals, and how to be responsible for themselves. Wings are about developing good decision-making abilities, self-confidence, and courage to keep going when life gets tough. Honestly, giving our children true wings means giving them the ability to live without us.

How Can We Achieve Both?

All parents define roots and wings for their children differently. There is no right answer here, only the answers that help you lead your family and your life the best way you can. Here are some ideas that have helped my family nourish my children into becoming the best they can each individually become:

- Let them succeed, but more importantly, let them fail.

- Guide them to find their own solutions.

- Know that consequences are a necessary pain.

- Choose your battles; they don't all matter.

- Decide whose homework it is.

- Know that one of the most powerful opportunities for life lessons and growth can be found in extracurricular activities.

- Set standards that empower.

I'll explore each idea more thoroughly in the rest of this chapter. But always remember, we have a far greater responsibility *to* our children than we do *for* our children.

Let Them Succeed, but More Importantly, Let Them Fail

"Mom, this was a bad, bad day.
I cannot find my Power Ranger, and I do not like my lunch.
I want to throw my toys away! I want to
step on them and break them.
I am so mad at them!"
—Parker (age 3)

Growing up today is different from when we grew up, but the basics remain the same.

Each child has skills and lessons to learn. We start with the simple stuff: learning to keep baby food in your mouth instead of spitting it all over Mom, learning to walk and not hit your head on everything as you fall, learning to not take away the Matchbox cars while your sibling is in the middle of playing with them, learning to not wrinkle up your schoolwork in frustration and throw it away just because you colored a little bit outside the lines.

In elementary school, kids must obey the rules, or they will spend a lot of time with their principal. They must take a shower every day *and actually use the soap and shampoo*, or they will smell bad. If they talk too much in the hallway at school, they will lose their recess playtime. Their new tennis shoes are not really what makes them fast—they do. Simple stuff.

It can become even more challenging for children as they get into middle school and high school. They begin to see that life is not black and white like it was when they were little. Life is actually gray. They will have to make decisions when there is not necessarily a clear right or wrong, only shades of right and shades of wrong. Values and integrity enter the picture in a big way. While they grow up and progress toward "gray," they will make many mistakes along the way. We all did.

Also, their failures get bigger from their bigger perspectives, and more difficult to manage:

- I failed my test.

- I lost the Student Council election (for the third time).

- I was not selected for a part in the school play.

- I did not place in the science festival with my project that took me a month to finish.

- I was the only girl in my class not invited to the birthday party.

- I did not make the honors band.

- I did not make the shot on the free-throw line in the last ten seconds of the basketball game.

As they go through all their stages, the question for us is this: *Do we let them go through those mistakes and fail?* Do we push them over their obstacles, or help them learn how to hurdle them on their own?

We spend a lot of time focused on helping our kids succeed, but it is interesting that, in reality, we should probably focus more on letting them fail. Consider Buzz Lightyear's famous "flying" entry in *Toy Story*, where he is convinced he can fly. Woody does not believe him, so Buzz demonstrates. Through an unlikely series of leaps, jumps, and falls, Buzz declares, "See, I can fly!" Woody corrects him: "No, you just fell with style." That is life—falling with style.

It is so much easier to clean up our kids' messes for them than to deal with trying to teach them to do it for themselves. But when we do, we let go of long-term results in exchange for a short-term solution. In other words, we all lose.

Life will send us all a series of problems and obstacles we have to overcome to move forward. They come at us at different times and in different forms. Some people have overcome what could have been life-altering situations. And they have achieved inordinate success in part *because* of those obstacles that appeared in their path.

Those brave souls who are willing to share their problems and failures with us teach us priceless wisdom. If we are paying attention, they also can save us the pain of some mistakes. Surprisingly, their words are often very simple. There are an overwhelming number of examples throughout history of good people failing, learning from their experiences, and going on to greatness:

- **Michael Jordan** was cut from his high school basketball team.

- **Walt Disney** was fired from a newspaper because they said he "lacked imagination and had no original ideas."

- **Steve Jobs** was thirty years old in 1985, actually very successful at that point in his life, and in the midst of it was forced out of Apple.

- **Marie Curie** (in the early 1900s) lost her oldest sister to typhus and her mother to tuberculosis. Russian authorities forbade her to pursue studies of lab science, she had no money, and so she had to educate herself. She overcame one overwhelming life challenge after another. Eventually in her research, she discovered the element radium, which created a new era for the treatment of diseases.

- *Chicken Soup for the Soul* authors **Mark Victor Hanson** and **Jack Canfield** were turned down by more than 140 publishing companies before one finally agreed to publish their first book. They have now sold more than a hundred million books in fifty-six languages worldwide.

- **Oprah Winfrey** lost her early job as a news anchor. They said she was too emotional and moved her out of the limelight to a small talk show in Baltimore.

- **Thomas Edison** was told by his teacher that he was too stupid to learn anything and that he should go into a field where he might succeed through "his pleasant personality."

- **Bethany Hamilton** lost her arm in a surfing accident at age thirteen, but she has gone on to inspire young people around the world to never give up on their dreams.

- **J. K. Rowling** was turned down by multiple publishers before finding someone to publish her now-famous Harry Potter series of books.

- **Vincent van Gogh** sold only one work of art during his lifetime, often starving to complete his paintings, which today sell for millions of dollars each.

What would our world be like in those different fields if any of these people had given up when they failed? Their eventual accomplishments are legendary. But at any point they could have let their failures stop them dead in their tracks.

How we deal with this issue for our children will leave a lasting impression on them. They are going to have successes. But if they are human, they will experience more failure than success. Understanding that our children's mistakes and failures are a critical part of their growing up is significant. It is easy to want to protect them. It is hard to see them struggling. What they really need is for us to keep encouraging them.

Our role is to love them even more when they are not perfect or when they mess up. Everyone's life is a series of failures. It is whether we learn how to get back up again that defines us. Helping our children learn this lesson early, while they are still under our roof, gives them the confidence they will need to face later inevitable failures on their life paths. History has taught us again and again that the real journey to success is actually through failure.

Once again the caterpillar and butterfly come into my life. What would happen if the caterpillar gave up and quit when it was at its darkest point in life?

"Just when the caterpillar thought the world was over...it became a butterfly." (Chinese Proverb)

The Butterfly's Struggle for Beauty

One day, as a young woman sat in her garden, she noticed a cocoon hanging from a nearby branch. Before long, a small opening appeared in the cocoon. The woman watched for several hours as the butterfly within struggled to free itself from the envelope in which it had recently been transformed.

Then it seemed to stop making any progress. It appeared as if it had gotten as far as it could and could not go any further. So the woman decided to help the butterfly: she took a pair of scissors and cut open the cocoon, from which the butterfly then emerged easily.

But to the woman's surprise, the butterfly didn't fly away. Instead it crawled out onto the branch and sat there. As the woman looked more closely, she noticed the butterfly's body was withered; its wings were tiny and shriveled. The woman continued to watch because she expected that, at any moment, the wings would open, enlarge, and expand sufficiently to support the butterfly's body. Neither happened!

In fact, the butterfly spent the rest of its life crawling around with a withered body and shriveled wings. It never was able to fly. What the woman, in her kindness and her goodwill, did not understand was that the restricting cocoon and the struggle required for the butterfly to get through the tiny opening were God's way of forcing fluid from the body of the butterfly into its wings so that it would be ready for flight once it achieved its freedom from the cocoon.

Sometimes struggles are exactly what we need in our life.

Susan Macauley
Creator and Curator of Amazing Women Rock
AmazingWomenRock, http://.amazingwomenrock.com/

SheQuotes, http://.shequotes.com/
CrackerJacks, http://amazingsusansblog.wordpress.com/
Facebook: https://facebook.com/AmazingWomenRock,
https://facebook.com/SheQuotes
Twitter: @AmazingSusan, @AmazingWomen, @SheQuotes,
@FindingPINK, @WhatLifeIs

Guide Them to Find Their Own Solutions

> "When Courtney eats more broccoli, then her brain will be bigger.
> Then she will be smarter and stop hitting me on the head."
> —Parker (age 5) talking about his three-year-old sister

So if the journey to a successful life is through a series of failures, then how should we help our children when they fail? Truly, this process begins at a very young age. It is easy to imagine the problems they will face in middle school, high school, and beyond. But the need to solve problems starts out pretty quickly in their little lives.

As early as two or three, depending on the individual child, children are making choices. And just as quickly, we can begin to guide them to find their own solutions. Obviously, some problems they cannot handle: they cannot get that drink cup high up in the cabinet without falling off the counter; if they eat the little Lego man their big brother left on the floor, they could choke. But other choices they can make. By five or six, as they are entering school, situations arise that can be quite upsetting to them: it is a problem if a classmate is taking their afternoon snack away from them; they will be upset if at school rest time they find that their special stuffed animal is not rolled up in their rest pad.

When do we get in the middle of their problems, and when do we support them to figure things out for themselves? That depends a lot on their age. Here are some ideas for beginning to guide them to finding their own solutions at different ages:

1. Toddlers:

When our children are toddlers, we are in the physical problem-solving business. We move the toy cars out of their way as they are learning to walk, we push the potty step stool close to the toilet so they do not fall in, we steady the bike handles as they are learning to ride, we move the plate of spaghetti close to them so most of it will hopefully land in their mouth rather than all over their seat and on the floor. They are learning about the physical boundaries in their lives and hopefully how to not hurt themselves in the process.

2. Kindergarten and elementary school:

It gets a little trickier when kids start going to school. Now they are interacting with other adults and other young children on a daily basis and in a structured environment. Beyond physical safety now, they have to learn how to handle the inevitable conflicts. When a classmate takes part of their lunch, or when the other child at their table is cheating off their test, they have to learn how to talk to someone—if not to their teacher, then to us, their parent. Teaching them the importance of communication and how to do it is critical in these years.

The best way to communicate? Be respectful of each other (no matter who we are talking about). Listen first and be sure everyone has a chance to talk. Find a resolution, then stick to it. Keep working through the problem when it shows up again.

When children's grades slip because they are not completing their homework, we have to be aware of it and counsel them on how they are managing their schoolwork and their activities. Find out if time management is the problem, or if they do not understand what they are learning. Teach your children how to go to the teacher to talk through the issue. Then ask your children about it and follow up with them until they have a solution to their problem. In these conversations, once we understand where they have fallen down, then we can teach them how to pick themselves up. This six- to seven-year window involves a huge learning curve for children.

3. Middle and high school:

I look at these seven years as our children's prep for life out from under our roof. They will take the problem-solving skills we help them learn at this age out into the world. If we solve all their problems during these years, they will not be able to solve them for themselves when they are out of the house. At this point, their problems and failures come more from their thought processes and their decision making. Hopefully we have begun the foundation for good communication skills—we will really need them during these years.

When our children fail a test, we have to find out why. If they cannot understand the teacher's teaching style, then we must teach them how to learn to work with all kinds of different people. That is life. They have to figure out how to be successful in different situations. When they are not selected for the volleyball team, we have to find out either if they really aren't skilled for that sport or if they need to seek out coaching and training to try again next season. When they are having problems with their friends, we need to guide them to find people who will like them for exactly who they are. Then we need to help them get together with those kids who will be good friends for them. We also need to be sure that our child is not the problem! They will all have issues and failures they deal with in these years. Our objective is to give them as many problem-solving skills as we can.

Is helping our children find solutions to their problems easy? No. Is it necessary to raising independent, self-sufficient children? Yes. Parenting is not for wussies. We usually know in our hearts, since we know our children best, when they need help. As soon as they tell us about a problem they are having at school, or when we hear about it through a conversation with them, that is the moment we need to begin helping them search for solutions that they can work through themselves.

Life is all about solving problems. No matter what our age is. At our work, we solve issues every day, whether we are a business owner, an accountant, a retail sales person, or a technology support person. By helping our children be creative in looking for solutions to the problems they face, we are arming them to be ready for their future lives.

Failures and problems for young children can mimic later "big" problems in life. If we're a shoulder to lean on, our children will learn that they can depend on us. If we're teachers, our children will learn that others can help them solve their problems. If we're coaches, our children will come to believe in themselves and learn how to go out in the world and find the solutions to solve their problems on their own.

Know That Consequences Are a Necessary Pain

> "Oops, I forgot that! My brain must be broken!"
> —Chloe (age 7)

When our children do not make good choices, the consequences are often as hard on us as they are on our children. They can be hard for us to enforce. They can be even harder for us to manage. It can be embarrassing to stand outside a restaurant with your toddler screaming by your side because you would not let her run around the restaurant and disturb the other guests. Yes—been there, done that. It is hard for us to get our work done and keep our child occupied if we restrict his or her electronics time. It is difficult for us to rearrange our schedule to pick them up after a detention at school.

But solving their problems for them or not being strong enough to hold them responsible for their consequences only sets them up to repeat the problem later in life.

Our children's darkest moments might not have the same impact on us as on them. For young children, not being included in the recess game of tag can ruin their whole day. Not winning the drawing contest, not being invited to the birthday party "everyone" else was invited to, not getting a great grade on a project they worked so hard on, not being chosen for first string of their team, not being invited to the prom, choosing the wrong group of friends—these can be painful experiences for them. I try to pull myself back down to their height for better perspective. From down there, we can more clearly look straight into their younger eyes, see their sadness or frustration, and remember what it felt like when we were young children.

The successes we experience with each child are moments to celebrate. But it is in the dark challenges of a failure or a discouraging problem that we really prove our parenting mettle. Perfect timing—as I am writing this, my teenage daughter just asked if she could close my office door and talk. What was I just saying a few minutes ago...?

> "When you get older, then your brain will be smarter.
> Then it will tell you to aim first so you don't
> keep hitting me in the head."
> —Parker (age 6) to Courtney (age 4)

Choose Your Battles—They Don't All Matter

> "Please be sure you do not tell any of my secrets."
> —Chloe (age 8) to little sister
> "No problem. Actually, after a couple days, I
> forget most of what you tell me anyway."
> —Elle (age 6)

We choose our battles carefully. As our children grow up, we will inevitably have disagreements with them—and some will be more heated than others. Often the topics involve what they are doing, or maybe what they are wearing. Some topics are important to argue over:

- Did you go in your brother's room when you were not allowed to and take his Legos?

- Did you lie to us about your real grade on that test?

- Did you talk back to me in a disrespectful and hurtful way?

- Did you go to that friend's house when we specifically said you could not?

  Other disagreements are over topics that really do not matter in the long run:

- Did I say you could flush your dead fish down the toilet?

- Did I say you could wear your blue dress backward?

- Didn't I ask you to take down that Happy Birthday sign that has been hanging in your room for five years?

How far do we battle on clothing? Do we insist that they dress a certain way that we prefer, or do we let them explore their own style? For Southern moms: do we make them wear hair bows after age eight? Often, children, even younger children, use clothes as a form of self-expression. They will tell us pretty quickly if they want to wear skirts or shorts, dresses or pants, T-shirts or button-ups. My son developed a passionate dislike of buttons one day, and it was more than eight years before he again wore a shirt with a button on it—and then only because he had to.

One of my daughter's young friends tells her that her mother still insists she wear girly clothes, even though she does not want to anymore. We each have to decide if this is a battle worth fighting. Sometimes it is. But whether her little outfits are girly and actually match (as much as we might like them to) will not determine whether she becomes a fashion goddess or a fashion disaster. And her current fashion sense could make for some great photos to show her future high school boyfriend.

Usually, as long as our children's clothing is clean and appropriate, it is not worth a battle. When they are young, we can use the "alternative choice" method: we select two outfits, both of which would work fine, then let the child pick which one he or she wants to wear. Our idea of cute is not necessarily theirs. In fact, choosing their clothes is a great place for them to exercise some independence.

One of my daughters loved to wear red Santa socks with her purple-and-green-leaf pants. Courtney insisted on wearing her clothes backward for about three months. I tried each morning to explain to her that they really were on backward, but she insisted that she liked them that way. I decided it would not really make a difference, so I let her go to school that way. After about three months, she got tired of it and began to wear her clothes the right way again. Elle wore a straw Hawaiian skirt everywhere for about four months until it literally fell apart. It actually disintegrated from so much use and had to be secretly thrown away. I had to buy another one, knowing how upset she would be. I was a bit sad when she lost interest in the replacement.

An opportunity for building stronger children is found in giving them room to make their own choices about less important issues. For example:

- When we give our children some space to express themselves as they are learning and growing, we give them confidence that we believe in their abilities.

- When we give our children some room to personalize their life through their room decorations or their clothes, we give them confidence that we believe in the person they are.

- When we give our children some room to explore different activities, we give them confidence that we believe they can become what they dream about.

Choosing the Battles That Matter

> "Mom, prepare for trouble!"
> —Courtney (age 3) looking at Parker (age 5)
> "Make it double!"

As our children get older, the issue of which battles we choose to fight becomes significantly more important. We also begin to enter "the gray area," where it gets quite interesting—here there are not necessarily rights or wrongs, just shades of opinions. We have to make critical judgment calls with them and for them.

What topics do we believe will truly matter over the course of their lives? Where do we draw the line in the sand? Where we will stand our ground, and where will we bend? Some common topics most parents agree should be handled the same way:

- We do not run across the street without looking for oncoming cars.

- We do not hit a sibling, a friend, or a pet dog—essentially, not much other than a baseball or the plastic hammer on the plastic workbench.

- We do not break the heads off our sister's Barbie dolls.

- We do not say mean things or treat each other disrespectfully.

- We do not play with matches to set army men on fire.

- We do not color on the walls with crayons.

- We do not step on the tail of the sand-sculpted mermaid that the talented gentleman spent four hours creating on the beach.

These and a few others are the kinds of battles most parents will fight until they win; our children must obey these rules for the health and safety of many.

Help Your Children FLY, Just Not in The Car

Choices are just that, choices. Choices your child MAKES not choices we think they should make. Our job as parents is to make sure our children have a good moral compass, and I am convinced that the first four years of life are when we instill right and wrong in our children. I have ALWAYS allowed my children to make their own choices, and they have never let me down.

Anytime you take choice away from you child, I believe you are telling them you don't trust their judgment. When you give your child free range of "choice," they take on the responsibility of the consequence of their choice. I believe our job from the day they are born is to prepare them to leave us.

With all that being said, my youngest of four (ages fifteen to thirty-six) did make a bad choice once. At age four, he decided to open the car door as I was driving out of the driveway. He thought (like the young man in the animated *Treasure Island* movie) that the car could fly and the door was the sail. It was the only time he was in a "time out." He didn't make that choice again. Let your children FLY, just not in the car!

Rebekah Rivers
Mother of four
CEO, The Rivers Team And North Florida Title Company
Operating Principal, Keller Williams Town and Country
Realty/Tallahassee
Keller Williams Success Realty/Panama City
Keller Williams First Coast Realty/Orange Park
Keller Williams Big Bend Realty/Jacksonville
www.ringtherivers.com
Facebook: facebook.com/Rebekah.rivers.73
Rebekah@ringtherivers.com

Friends—An Influence We Cannot Ignore

When we consider what battles are worth fighting, being sure that our children have good friends is one of them. Outside of our family, our children's friends are one of their most significant influencers. We know the impact friends have on our children—good and bad. Teaching them the importance of having and building solid friendships is a critical part of their childhood. The impact of these relationships can support them or cast a shadow on their lives for years.

With each of my children, we have had several issues with young kids not being nice and not being good friends. One daughter experienced a girl behaving very badly toward her in kindergarten. I did not expect to have to deal with a bully at such a young age, but it escalated to the point where I had to call the school principal to get the situation handled. This was a battle worth fighting and one she still talks about years later.

The relationship training we give them at a young age is the foundation from which they will make their choices later. My husband and I spend a good amount of time on this topic with our children, even when they are very young, helping them build the self-confidence from an early age that they are worthy of good friends.

When something goes wrong with one of our children's friends, we take the time to talk about it right then until he or she has a solution he or she is comfortable with. We have always counseled our children that they are better off having a few good friends than allowing people into their lives who do not treat them well. If we can help them choose their friends carefully when they are young, they will have more confidence to choose well as they grow.

We can argue and disagree over almost everything if we choose— we are all different people with different interests. Or we can make our parenting path much easier by choosing our battles carefully and only fighting for the issues that really matter in the long run.

> "Mom, what are they doing?"
> —Courtney (age 6)
> "They are praying."
> —me
> "How do you do that?"
> —Courtney
> "Bow your head and talk to God."
> —me
> "What do you say?"
> —Courtney
> "I ask God to help me be a better person."
> —me
> *Courtney prays.*
> "I asked God to give me a lot of presents."
> —Courtney

Decide Whose Homework It Is: Creating Self-Sufficiency

> "My hands were too sweaty to hold my pencil,
> so I couldn't do my homework."
> —Courtney (age 10)

In addition to the challenges of helping our children find the gift in a failure or go through the pain of consequences from their poor decisions, we parents can also feel pressure from our children's schools on how much the school believes the parents are responsible for.

I caught myself just in time one afternoon several years ago as I was about to begin a big project for the kids. I was sitting on the floor in the hallway, in front of a large corkboard wall I'd put up. All the supplies I needed were spread out around me: poster board, markers in every color, fun stickers to decorate. I thought my sweet little children could not possibly keep up with all of their school projects. It was just way too much.

I was going to create a large calendar on which I could write all of their school projects, tests, and papers. So *I* could keep up with them *for them*. Clearly, lack of sleep interferes with good thinking. Thankfully, that moment of insanity passed quickly. If I "fished for them," they would not learn how to fish for themselves. I put away the huge calendar and all my supplies and told the children that night at dinner that their homework was just that: *their homework*. Ten years later, I know it was the right decision. They learned to manage their school responsibilities on their own, all of them getting solid grades in their classes. On their own. It has worked—with all four of them!

I have had some backlash on this belief from teachers, and even other moms, who feel that parents today should be more involved in their children's work. Some moms will stay up until two or three in the morning helping their child with a project. At one daughter's sixth-grade concert, the mom in front of me was completing her child's math homework. I know many parents who will drive back home to get the forgotten homework and bring it to their child back at school. I have even had a middle school teacher e-mail me to tell me I should be doing more to manage my daughter's classwork.

I apologize if I am offending you. You may be one of those moms. If you are, I must respectfully disagree on this. I do not believe that my children's homework is my responsibility. I believe that if we are constantly reminding them to do their work and helping them complete it, we are *not really* helping them—we are handicapping them. What if our handling this for them is actually keeping them from growing up? Is it possible that our completing their projects for them is robbing them of learning important life skills? They are not learning how to prioritize their homework over play, how to manage their time when they are involved in sports, or how to take responsibility for learning. Instead, they are learning to wait for someone else to do it for them.

> I have seriously smart kids.
> Two-year-old's response when I explained something
> to him that he knew nothing about:
> "I already knew that."
> Fifteen-year-old's response when I explained
> something to her that she knew nothing about:
> "I already knew that."

This responsibility evolves as our children grow. When they are young, we know what their schoolwork and project responsibilities are. But as they progress through elementary school, we need to pass it off to them pretty quickly. We can teach them to learn the calendar and understand when their work is due. We can give them ideas on how to study, quiz them for their vocabulary test when they come to us with their flash cards, or brainstorm with them on how to creatively decorate their art-project poster. But then we let them do it.

If we are not careful (even though we act out of love for our children), we will get the opposite results from what we want. We can make our children dependent, and even lazy, while they wait for someone else to do their work or solve their problems. Our children will grow up believing someone else should keep up with their test dates, know when their projects are due, and be sure they have the right markers, glitter, glue, and poster board for their project. If our goal is to raise self-sufficient, independent adults, then we are handicapping them by managing their responsibilities for them.

Becoming self-sufficient is a critical life skill children will have to learn at some point. Some parents today think this approach is too tough. But it is easier to help children develop good habits early and when they are in the safest time of their lives—under our roof.

My husband and I hold our children accountable for one thing: results. If they have good grades (mostly As and a few Bs), then they earn a lot of freedom. If their grades slip, they lose freedoms and we implement tighter accountability from them. We ask them very specifically about projects, quizzes, and homework. They lose privileges that are important to them. It is not easy for them or for us. They would much rather that we do their work for them, clean up their messes, or take care of their last-minute problems when they did not plan ahead.

So far, all of our children are highly self-motivated to do well. They take pride in managing their responsibilities, in doing well at school, and in getting good grades. Our big kids have managed their schoolwork since elementary school. While I know when they have big projects due or a big exam, they understand that this is their schoolwork, their opportunities, and their life.

By the way, I e-mailed back to that teacher who thought I was not managing enough of my sixth-grade child's work for her. I respectfully told her that I believe micromanaging my daughter's work would be the greatest disservice I could do my child. If I solve my children's problems, fix their low grades, turn my life inside out to accommodate theirs, what am I teaching them? My responsibility is not to catch the fish for them but to teach them how to catch it themselves. I did not hear back from her, and Courtney's final grade in her class (which she earned all of her own accord) was a high B.

Know the Power of Extracurricular Activities

"It is very different watching football versus watching gymnastics. In football there is a ball!"
—Elle (age 5)

Our children have many significant dimensions to their young lives when they are under our roof: family life, school life, and extracurricular activities, to name a few.

In terms of extracurricular activities, I have to pause here and give credit where credit is due: My husband has been an enormous supporter and believer in the benefits of athletic activities for our children. When I have been at times overwhelmed by the endless hours of driving our children to and from the seemingly hundreds of practices and events (multiplied by four active kids), he has never complained. He encourages our children in their athletics. He disciplines our children through their athletics. He prods them and pushes them to give it their best effort—every time. When I was too tired and stretched, or wanted to go easy on them, he never gave up on them. To his credit, I believe many of our children's successes have and will come from his support and belief in the power of these activities. Now I am a full-fledged, if still tired, believer. I have seen the powerful impact of his efforts—and our children's—firsthand.

Extracurricular activities offer rich opportunities for children to develop different aspects of themselves, explore activities they may (or may not) like, and find special talents they build into lifelong skills and lessons. From arts to athletics, we cannot always predict how our children will develop or where their paths may take them. We also cannot judge them by their early experiences or reactions.

One year, we were all packed to go to the beach for spring break. Our two young kids were bouncing off the walls with excitement. We had jam-packed the mama-van with all the necessary just-in-case-anything-goes-wrong kid paraphernalia, had put the bikes on the rack, and were ready to go. The only thing stopping us was our son's soccer game. We were fine with that; he was not.

So we pulled him along all the way to the soccer field, little sister in tow, as he cried and declared that he would not play his game. He refused. Short of throwing him at the soccer ball in the middle of the game, we could not get him to budge. He sat on the sidelines and cried. We were so not proud. All the parents stared at him, then us. His teammates did not know what to do with him, so they ignored him. His coach tried to coax him, then cajole him, then had to ignore him. We wished we could have ignored him and even pretended he was someone else's difficult kid.

Fast-forward twelve years, and that same child lettered four years in two of the toughest varsity sports (football and wrestling), placed in state in wrestling, and achieved his childhood dream of playing football in college. Who would have guessed that back then, on that difficult Saturday morning as we stood on the soccer-game sidelines with our incessantly crying child curled up on the ground?

For children's critical personal development, their extracurricular lives provide rich opportunities to guide them and help them learn life skills they will need when they grow up. These life skills directly affect our children's ability to overcome the obstacles life will undoubtedly throw at them. Extracurricular activities *teach* so much more than just the activity. Children learn:

- About the power of repeated practice to develop a skill
- That if they mess up with their responsibility, it can affect their whole team
- That some coaches yell a lot and some coaches inspire
- About self-sacrifice toward a common group goal
- About time management and the power and impact of discipline
- About working hard to accomplish goals
- About winning with grace and losing with dignity
- About the impact of the lack of any or all of these skills

Sometimes children learn unimportant things from their siblings' activities, such as, the best way to cool off at your big brother's hot and humid August football game is to eat cup after cup of ice from the concession stands. They learn to charge their electronic games the night before so they have playing options sitting in the stands. Parents also learn: we learned that Ring Pops stop a little girl from complaining if she is bored at her sister's cheerleading practice, and soft pretzels fill their tummies to tide them over during a late-afternoon soccer game. Yes, we have years of unexpected concession-stand purchasing expertise to top it off.

What If They Don't Like Anything—or It Seems They Are Not Good at Anything?!

We can worry if our children have a hard time finding their "place." Some kids home in on it very quickly. Parker told me at age four that he wanted "to grow up to be a football player who tackled those guys trying to make touchdowns." He grew up to do just that.

Courtney tried several different activities in searching for her "place." We tried gymnastics, soccer, cheerleading, and dance classes. She did not find one thing that she stayed with for more than a year or two. We were worried she would not find something that she could excel in.

Then Courtney decided to take tae kwon do, and was moving her way up through the different colored belts. One early Saturday morning, she participated in her tae kwon do studio's tournament. We did not know what to expect for our little fifty-pound eight-year-old. Somehow, she completed what they wanted her to do, competed with some other children, and won. We were so thrilled for her. The "Master" presented her with a trophy that stood taller than she did. I tried to hide my disbelief as Courtney stood so proudly next to it to smile for her photos.

For the next two years, anyone who came to visit our home was shown the trophy within five minutes of crossing our doorstep. Even though Courtney did not pursue tae kwon do beyond a few years, that trophy is still in her room today. Successes in extracurricular activities can stay with children for the rest of their lives.

We actually knew very early that Courtney was a gifted runner and jumper. Playing in the yard or on our cul-de-sac, she always ran fast, looking more like a gazelle gliding through the air. But we could not find an organized running program or team until seventh grade. In the meantime, she did so many different activities that we became concerned for her—we wanted each child to find his or her "thing," the opportunity to shine and build that early self-confidence.

As soon as Courtney was old enough, she started in the running program. We have not looked back since—we knew she had found her chance to shine. Now in high school, she is learning and earning ribbons on her track team, qualified as a sophomore for the state competition in the long jump, and placed at state in her junior year in the triple jump and 300 meter hurdles.

The intent is to help our children find their opportunity to excel. Every child has his or her own path. But ultimately, it does not necessarily matter what activities our children select; any activity has dimensions that they will learn from. The important idea is that they have an activity. In this part of their life, they will gain life lessons and self-confidence that we would have a difficult time teaching them otherwise. If I asked our older children about some of the most important things they had learned so far in their young lives, I can promise you they would say those lessons, in many ways, were coming from their extracurricular experiences.

Set Standards That Empower

> "I don't want to pway soccer.
> When I am a mom, if my children don't want to pway soccer,
> I won't make them!"
> —Elle (age 7) when she wanted to quit
> midseason and we would not let her

In many areas of their young lives, our children need boundaries and rules to guide them. We have standards for their extracurricular activities that provide the framework for them. Without these rules, we weaken our children and their future abilities to handle much that life will throw at them. These are our standards:

1. Don't quit.

My children are not allowed to quit once they have signed up for an activity. Their team or group is depending on them to fulfill their role. We teach them early that they do not quit on a commitment. Once they fulfill their commitment, then they can change their activity next time or next season.

Without this standard, we would be teaching them that later in life it is OK to quit on big things that matter. We would be saying it is OK to quit their business team when those peers are depending on them to fulfill their role. We would be saying it is OK to quit when the going gets tough in any aspect of their life. And we would not be teaching them how to fight through the difficulties that will inevitably come into their lives. We would not be equipping them to fight until they achieve their objective. We do not quit.

> "In the game of football, there is a winner and
> a loser at the end of the last quarter.
> In the game of life, you only lose when you quit."
> —Gary Keller

2. Practice, practice, practice.

Each activity requires different time commitments, depending on many factors. So whatever our children focus on, they make a commitment to the time it takes to be good at that activity.

No one will be good at anything that he or she does only occasionally. A great book on this topic is *Outliers* by Malcolm Gladwell. He shares example after example of people who found success in different areas not only because of opportunity, but also because they had put in "ten thousand hours": "An outlier's recipe for success is not personal mythos but the synthesis of opportunity and time on task." Most highly successful musicians and athletes are obvious examples of this: they have honed their skills through consistent and unrelenting practice. I calculated that our son, an exceptional football player, had put in almost ten thousand hours to learn and practice the sport of football when he was recruited for and earned the privilege of playing in college.

In his young years, as most kids will, Parker complained many times about having to practice so much. In fact, this was a topic of conversation with all of our children at a family dinner recently. Our youngest did not want to go to her practices. We had the other three older children counsel her with their thoughts about practice. Their words had much more impact than ours would have had. Each of them is an accomplished athlete now. And all of them, in their own ways, explained to our youngest that even when they did not *want* to practice, they found a way to make the best of it because they understood the power of consistent practice. Any person who wants to become very good in his or her chosen field has to practice over and over. Practice a little: have little results. Practice often and with focus: enjoy significant results.

3. They communicate with their coaches.

> "Son, do you want me to talk to the coach
> about the problems you are having on the team right now?"
> —Bryan (my husband)
> "Dad, I don't want you talking to the coaches.
> This is between me and them. I will handle it. I got this."
> —Parker (age 17)

The above quote came from a very difficult situation for our son, and it was hard for us to stand aside. But we believe in the importance of teaching our children communication, self-reliance, and problem-solving skills. We explain to our children how to think from their coach's (or teacher's) perspective: what might the coach be thinking? Their perspective is important for how they are addressed. Instead of assuming that the coach "doesn't like our child," we first assume that the coach cares for our child and is trying to get him or her to be the best he or she can be.

Why do most teachers teach and coaches coach? Maybe it's because they want to help children learn and grow in their activities and carry those lessons with them for the rest of their lives. We teach our children how to talk with an adult, and then we hold them accountable for the discussion. Parker earned his coaches' respect by working through that problem with them himself that season, instead of us trying to do it for him. Now he carries those life lessons with him. We know that he will—as all of our children will—need those lessons many times over the years.

We teach our children how to communicate when they are having a problem with their activity, instructor, or coach. Nine times out of ten, we do not go to the coach ourselves. We do not "helicopter in" when we disagree with a coach or when they have done something we do not like. The earlier we start this with the children, the better. Certainly in the elementary grades, we can begin working through our child to help them learn how to communicate.

This can be very hard to do, especially when our child is disappointed, hurt, frustrated, and confused. I did not say we are uninvolved. This approach actually takes a deeper involvement. It is easy to call a coach and complain. It is easy to blame someone else for our children's problems. It is much harder to teach our children, guide them, consult with them, and coach them through these situations. We are very involved, but our involvement is with *our child* and not so much the coach.

Instructors and coaches come and go in our children's lives. Some will be great, some will be all right, and some will not be good. But isn't that life? When our children are grown, won't they have different people they work with and different managers? We know some will be great, some will be all right, and some will not be good at all. We know our children have to learn how to work with and communicate with each kind of personality.

4. Teach them to fish for themselves.

We want to empower our children and build their self-confidence. Teaching them how to do things for themselves is one of the greatest ways to accomplish that. As with my decision to *not* manage their homework for our children, we have continuously looked for opportunities to teach them to fish for themselves.

For example, if they do not understand a word they are reading, I suggest they go find an online dictionary. If they are having a problem with a friend, I will give them some things to think about, then I usually suggest they ask their bigger brother or sister how they handled that situation themselves.

I have so many kids that now when the little ones have a problem or failure, I can refer them to their big siblings for answers and suggestions. The little ones like the ideas their big brother and sister have, and often so do I.

When you do not have older children to help your younger ones (which I did not have at first either), then look for the simplest way to empower them solve their problem. Ask them questions they know the answers to that could lead them to their solution. Show them a resource they can learn to use so that the next time they have a problem, they can use that resource; this could be as simple as instructing them on where to find the extra tissues in the house so they can replenish their own, or as complicated as having them learn how to change a tire on their car.

Teach them to think about who might be able to help them. Then teach them how to ask. Ask. Ask—until they find the answer to their problem. Learning how to ask is one of the greatest life skills we can teach children that will enable them to solve problems later.

I Don't Want to Worry about You Being Helpless

When I was a grown adult in my early thirties, I realized how often my friends would call me for advice on how to best "do" things or to figure out how to "do" things. I asked my father one day when I was visiting, "How is it that I know all these things and my friends don't?" His reply: "Your mom and I made a conscious choice to teach you how to do things, and accept that it might not be done right or the way we wanted, OVER just taking over and doing it ourselves [which would have been easier, he said], because we wanted you to learn."

This reminded me of the era before cell phones when I turned sixteen and he took me outside to my sister's '69 Camaro that was being passed down to me. He said, "I don't want to worry about you being helpless, broken down on the side of the street. Before you can have the keys, you must change the oil, check the water in the radiator, and rotate all four tires with only the tools in the trunk of the car." And thus the training exercise of the day began. Years later, I remember rolling a jack across the street and helping my neighbor change her flat tire because she was stranded and did not know how to do it. Training worked!

Patti Martinez
Mother of four
Realtor, Keller Williams Realty Atlanta Partners
www.PattiSellsAtlanta.com
PattiMartinez@kw.com

For years now, whenever my children have come to me with a question, I have replied, "I am not sure. Google it." My children were first a little annoyed that I could not or would not answer their questions. They rolled their eyes when I said, "Google it." But I stood firm so they would learn how to search for the answers to all sorts of questions.

Our practice of teaching our children to go find solutions to their problems and help them become self-sufficient has had an amazing payoff so far. All of our children are well behaved, respected by their peers and teachers, choosing solid friends, getting good grades, and performing at a high level in their extracurricular activities.

Don't quit. Practice, practice, practice, practice. Communicate. Learn how to find solutions yourself. These rules are demonstrating very positive results in my children's lives so far.

Ultimately, no one as a child is perfect, and no one as an adult is perfect. It is interesting that so many CEOs were "C" students—maybe it is because they learned how to deal with failure and fight through it. How many people do we know who have the "perfect" life as adults? No one does. Do not set your kids up for a "perfect life" that does not exist. Set them up with skills to work through their inevitable problems, and you empower them for real life.

Before Our Children Leave: Creating an Eighteen-Year Plan

In our overloaded lives, as we have discussed, we have to make hard choices. But our choices are seasonal over our lifetime: what we have to let go of today, we could absolutely choose to do again later in life as our family grows up. So what can guide us best while our children are living at home? A plan. A plan composed of our family's priorities that gives us a framework to guide and keep our focus on the most important activities during those years. A plan to ensure that we both build roots and give our children wings during their years under our roof.

I came up with my first Eighteen-Year Plan when we added our last two children to our family. I was living absolutely overwhelmed, as our professional life was running at two hundred miles an hour all the while I was chasing a ten-, an eight-, a three-, and a one-year-old around. Desperate to keep my head above water, I would try to talk with my husband about what life might be like in the years ahead as the children grew. In other words, we were trying to hold onto our sanity by thinking about a future in which we could once again actually sit down together and share an uninterrupted cappuccino and be able to finish a sentence.

Little did we know, as young parents, how much the stages our children were in would affect what we had the freedom to do or not do. I could not spout, off the top of my head, how old all the kids would be in the different future years. Yet their ages, their school years, and their siblings' ages would all dramatically affect any plans we wanted to make. So—I made a spreadsheet.

That was the first time I saw on paper what the next eighteen years of my life would look like with each child, based on the children's age progressions. Wow. It was then that I also realized that the oldest child, who was already ten, would be out of the house in eight short years. Only eight years. It was quite a shock, honestly, to see that in black and white.

I decided that day that I had to be intentional in my parenting on all levels. I only had eight more years with the oldest one at home. Then he would be off to college and beginning his life as a young adult. I had no time to waste. My Eighteen-Year Plan had to include both roots and wings, for them and for myself. It had to allow for my weaknesses, and it had to build their strengths. It had to give them values that would help them through the *TILT* that would undoubtedly come in their lives. It had to set boundaries and be tough. It had to teach and enable them. It had to celebrate their lives and our life together. It had to be fun and funny. It had to love them every single day. It had to be memory rich.

My Eighteen-Year Plan is far exceeding our original expectations and hopes. Rather than being tossed around in the winds that blow through these years of parenting, we have a sail we can hoist or close depending on our objectives during that season with the kids. They are each developing into unique, awesome individuals. They are their own people, and they are learning their life lessons right alongside us as we are learning our own.

Once we had a big-picture view and awareness of our children's progression over their time at home, we were more prepared for them. We did a better job of making the most of each year with our children. I do not want to be blown around by the whims of life. My life with my husband and children and my personal professional objectives are all too important to me.

Writing Your Own Eighteen-Year Plan

Annual goals, or an annual perspective, help us better manage and choose from all that we could do. Below are just some of the goals we have for the eighteen years when our children are under our roof. Use these to help you write your own plan for the years your children have left under your roof. Define your plan based on your time and objectives. Some moms might find my examples too simplistic. My list is not Martha Stewart's list; it is just my own. Plan your annual goals based on your values and your life. Just do it. Once your children leave home, your relationship shifts. What you choose to do, or not do, will become the foundation of their lives and their memories of their childhood and growing up with you.

Above and beyond the necessary (school, food to eat, clothing, etc.), the five areas where I have found our opportunities to make memories are the following:

1. **Traditions over Time**—repeating traditions that have meaning to us

2. **Exceptional Extracurricular Experience**—focusing on this incredible opportunity for life growth

3. **The Written Word**—being sure that our children know how much they are loved

4. **Celebrations and Vacations**—celebrating our life together and enjoying family fun

5. **Community Service**—giving to those less fortunate, which helps everyone involved

Earlier, for example, I shared many of our silly family traditions with you. I am careful that each year I include those on my calendar. I have a list for each one in my task manager app, and I date it about thirty days before the event so I have time to plan for it and pick up what I need when I am already out and about. I make notes to myself on how to make our traditions more fun for the next year. Then each year I make those special moments happen.

With the written word, likewise, I am very intentional with each of our children (and my husband): leaving them hidden love notes, mailing my son packages to college, e-mailing my daughter flowers from my flower app, and leaving special surprises in her locker throughout the year. I know how many times I want to do it for each of them, and I manage it with my task manager.

Your Eighteen-Year Plan can be as simple or as complex as you want it to be. We have additional layers to ours for each of our children. The layers are related more to memories that matter, however, than they are to the mundane—such as clean socks.

This planning includes asking yourself a few questions about what is important to your family. If you have the elements that matter to your family on your calendar for the next year, building toward your child's eighteenth year, then you are on the right road. Keep going! We plan in October for the following year. It is never too late, no matter what your children's ages are, to have a plan to make the most of their years at home with you. Do it today. Here is a very simple version, an easy way to start:

1. Think about what is happening in your child's life in the next year based on her age. Plan one special event related to his or her age to do with him or her alone.

2. Be sure your child's birthday celebration is on your calendar well *before* the birthday. Make him or her feel special.

3. Make sure your child has an opportunity to explore his or her abilities through one extracurricular activity.

4. Add a task to your task manager to remind yourself at least four times over the year to do a little something special for your child that reminds him or her how much you love him or her.

5. Be sure your family vacation or staycation is on the calendar. To add to the excitement, talk about it in the months leading up to it or put up a poster with photos about the trip.

6. Find at least one thing your child can do to volunteer or help someone else. Go with him or her if you can.

There is a lot you could do. The essence of the Eighteen-Year Plan is an awareness of where your child is at as he or she approaches the age of leaving home. Over and over, we are told how quickly it happens. Now I am one of those moms saying it also: the years with our children at home go by very, very quickly.

Live your own plan, and leave guilt behind. The plan helps push away frustrating feelings by empowering us with action choices for each child. We are not perfect, and we will not be able to perfectly follow our plan. But it gives us direction in each part of our children's childhood, so we can consciously focus on the parts that impact them the most *in each phase.* Find your moments—and make the most of them.

We also do not want to simply survive our children's years at home. We want to really live and be present during that time. I do not want to only share ideas on how to make it through each week, how to try to keep the clothes mostly clean, how to attempt to feed everyone more than spaghetti and meatballs, or how to avoid being the team's soccer coach when we are overwhelmed. These are important survival techniques, but only to get us to the bigger purposes of our mom lives and our personal lives.

Our children will carry their young experiences with them for the rest of their lives. Those experiences can support them and positively influence them, and they will ultimately be the foundation on which our children will build their future lives with their families. I am pretty sure I am coming this way only once. So I am not willing to let these years pass without giving them—my husband and our children—*and myself* my best effort and focus.

> "When I am ten, then I won't wear hair bows anymore.
> But don't worry, Mom, I will always love you."
> —Chloe (age 5)

OUR MOST IMPORTANT BEQUESTS
Giving Ourselves Wings

There Is No Greater Gift That Parents Can Offer Their Children

For parents, the most important step in giving their children wings is to give *themselves* wings. Children patiently await their parents' freedom from old wounds, hidden beliefs, and denied emotions that often disallow authentic joyful self-expression. As parents, few of us understand who we *really* are as intuitive, creative, powerful, spiritual beings, and therefore do not reflect the truth of our magnificent identity back to our children. Despite often well-meaning and loving intentions, instead of children observing and, more importantly, feeling wholeness, authenticity, self-love, personal truth, and presence and oneness reflected back to them from their parents, they often see a diminished version of the total well-being of the parent, and therefore a diminished version of the total well-being that is possible for *them.*

Parents give their children wings when they become a clear mirror for what living with wings truly means. As parents become able to fly freely, they simultaneously give their children permission to do the same. There is no greater gift that parents can offer their children than their own awakening.

Annie Burnside
Mother of three
Soul Nurturer and Author
www.annieburnside.com
facebook.com/soulnurturer
Twitter @annieburnside
annie@annieburnside.com

In parenting we come to realize that we cannot hold onto our children too tightly; we have to let them grow up with all the bumps and bruises that come with it. In fact, holding onto them too tightly only adds to the *TILT* in our lives. As hard as it is, we know that letting them go is critical to their independent development. It's not only our seesaw that goes up and down irregularly and at inconvenient moments—so does theirs. Part of our parenting responsibility is to help them learn the skills they need to manage that ride and, ultimately, how to live without us.

In giving our children wings, we also give wings to ourselves. As we raise independent, loving children, we also empower ourselves to live a fulfilling life. Our lives are as worthy of happiness, dreams, and accomplishments as anyone else's. It is within our reach to grasp for what fills our hearts. We can also soar; in fact, we should soar while we help others fly high as well.

How are you doing so far on your journey? Are you happy with yours? What would you change? There is still time, no matter where you are in your life. You have the power to take a step (or a couple of steps) forward today if you choose. It is never too late to become the mom and the woman you always wanted to be.

My hope and goal is to help moms think from a big-picture awareness of the years we are fortunate to have: the years we have for our own lives and, within that framework, the years with our children at home. I hope moms who read this book will consciously select a few things to accomplish that matter the most to them. We want to live the best life we can, as we find the fun, enjoy the humor, and learn as we grow. We want to be proud of the results of our heartfelt efforts and investment in the lives of our children.

When my children reflect on their childhoods (so far), they remember our silly unique traditions. They talk about our loud, irreverent, and goofy family dinners. They remind me about all the poor hamsters we could not keep alive. We laugh about our silly kids' quotes. They reflect on their birthdays and how they are convinced that I must be our Saint Patty's Day leprechaun. Almost all the memories they cherish (except all my mistakes and burnt green beans) were planned into our eighteen-year objectives with our children.

As we mature, we come to understand that in our final hours on this earth, we will not be as concerned about how many toys we accrued in our life. Toys can be great fun, but we cannot take them with us. Instead, it will be the lives that we touched in a positive way that matter. It will be the relationships that we built, fostered, and inspired that will last for generations and will be our true life legacy.

My sixth life lesson is about ensuring that we give our children roots and give them wings. Our efforts for our children ultimately lift us up as well. We can choose to inadvertently hold ourselves and our children back, or we can consciously choose to empower. In each of our *TILTed* momoirs, being the wind beneath our children's wings will become one of our greatest soul-satisfying accomplishments.

Recap of Chapter 6

- ✓ Giving our children roots (core values, traditions, memories) and wings (the ability and confidence to live independently of us) are two of our greatest parenting gifts.

- ✓ Helping our children learn from failure, and sometimes the consequences of it, is a great opportunity to grow.

- ✓ Rather than solving our children's problems for them, we enable and empower them when we instead teach them how to find their solutions themselves.

- ✓ Parenting can inevitably create conflicts between our children and us. We need to choose the battles that matter and let go of those that don't.

- ✓ Our children's homework is not our homework. Teaching them early to manage their workload creates self-sufficiency skills that they need in life.

✓ Outside the classroom, their extracurricular activities can be a powerful teacher of discipline, practice, focus, teamwork, time management, and much more.

✓ Set standards to encourage and empower your children.

✓ Before our children leave, creating an "Eighteen-Year Plan" gives us a big-picture view of what is most important to us to have happen before they go to college.

✓ In giving our children wings, we also give wings to ourselves.

Personal Profile in Mom Courage:
Give Them Wings

I have been a single mother for a little over twelve years and have been blessed with four wonderful children. When my children were thirteen, eleven, six, and five, sadly my marriage ended, and my children's father moved away to be with his newfound love.

During those first few years, the challenges of being a single mother of four were many, between working a full-time job and caring for my children. The only thing that kept me going was the amazing love of my children and the closer relationship I was able to have with each of them. My children visited with their father two days a month, which, as I watched, was not nearly enough, and my heart just broke for them. The days that I held them close and assured them of his love were the hardest.

When my oldest went off to college, I searched my heart and knew that the greatest gift I could give my children was to move them closer to their father and his new life. Children are innocent, and it is not their choice, nor is it their fault, when parents divorce. All of our lives changed with that move, which was now six years ago. The memories that all of us have shared as a family since that move are difficult to put into words. I made the choice then to be their mother and to focus on them and all that they had going on in their lives.

I never imagined the love and the closeness that I developed with each of my children, even if at times I thought I would never make it through. Their father has forever been thankful, and he was able to experience a greater part of their lives, and I believe his life has also changed. My youngest has just started her freshman year in college, and I find myself now with a quiet house and ready to begin the next chapter of my life.

Never let circumstances determine your life; make the choice to do the best you can, and be happy, for you never know what tomorrow will bring. The memories of happiness and times cherished with your loved ones are worth every moment.

Michelle Steele
Mother of four
Director of Operations and Regional Operations Manager, Pinnacle
Partners Group

GUILT-FREE TIPS –
Ten Ways to Let Your Children Grow Up and Give Them Wings

1. Start early with rules and boundaries. Do not give your children everything they ask for regardless of the expense (or lack thereof). Children who are given "every-thing" often struggle later on in life when they believe they deserve it all.

2. Instead of ordering for them, teach your kids how to order their own meals when you eat out. They will do a fine job asking questions and asking for what they want. Empower them!

3. Have kids read the books that will give them a big-life perspective. Remember, they are smarter than you might think!

   - If they do not like to read, give them a "carrot." Tie something that they want to their successfully finishing certain books you assign to them.

   - If that does not motivate them to read, pay them twenty dollars for every book they read off your preapproved list.

   Here are some books we have had our children read:

   Think and Grow Rich, Napoleon Hill

   Tuesdays with Morrie, Mitch Albom

   How to Win Friends & Influence People, Dale Carnegie

   Richest Man in Babylon, George Clason

   7 Habits of Highly Effective Teens, Sean Covey

   Success Principles, Jack Canfield

QBQ, John G. Miller

I Can't Accept Not Trying: Michael Jordan on the Pursuit of Excellence, Michael Jordan

Rich Dad Poor Dad, Robert Kiyosaki

Cash Flow Quadrant, Robert T. Kiyosaki

Million-Dollar Habits, Robert J. Ringer

Soul Surfer, Bethany Hamilton

Acres of Diamonds, Russell H. Conwell

Lincoln on Leadership, Donald Phillips

Anything written by Jim Rohn

4. Teach your children to be respectful of others. Show them how to behave and hold them to those standards, no matter how hard it may be. One easy way to teach respect is to teach them the powerful phrase, "thank you." Those are two of the most powerful words they can use throughout their entire life.

5. Help your children get on their feet, but DO NOT BE THEIR FEET. When they are young, send them back to their rooms to get things they forget rather than getting those things for them. When they are older, make them be the direct liaison for discussing issues that are important to them, from figuring out computer problems with tech support to meeting with their high school guidance counselor.

6. Let them choose their clothes to wear. When they are young, give them three acceptable choices to choose from. Once they are in elementary school, let them express themselves and their style (within reason) through their clothes. What you like may not be their style.

7. When it is time to return the library books, give your children the list of books checked out and a bag. Have them gather the books themselves and bring the full bag and checked-off list back to you.

8. Have them pack their own suitcases for sleepovers or trips. When they are younger, give them a checklist to use to remember the important things they need to take—otherwise they tend to forget toothpaste!

9. Help your child get to know an older child that they look up to who has had success in an area that is important to your child. Whether it is helping your child score a soccer goal or write a college essay, encourage your child to cultivate the relationship and get tips and tricks from their peer.

10. As they grow, help them set age-appropriate goals. Nudge them and support them into accomplishment. Then remind them (often) that they accomplished their goal. Goal achievement now (no matter how small the goal) will equate to self-confidence and more success later.

7

Wisdom from Women: Life Reflections from More Than 50 Wonderful Women

"I do this ALL BY MYSELF...now you help me."
—Courtney (age 4)

Mom Quiz #7: "Now I Do This All by Myself"

Check if anything below applies to you!

☐ You have cried alone, late at night, feeling overwhelmed by this little person(s) you brought into the world. You love her like crazy, but you are scared to death of how to take care of her properly and even more scared of the responsibility you have just taken on.

☐ You did not have time to read all the e-mails in your overflowing e-mail inbox. So you missed the one that told you to send in cookies for your child's very special class party. Every *other* child's mom read that e-mail and sent in a treat. Except you.

☐ You have no idea how to keep all these kids fed all the time, let alone with healthy food. You really wish you could go to the grocery store only once a week but end up going there four to five times in seven days. And you still have to feed them fast food to keep them from starving.

☐ You have wondered with a heavy heart if you said the wrong thing to your teenager. You worry if you are guiding her to the right path. But you do not go back to talk with her, nor to other moms you respect, for fear that it will show weakness or indecision on your part.

☐ You worry about sharing your crazy love and longing for your children in your workplace. Many of your coworkers do not have kids and might think you are distracted and loony.

☐ You worry and have no idea what sixth grade will be like for your child. How will she get along with so many different teachers? How will she make friends with so many different classmates? How will she zigzag in between classes and get to the next one on time? But you do not ask anyone for help because you think you should be able to handle this on your own.

☐ You never ran "track" growing up. So in your child's first season, she is talking a foreign language to you. You did not understand that she would participate in several events at each meet, so at the first event, you miss seeing most of them. You are there, but you are clueless. You mean there are different kinds of shoes *for each event?!*

Mom Hazing to Mom Amazing

I was checking out in a department store a few years ago when a nice young woman commented on my hair. "Oh," she said, "I love your hair color! What *is* it? Ash-blond? Blond-ash?" I do not know exactly what she called it. I had to think for a minute because I had never colored my hair, nor had I taken much time to pay attention to it beginning to change color.

I looked at her and told her my hair color was "four-kid gray." I said, "You cannot buy this color; you have to earn it." I wasn't sure she wanted to go down that road; it would be easier for her to buy my hair color off the shelf. Maybe that should be my next business endeavor: sell "Four-Kid Gray" hair color, although there may not be a large enough demographic interested in it.

The funny thing is, my kids do not care what my hair color is.

Being a mom is a humbling experience. No matter what we might have accomplished in our lives, once kids are here, we are brought right back to earth like our first day on a new job. Maybe we went to the new-parent classes and read the new-baby books, but real life always has a way of surprising us and humbling us with how little we really know about it.

I actually realized my seventh life lesson the first day our first child arrived—my world was drastically *TILT*ed within hours of his birth, and I needed some real moms to help me through it. Our son was born early in the morning after a difficult delivery and an emergency C-section. Just a short time later, I realized that everything I thought I knew from reading about how to take care of a newborn was of little value in the real world. This was a real child—who cried, who was hungry at strange hours, and who was quite heavy to hold (nine pounds, one ounce). That extra head roll for the car seat did not even fit—he was already too big for it.

Thinking I had my seesaw straight, balanced, and in control was, of course, not true. I was not ready for what was coming, as I had thought.

The mom *TILT* had begun. Reading about how to care for a baby was very different from reality. I would end up learning much more about parenting from the experiences of great moms around me.

From Mom Hazing...

> "Mom, I will share my new mirror with you.
> But I do not know how you will fit your big hair into it."
> —Chloe (age 6)

I will never forget that boardroom meeting when my big prego belly hit the table and spilled several cups of coffee. Over twenty years later, I still remember that moment like it was yesterday.

So if our mom hazing really begins during our pregnancy, and proceeds to taunt us after delivery, through walking, talking, and potty training, into adolescence and teenage years—can we ever look forward to taking the step from mom hazing to mom amazing?

Yes. Understand that the hardest parts of being a mom are when we have no idea what we are doing. Maybe our child is about to start walking and we are worried that the house is not properly child-proofed. What cabinet locks should we buy so we can keep the baby out but still get in ourselves? Maybe our child is about to enter sixth grade and we have no idea how he or she is going to deal with the higher levels of independence and responsibility, let alone how to get the locker open between classes and still get to the next class before the bell rings.

The questions continue as the years progress and we come to new stages. Who is going to have the "birds and the bees" talk with our daughter? When should we tell her that, no, you do not "poop out a baby"? What is the difference between jazz and hip-hop dance, and why should our daughter do either? What is DXM, and how do we know our kids are not messing with that? What classes should our high-schooler take to be sure he meets college entrance requirements? How do we help our high school child through the college search and admissions process? What do we say if our child tells us he or she does not believe in God?

The hazing is in the not knowing what to expect. We can do our best to be prepared, but we will undoubtedly still slip up.

My first delivery in the hospital was so hard because I did not know what was coming next. I did not know what to expect. I had read *What to Expect When You Are Expecting*, but I still did not grasp all that I was expecting. Birthing a child is no small or simple experience.

Some of us are further along in our mom lives. Some of us are rookies, being hazed in our first year of motherhood. Who do we turn to for help and answers to our toughest mom questions?

To Mom Amazing!

This life lesson is about finding mom mentors who can help us clear that next hurdle. We can find help to strengthen, inform, and prepare us for the next stages in life with our children. Our amazing mom is in us, waiting to be discovered, even if she is buried under layers of wet crib sheets, larger-than-life school art projects, or clothing our child outgrew two months after we bought it.

Wherever we each are in our journey, there are working moms who have successfully gone ahead of us. Reaching out to smarter, wiser people for their wisdom can alter our life decisions—forever.

One such person shared his wisdom with me, and I have never forgotten it. I used to have my hair cut by the owner of several successful hair salons. I loved to go to him to learn from him (and his haircuts were pretty good, too). His family was very close, and I have always admired those who could keep a close relationship with their children over time. As Christmas was approaching one year, I asked him what they were going to do for his kids. I knew he could afford to do anything he wanted. He told me, "Oh, we do not give our children gifts."

Since ours were still so little and life was *all* about Little Tykes, Matchbox cars, and Legos, it took me a moment to digest what he was saying. Then he finished: "We give them memories." Honestly, I was quiet as I absorbed the depth of what he had just shared with me. I have never forgotten it.

A few years later, I am very sad to tell you, his grown daughter tragically passed away from cancer, leaving behind a small son. The owner's family will grieve for her forever, but I also know how much he cherishes the memories they created together before she was gone. It is profound that he focused on the memories long before he ever knew she would be gone far too soon.

Balance in life is truly impossible. I have searched for it high and low; I cannot find it. I have actually searched for it since the day I became a mom—over seven thousand days now and counting. But my salon owner found a way to bridge the gap. Balance is impossible; memories are better.

Seeking wisdom from those who have gone before us, whom we respect, can help us solve an "unsolvable" problem, can help us overcome sadness and failure, and can inspire us to reach our potential. I learned that real-life knowledge was by far the most valuable and practical—the more we learn from experienced moms about what is coming, the easier our lives can be. We cannot underestimate the wisdom of experienced women.

Where Can We Find the Best Mom Advice?

"I can't wait to grow up and have kids, Mom.
I want to get all my tips from you—you are the best mom ever!"
—Chloe (age 10)

It is OK to ask for help. Mom mentors can clear up our confusion, liberate our guilt, and help us laugh (instead of cry) about the day our child was the only one not wearing sixties clothes to school because we forgot. They understand. They have been there and done that. Or they are in the middle of it right now, just as we are. This village of mom mentors is powerful. They know the heartache, they have lived in the carpool lane, their children have cried on their shoulders, and they have experienced the deepest joy in their children's love. Do not underestimate the power of the women all around you. Reach out and ask for help.

Who should we ask for good advice? We can seek it from many people: teachers, pediatricians, our moms, neighbors, family members, dads, school child psychologists, business coaches, soccer coaches, other professional working moms, or anyone whose shoulder we can lean on long enough. There are working moms in every industry, thankfully, so there are many out there whom we can ask for their insight and experience to help us as we raise our children.

And more often than not, in our search for answers on how to parent, we find that many of our answers are inherent within us. Sometimes we just need to hear how others have done it before us to realize our way works best for us. We expect that others, who are "successful," know more than we do. Yet, many times, in the depths of our hearts and souls, we, in fact, hold some of the answers we need.

As we each go through our mom years, we have to find people who are like-minded, who have the same values and parenting philosophies we have, whose children are doing all right or even excelling in life. Listen to their advice, not to the ideas of moms whose children have to call their secretaries to request an audience with them. While there may be some women in the world who need or want to live that way, that is probably not a solution for most of us.

Being Ready for What Is Coming

> "Don't use big words right now. I am on vacation."
> —Courtney (age 12)

Our poor first child: everything was trial and error with him. I made many of my rookie-mom mistakes raising him. I just have to hope that I will be a brilliant mom to the rest of them as a result of it.

A few days after Parker's fifteenth birthday, he told me, "You know, I could already have my driver's permit." My response, "What?! You are just a kid!" Then I found out he was right. I had no idea. We went out a week or so later, and he passed the tests for his permit. I learned that all the *cool moms* already knew that and took their fifteen-year-olds to get their driving permits on their fifteenth birthdays. I have long ago resigned myself to the fact that I am just not one of the coolest moms. Poor first child.

Now with our other children, I am *so* much smarter. I might even have a shot at being a cool mom, because now I know that taking them to test for their driver's permit on their actual fifteenth birthday means you rock as a mom.

Many sources can advise us on our next stage in life with children, including social media. Books, parenting newsletters, and websites put information at our fingertips. Yet still the simplest and most relevant resources are often our mom friends. Not just any mom friends, but the ones who are in alignment with us and who live similar lives, since they will give the most relevant advice.

If you work full time out of the home, talk with those moms—they are juggling the same schedule you are. They have had to find solutions to get the basics done, get to work, and find ways to fit in the bonus fun. Likewise, if you work part time, if you work from home, or if 100 percent of your work is mothering your children, then ask similar working moms for their best ideas.

I love to ask parents with children older than mine how they handled things that we still have coming. In the following pages are some of the ideas they shared with me.

> "When your tummy hurts, that means you need to go to the potty."
> —Elle (age 4)
> "Eewww—TMI!"
> —Chloe (age 6)
> "What does 'TMI' mean?"
> —Elle (age 4)
> "Too much information!"
> —Chloe (age 6

How to Handle Coming-of-Age

1. For your kindergarten child:

For those whose children are the youngest in class or near the youngest, or who show lack of maturity, consider starting them one year later or holding them back in school. It really cannot hurt them to give them a chance at maturity or to be the oldest in the class. When I was considering this for one of our children with a summer birthday, the only moms I spoke to who regretted their decision were the ones who did *not* hold their children back.

2. For your sixth-grader:

Moving from elementary to junior high is a big shift in our children's lives. Not only will their class environment completely change (going from one main classroom and teacher to several), but they and all of their friends are entering puberty. This is no small change. I learned after my first daughter to spend a lot of time from third grade on preparing my girls for what was coming: how the kids start to focus on more than grades or who is the fastest in the class, how the boys start to look at girls differently, how the girls start to look at each other differently. Communication on the front end makes this big transition easier in their awareness of what is happening. It also helps them be prepared for it.

3. For your thirteen-year-old:

On the thirteenth birthday, consider taking just that one child on vacation somewhere, anywhere. At this age it helps strengthen the bond you have going into what may be some tough years. They will remember the time you spend with just them. Frommer's little book, *100 Places to Take Your Kids before They Grow Up*, is full of great destination ideas.

4. When your child gets his or her driver's permit:

Let them drive as much as possible with you in the car (white knuckles and close calls included). My mom-of-five friend shared this with me. The more they drive in the car early with you, the more prepared they will be to drive alone.

5. For your eighteen-year-old:

Do not think that just because they are older, they do not want or need your attention. Children love to be loved by their parents at any age. Pay attention to what is important to them and connect with them there. Whether it is listening to their favorite music and gifting them a song through iTunes or texting them good luck when you know they have a big presentation for their class, keep paying attention, no matter their age.

Insights from Seriously Cool Moms Who Have Been There and Done That

I have come to understand that life is about continuous learning, not a moment at which we "arrive" and have all the intelligence we need. As we progress through our lives, we learn how truly little we know or understand. The meaning of life, why we are really here, and *what are we doing* having these children in our lives are daunting questions. They are difficult to answer. Yet in seeking those answers, we can find the fulfillment in our daily struggles.

To help us all on our mom journeys, I asked women around me if they would share their experience and wisdom with us. Some of these women I know very well, and some I have gotten to know recently. But all of them have worked, all have braved the world of momhood, and all have come out the other side a survivor. Many graciously shared with us. Some of their thoughts I have scattered throughout the book; some are included in this chapter.

Enjoy this part of the book. It is a blessing to have the wisdom of so many amazing women who have shared their hearts with us to enrich our lives and those of our families.

"If I Knew Then What I Know Now, I Would..."

1. If I knew then what I know now...

I would have had more confidence that I was doing the best for my children, my family, and myself in meeting my own goals. My priority was to provide opportunities for my children that I did not have during my childhood. As a working mom, I tried to set the stage for my children to be better people and to be more accomplished than me while finding happiness as adults. I was once asked by a mom who did not work outside the house: if I had had the same financial stability without working, would I quit my job? My answer was no. Part of my persona was the satisfaction that came from the experiences provided by my career. I believed then as I do today that the quality of time spent far exceeds the quantity of time, regardless of the endeavor.

Mary Nance
Mother of two
Grandmother of four
My Loving Mom
Retired Executive Vice President/Controller

2. If I knew then what I know now...

I would have relaxed, loved more, and stressed less. Our children learn more from the difficult times (maybe when we weren't at our best) than when everything is right and we're trying for perfect mom/perfect family. Life lessons work that way and better prepare all of us to be thriving adults.

Prior to my children reaching their high school years, we lived in four foreign countries. I had little control over anything—no supermarkets, only one English school, no choice of teachers, no after-school activities, and no TV they could understand. Guess what? They have grown into amazing adults! So...relax, enjoy, and give them your best, then let go!

Linda Fair
Mother of two
Grandmother of five
Operating Principal, Keller Williams Realty—Cary
lindafair@kw.com

3. If I knew then what I know now...

I would not have wished the time away. At every stage, I wanted to already be past it. During potty training, I could not wait for that to be done. Then when we made it to adolescence, I wished we were back at potty training! Now, years later, I am so sorry that I did not enjoy each stage as I lived through it. Those stages are gone forever.

Amy Sperr
Mother of two
Owner, One Incredible Life Salon
Facebook.com/AmyMorrisonSperr
Amyhair16@bellsouth.net

4. If I knew then what I know now...

I would have saved that first pair of grimy tennis shoes,

I would have framed every poem ever written for me,

I would have said "yes" even when it scared me to death,

I would have taken a picture of the proud son who brought that snake home, instead of screaming and running,

I would have not missed a single occasion that each of them wanted me to attend,

I would have scratched each back *every* time they asked,

I would have snuggled more,

I would have told them how proud of them I am each and every day and NOT have forgotten a single one!

Love is a powerful thing...and I must say that my three kids are the best part of my life!

> **Kathy L. Larrabee**
> **Mother of three**
> **Grandmother of one**
> **Team Leader, Keller Williams Realty Augusta Partners**
> **larrabee47@gmail.com**

5. If I knew then what I know now...

Actually, I would not do ANYTHING differently. I think the knowledge of who I am at this point in my life and what I've become is shaped by the many years of making choices, choosing paths, and venturing into uncharted territory. What a pleasant ride it has been to find myself in the place where I am now, not encumbered by the question of how I got here but simply enjoying the fact of being here. I can honestly say that I think my wrong turns have been as important to this process as my right turns, which is why I say I would not do anything differently. And there's so much more to look forward to on this journey!

> **Linda Gifford**
> **Mother of four**
> **Grandmother of six**
> **Vice President, Retail Operations, Rosemary Beach Retail Company**
> **www.rbtradingcompany.com**
> **facebook.com/RosemaryBeachTradingCompany**

6. If I knew then what I know now...

I would realize the past and the future live inside of my head. Therefore, I get to remember and create anything I choose. Since my thoughts determine how I feel, how I act, and how I treat my children, I would have watched my thoughts more carefully.

I always have and always will see my children as powerful beyond measure because how you see your children is how you will treat them, and how you treat them is who they will become. It has proven true because both of my sons are powerful men.

Dianna Kokoszka
Mother of two sons and one stepson
Grandmother of four
CEO of MAPS Coaching & Keller Williams University,
Keller Williams Realty International
mapscoaching.kw.com

7. If I knew then what I know now...

I would not change a thing! I think back to the time in my life when I was teaching and raising my children and remember that even though there were ups and downs, the decision to continue teaching was without a doubt the one that was right for me and my family. I was a better wife and mom because I was fulfilled with my own career goals. I am blessed with a supportive husband and three fantastic children who have grown into adults who inspire me every day with their character.

Kathy Ramos
Mother of three
Grandmother of two
Retired Teacher, Gwinnett County Public Schools
clkaramos@gmail.com

8. If I knew then what I know now...

I would have lived in the present more! I wouldn't have worried about pleasing others but instead just focused on my immediate family! It is true that our lives are no dress rehearsal...LIVE it now! You'll be watched, you'll be judged, you'll be gossiped about, you'll be admired, you'll be envied—but you'll end up on top of a beautiful world if you listen to your heart and live YOUR dream. Happiness in the end is what it's all about! If you have it, you will give it—to your family, to your community, and to our world...It will make for a better place. Don't listen to anyone other than yourself and your family in deciding what works for you! It's OK to be "outside of the box"! Your life should be a fun, exciting adventure, and you need to make the most of your journey. You cannot do it all or be it all! Just live your dream and decide to BE HAPPY. At times there will be bumps in your road, so embrace those bumps and move on. These bumps might be changing careers, a divorce, managing your home while dealing with aging parents, children struggling in school, cancer in your family—lots of things can "throw" us! Remember that it's all creating puzzle pieces of YOUR life. Make your final puzzle one that stands out and one you're very proud of!

Ann Hartley
Mother of three
Owner, Hartley Restaurant Group
Georgesatalysbeach.com, Seagrovevillagemarket.com,
Lacocina30a.com
Facebook.com: George's, Seagrove Village Market, La Cocina
Mexican Grill and Bar
Twitter: Georgesatalysbeach, Seagrovevillage, Lacocina30a
Annhartley1@gmail.com

9. If I knew then what I know now...

I don't think I appreciated my children, especially my oldest, as a little being that was not just "my child." I was young and very busy making a career for myself and for her. I was divorced when she was two and was primarily responsible for us. I think I would read more about what connects for children, like how to listen to them more carefully and how to make sure they are honored and feel important. She went with me everywhere, but we seemed to always be rushing. I would rush less, listen more, and read more about how to be a great mother, instead of being a mother on the run.

Beverly Steiner
Mother of two
Grandmother of one
Operating Principal, Keller Williams Realty Danville and
Walnut Creek
Partner, Keller Williams Realty Northern California and Hawaii
www.donthang-climb.com
www.donthangclimb.wordpress.com

10. If I knew then what I know now...

I wouldn't have wasted one precious second struggling with our lifestyle decisions and sacrifices; to buy the smaller house, drive the used car, wear the "non designer-label" clothes. We made those choices in order to gain more freedom and time to invest in the lives of our children. They are grown and married now, and we can finally have any of those things. Funny, what once seemed so attractive to me now seems so trivial. I have all that really matters, relationships with our children and amazing memories of the times we shared.

Mary Jane Rogan
Mother of three
Grandmother of one
Mentor / Counselor
mjrogan@bellsouth.net

11. If I knew then what I know now...

I would grow more alongside my children. As parents we sometimes want to control or shape our children as we want so very much for them. I would nurture their innate abilities and value them so much more for who they are rather than who we want them to be. Our children are important because a loving God individually shaped each one from the moment of conception. We need to allow them to blossom into the beautiful beings that they were designed to be.

Debbie Tufts
Mother of three
Real Estate Consultant, Keller Williams Realty Atlantic
Partners–Jacksonville
www.dtuftsandcompany.com
Debbie.tufts@kw.com

12. If I knew then what I know now…

I would do it all over again the same way. My mother went to work for the first time in her life when I was five years old and she was forty-five. She was so happy working and was very successful. She became a role model for me, influencing my attitude about working in a positive way, but I didn't really like having her away so much. That impacted my feelings about family and work. So I worked around my children's schedule, negotiating work hours that were unique for that era.

It worked out well for me, and when they were older, I was able to really focus on a great career in real estate. It was one of the advantages of being young when I had children. Real estate provided great flexibility, great earning potential, and some control over my schedule, which allowed me to be present at all of their events with planning. I have never regretted putting them first. I was still young enough to go for it when they went to college.

Kay Evans
Mother of two
Grandmother of five
Regional Co-owner, Keller Williams Realty–Southeast Region and
North Florida Region, kayevans@kw.com

13. If I knew then what I know now...

I would not have protected them as much as I did. My childhood was far from perfect so I was determined to give my three children opportunities, education, structure, and lots of fun. Along the way I found myself sheltering them from situations with negative outcomes. In my quest to protect them, they were spared many times from the hard knocks and tough decisions that we can sometimes face during childhood.

My children are well-rounded, wonderful young adults now. However, in retrospect those hard knocks might have made it a little easier for them as adults, when they inevitably have tough decisions to make or when they hit that proverbial brick wall.

Julia Nelson
Mother of three
Grandmother of one
Operating Partner, Keller Williams Realty Atlanta Partners
www.youratlantahomeguide.com
Twitter @julianelson5
julia.youratlantahomeguide@gmail.com

14. If I knew then what I know now...

I would be sure to take care of myself first. It may sound selfish, but if you don't take care of you, you cannot help and take care of others.

Connie Wiggins
Mother of two
Grandmother of three
President, Gwinnett Clean & Beautiful
www.gwinnettcb.org

15. If I knew then what I know now...

I would have let my kids struggle a little more, and I would have had them get jobs (and not made excuses about how they were too busy with school activities) so they would have been better prepared for the real world. I would have had them spend more time serving others. I would not have made it all about them. In the real world, it is all about others.

Linda McKissack
Mother of three
Grandmother of three
Business Owner and Wealth Building Coach, Keller Williams Realty
Regional Owner, Keller Williams Realty, The Ohio Valley Region
Author of *Presentation Mastery for Realtors* and
HOLD: How to Find, Buy, and Rent Houses for Wealth
LindaMcKissack.com
@Linda_McKissack
McKissack@kw.com

16. If I knew then what I know now...

1. I would have provided more opportunities to have my children participate in the arts from an early age.

2. I also would have exposed them to more charitable-giving opportunities. Serving the underserved can be a wonderful experience in teaching children to respect and care for their fellow man.

3. Having always volunteered with our children's extracurricular activities, I wish I had protested more aggressively against trophies for everyone, every time, no matter what. The ability to learn to accept failure is most important to children's ability to motivate themselves as they develop life lessons. To try harder next time teaches them to try harder in life.

4. Lastly, I realize how important it is to accept the fact that as a young parent "YOU DO NOT NEED TO KNOW EVERYTHING!"

Remember, these lessons are what make grandmothers amazingly smart!

Judy Waters
Mother of two
Grandmother of four
Executive Director, Community Foundation for Northeast Georgia
www.cfneg.org
jwaters@cfneg.org

17. If I knew then what I know now…

I would have invented the Crock-Pot…and used it. On a serious note, I might not have been in such a hurry…If I financially could have, I would have preferred only working part time until he started school—not so much for his sake, since he turned out fine, but for my sake. I missed out on some important moments that can never be recaptured.

Sherry Lewis
Mother of two
Grandmother of seven
Regional Director, Keller Williams Realty—Oklahoma Region
sherry@kw.com
Facebook: Sherry Phillips Lewis

18. If I knew then what I know now…

I would have spent more time teaching my kids how to be grateful for the simple things in life. If I could have a "do-over," I would spend more time focusing on the importance of gratitude because it requires us to see how we've been supported and affirmed by other people… Gratitude encourages us not only to appreciate gifts but also to repay them (or pay them forward). Gratitude is so good for our bodies, our minds, and our relationships, and helps keep us from having an "entitle-ment" mentality.

Linda Cooke
Mother of two plus three bonus kids
Grandmother of eight
Retired Business and Life Coach, My Coaching Advantage

19. If I knew then what I know now...

Working moms, stop beating yourselves up! It is not about stay-ing at home with your children; it is about "being home" when you are there. The quality time you spend with your children is far more important than the quantity of time. Stay focused on them at home and focused on work at work. You cannot be in two places at once. We get no "do-overs" with our children, so make everything count!

Nikki Ubaldini
Mother of two
President / Director of 6 Companies, Keller Williams Realty South
Florida Region
nikki@kwopportunity.com

20. If I knew then what I know now...

I wish I had asked my children more probing questions rather than being so quick to offer advice. It is better for them to think through their problems and come up with their own solutions rather than for me to try to solve them in my way. Who knows—they may have had better ideas!

Norma Biggs
Mother of three
Grandmother of seven
Former Senior Technical Analyst, IBM

21. If I knew then what I know now...

I would definitely take more pictures and lighten up a bit when I was confronted with an unexpected dilemma. One afternoon my son Nick (age three) went to his bedroom to take a nap. I found him thirty minutes later completely nude and covered in magic marker body art because Razar and Tokar (the villains from Ninja Turtles) had obviously attacked him.

This was actually one of the fortunate moments that I took a deep breath and a few snapshots. Now we still pull out that picture on occasion and laugh. As I look back, I realize that very few "situations" were as serious as I took them. I would have had a lot more fun with their mischief!

Deb Nardy
Mother of two
Team Leader, Keller Williams Realty Atlanta Partners
debnardy.com
debnardy@facebook.com
deb@debnardy.com

22. If I knew then what I know now...

I wish I knew the most meaningful things...

I wish I knew how intensely rewarding and challenging motherhood truly is. It redefined me as a person in a million little ways and countless big ways, from expanding my hobbies and interests based on my kids' passions to learning how to fiercely advocate for my children when they needed me—when Mama Bear comes out, watch out!

I wish I knew that balancing the demands of motherhood and growing myself as a person would be a great challenge. It would stretch me to the highest highs and the lowest lows.

I wish I knew that growing in faith and praying for my children was more important than anything else. Prayer leads to partnership with God and ultimate wisdom (not to mention sanity). Ultimately,

God brought our kids into the world and HE is their heavenly Father forever. When my eldest son left for college, my heart felt like it was being ripped out of my chest, yet I KNEW God was going to be with him forever. I could let go. God guides and loves each of us, but we have to trust and stay connected to HIM.

I wish I knew what a sacred calling motherhood really is and how it is our chance to cocreate life with God. We leave our greatest legacy on the earth through the loving eyes and hearts of our children. The love we pour into them lasts for generations to come.

> Christine Martinello
> Mother of three
> Owner, Training Solutions International
> Author of *Atlanta's Real Women* and
> *The Momager Guide: Empowering Moms to Leave a Loving Legacy*
> www.christinemartinello.com
> www.momager.com
> Facebook.com: Christine Martinello and/or Momagers

23. If I knew then what I know now...

I would plan more uninterrupted family time for us to do things together. I would put it on the calendar and do it, not wait for it to happen, because it never did to the degree that everyone needed at the time. That way we would have had no regrets of "I wish we had done..." We would have just planned it and done it no matter what. Work will be there tomorrow, but the time with the children will not be.

By the way, some of us working moms are also working grandmoms now, and the same holds true—plan it and do it. They grow up even faster than our children did.

> Kathleen M. Teare
> Mother of two

Grandmother of three
Director of Property Management, Atlanta Partners Property
Management
www.atlantapartnerspropertymanagement.com
kteare@ppmmail.com

24. If I knew then what I know now...

As a mompreneur and wifepreneur, the biggest challenge you'll run into is balance, balance, balance. Balance as a wife, balance as a mom, and balance as an entrepreneur.

As a wife, mother of five children, and grandmother of three grandchildren, I have to prioritize my daily schedule, making sure that it has balance. Making specific work times has been a must for me, and allowing myself a certain amount of time to accomplish my work tasks within the set-aside time frame has helped me to maintain my focus. But I still struggled with feeling guilty about whether or not I was spending too much time on my business and not enough time with my family. The thing that freed me up from this was including my family in my weekly calendar. This has helped me stay balanced, and most importantly, it has helped me not to forget those things that are important to my husband and children while growing my business.

Danette Moss
Mother of five
Grandmother of three
Author, Business Strategist, and Radio Talk Show Host
www.LetsTalkStrategies.com
www.DanetteMoss.com

25. If I knew then what I know now...

There was a point in time when my daughters both shared with me that I was their role model. I wish I would have embraced those words and spent more time being their mentor rather than just a teacher. As a mom, we teach our children the basic life skills that we have mostly adopted from our parents and them from their parents and so on. We teach them the normal behaviors that are acceptable in society in preparation toward becoming good citizens of our communities.

But as a mentor we can expand the dialogue around the kitchen table, explore life's possibilities outside of our own comfort zones, and challenge our children to be more than good citizens within their respective communities, but also global citizens and leaders of the world who will some day become great contributors to the human race and mankind.

The things I have taught my children have enabled them to get out of the nest to fly, but I wish I would have mentored them so they could not only fly but SOAR into their highest potential. My nest may be empty today but my mentoring has just begun!

Trinita Patten
Mother of three
President and CEO, Ladybug for Girls Foundation, Inc
www.ladybugforgirlsfoundation.org
Twitter @ladybugforgirls
Facebook Ladybug For Girls Foundation
tpatton@ladybugforgirls.com

26. If I knew then what I know now...

I would probably make the same mistakes all over again.

Patricia Hermes
Mother of five
Grandmother of eight
Patricia Hermes Writes
patriciahermes@snet.net

27. If I knew then what I know now...

I would have listened to all the people who said, "Be careful, this time with your children will go by before you know it." I heard that so many times, but it seemed when my children were little that the time would last forever. Now my children are grown up with lives of their own, and I would give just about anything for even one day back when they were three or four years old to play with them.

I was visiting with my kids the other day, and we were discussing their childhood. I told them I wish I had been more relaxed and listened to the book *Don't Sweat the Small Stuff...and It's All Small Stuff.* I was specifically thinking about a time when Brooke's dad let her paint her own bedroom. She was only eleven years old. Now, at that time I was a single mother and divorced from her father. He was watching the kids that night and let Brooke pick out all of her own paint, gave her the supplies, and said, "Have at it, Brooke—paint it any way you like." I was really upset about that. I felt she needed guidance, she was going to make a mess, she was going to mess it up, and on and on. Now looking back, it was such a wonderful treat for her to be able to do that—and he gave her the freedom to "mess things up." It was her mess though. We laugh about it together now, but then it really stressed me out. I needed to let go of the unimportant.

My son, James, still remembers me rocking him to sleep at night when he was a small child. How precious that memory is! I would have never have guessed back then that he would think about that time as a child with his most fond memories.

For moms out there with children at home: Cherish every moment to hold, tickle, and snuggle your children. They will remember it. Focus on the most important things with your children—character, goals, direction, belief in God, and all else will fall into place. This will set their direction in life.

Being a business owner, I was always pretty busy. I have no regrets per se, but there are things I wish I had done more of, and some I wish

I had done less of. Now that my children are grown up, I do get to enjoy the time with them even more. Now we are good friends. One thing is for sure, I will be much more relaxed and fun with my grandkids. I can hardly wait for that time!

Wendy Patton
Mother of two and stepmother of three
Operating Principal, Keller Williams Realty
www.WendyPatton.com
Facebook.com/wendypatton
Wendy@WendyPatton.com

28. If I knew then what I know now...

I would have been more readily accepting of the help that was offered to me by others; mothers who raise their children alone are often reluctant to ask for any assistance because they want to be perceived by their friends and family as being a strong and competent parent. I have learned that accepting help does not make you a weak mother, and having a plethora of support and loving individuals in your and your child's life will give your children a strong, solid foundation to know how to learn, love, and grow.

Donna Marie Ardolino
Mother of two
Grandmother of one
Realtor®, Keller Williams Realty Atlanta Partners
www.ArdolinoRealty.com
Facebook.com/Donna Ardolino
DonnaArdolino@aol.com

29. If I knew then what I know now...

This has always been one of my passions—always being a working mom with all three of my kids. My advice would be to make sure to spend quality time with your children—reading with them, listening to their day, and asking questions. I always participated in field trips and showed up for events at school or in their classroom. I would pick each one of them up once a month for a quick lunch "off campus" or have lunch with them at school. Making special one-on-one time where you can focus only on them is so important.

Jennice Doty
Mother of three
Grandmother of one
Owner, TCT Property Management Services
www.tctproperties.com
jennice@tctproperties.com

30. If I knew then what I know now...

I would have simplified my life so that I could have treasured each moment with my children. Before I knew it, I was taking my kids to college, adjusting to a quiet home, and sitting at my dinner table with too many empty chairs.

Roxanne Formisano
Mother of three
Broker, Keller Williams Towne Square Realty
www.roxanneformisano.com

31. If I knew then what I know now...

Looking back, I would relax, enjoy more, and stress far less about all I thought I was taking from my boys by trusting in nannies while I went to work. I would laugh—not cry—as I was teaching a son to wash and dry his clothes at age twelve over the phone. Today, my sons are quite capable of managing all those household chores, without complaining or feeling imposed upon. They are as comfortable in the laundry room as in the boardroom.

I remember the guilt of missing a field trip or soccer game, and the worry that I was making the wrong decision. Today as adult men and fathers themselves, my sons remember all the events I attended and not the ones I missed. The few I missed loomed so large to me, yet to them were hardly noticed. I certainly wish I could have saved myself the guilt!

I wish I could have known then that I was not only teaching them basic life skills, but also the invaluable ability to support and encourage the women in their lives to follow their dreams. Yes, I would do it all over again!

Peggy Slappey
Mother of two
Grandmother of four
Broker/Owner, Peggy Slappey Properties, Inc
www.psponline.com
peggy@psponline.com

32. If I knew then what I know now...

My father gave me the best advice when I had my first child, Elizabeth. He said, "All children have their own timetable. Don't rush them and don't rush too quick to judge them." I didn't fully understand the impact of his omniscient wisdom until a few years later. He was so right! We are too quick as people, and especially as parents, to put a "label" on others. It is difficult as a parent to not label your children; after all, they can quickly demonstrate their personality traits at a very early age; however, they are still developing, and our reaction to their behavior as parents can manipulate them.

My children, now twenty-one and eighteen, are very different as adults than they were as youngsters. My son, JT, was an extremely shy boy who is now an incredible people person and very outgoing. My daughter, Elizabeth, was very bossy and not at all diplomatic. She is now a very refined young lady. I will admit that both "developments" in my children came from great coaching from my husband and me! Through constant conversation with gracious words, we explained to them how to treat others and, most importantly, taught them to look at situations from another perspective.

I have two famous expressions in our household, and I will share them with you. My first one: *With responsibility comes freedom.* I told my children that if they studied hard and received good grades, they would have the freedom of choosing any college they wanted to attend. If they always did what they told me they were going to do, then they would have the freedom with me to do what they wanted. If they ever lied to me (and I would always find out), then they had no freedom with me. As each one entered high school, John and I sat down with them and explained how their responsibility would affect their freedom in high school, including driving privileges. Their actions, study habits, and communication would affect whether or not they had freedom or confinement.

My second expression: *Your home is not a democracy; it is a dictatorship, and your dad and I make the rules.* My children learned quickly not to ask one parent and not the other. John and I are a team, and my children understand that now...It took them a while! Children seek out structure and discipline, but parents can tear that down by playing one against the other. The greatest gift you can give to your children is a great marriage. And that means two people work together to raise their children without raising their voices and to allow their family to grow together as one. We are all different and unique. Once we truly understand that and embrace all of our differences and accept them fully, and even make fun of each other (which we do...a lot in our family), we are teaching the great lesson of life—living together and loving together in spite of our differences.

Tara Locke
Mother of two
Team Leader/Managing Broker, Keller Williams Realty Atlanta
Partners
Tara.locke@comcast.net

33. If I knew then what I know now...

I would listen more, love more, and make my kids work harder for the things they want more!

Leslie Thebaut
Mother of three
Grandmother of one
Tebo Dental Group
tebodental.com
lthebaut@tebodental.com

34. If I knew then what I know now...

Life lessons are always important: how to talk to adults, interview for a job, even sew on a button, et cetera. The one life lesson that we have focused on for our grandchildren is money management. We focus on reading and mastering Dave Ramsey's *Total Money Makeover* and being able to discuss it to help our grandchildren have a healthy financial life.

In addition, our children were raised going to church, and they have raised our grandchildren the same way. Their being raised as believers has greatly reduced the stress we would have experienced and has made it much easier to teach them Christian principles. Our goal has been to raise a family that is "part of the solution, not part of the problem."

Mary Bennitt Harker
Mother of three
Grandmother of eight
Founder, Harker 5 Star Real Estate Team
mary@maryharker.com

35. If I knew then what I know now...

In Honor of Mary Harker's Amazing Mother, Who Adopted Her:

"GG" lived each day to the fullest, "extracting the preciousness from the vile" in all circumstances. She was easy to be kind to, as she had a word of encouragement or inspiration or kindness to all she touched, wanting so much to "bring out the best" in each one. One of her favorite sayings: "If you laugh, the whole world laughs with you! If you cry, you cry alone!"

I would call her at the retirement center each morning and say, "Good morning, Mom! Are you going to have a good day?"

"Why, Mary, of course I'm going to have a good day! I don't have enough hours left in my life to have a bad hour, let alone a bad day!"

Nola Belle Heald Bennitt, 1905–2001
Mother of two
Grandmother of four
Great Grandmother of ten
Concert Pianist, Piano Teacher

36. If I knew then what I know now...

I wouldn't sweat the small stuff. I wouldn't waste any time worrying about whether I was doing a good enough job with my kids. In my heart, my children have always been my priority. I would focus more on what is happening right now and let tomorrow worry about itself.

Marie Sapienza
Mother of three
Grandmother of one
Laser Technician / Medical Esthetician
mariesapienza@yahoo.com

37. If I knew then what I know now...

I am thankful to say that even after many years of raising two very active boys, I really have few regrets. The only thought I would consider is to have put some of my work on hold and given more focus on what was important to my children at the time.

Today my grown boys say that they can remember going on vacation to the beach and that while they would be out in the ocean or at the pool, I was back in the room on the phone taking care of customers. THAT was a huge mistake. Kids can have all the toys, clothes, and things you can buy, but what they want most is your TIME—time just to sit and listen to them, to tell them stories of your youth, to tell them what made you smile when you were young—TIME AND ATTENTION.

While my boys were never embarrassed by me, as I always heard other parents say about their children, they did wish that I had been a room mom or had gone on more of their school field trips. My missing those was a BIG MISTAKE. Those REALLY mean so much to a child—believe me, I still hear about it today. But through it all, I never missed but one ball game for each of my boys throughout their whole recreation, middle school, and high school years. I didn't realize until middle school how important it was to them for their mom to be involved, so at that point I was team mom, booster club fundraiser, team photographer, et cetera, until they both graduated from high school.

I can remember the day my oldest, Jeremy, walked into high school and I thought to myself, "Wow, here comes a long four years." Boy was I ever wrong—those were the *shortest* four years! Thank goodness that by the time his brother Jayson came in behind him three years later, I realized the days were passing by quickly, and that I wanted to help him live them to the fullest (to a point, of course).

I remember early in our oldest child's life, we were young and poor. We did without supper so that Jeremy had enough food to last through the next payday—thank goodness that was a short period of our life. Now my boys have grown into what I consider great men, sons, husbands, and fathers, and they make great contributions to our society. My husband and I did nothing without first, of course, seeking what

God's will was for us as parents and for the boys, and then we did the best we could.

Cindy Davidson
Mother of two
Grandmother of five
Associate Broker, Keller Williams Realty Atlanta Partners –
Peachtree City
cindydavidson.com
cdavidson@kw.com

38. If I knew then what I know now...

I would not have worried so much. I would have enjoyed spending even more time with my children instead of thinking about all the chores that had to be done.

As it turns out, the laundry, the cleaning, the food shopping, and the cooking somehow get done. The time I spent can never be replaced. I am grateful that I did a lot of fun things and spent a lot of time caring.

Adele DeMoro
Mother of five
Grandmother of six
Operating Principal
Keller Williams Realty West Monmouth
Keller Williams Realty Monmouth/Ocean
Keller Williams Realty East Monmouth
adele.demoro@verizon.net

39. If I knew then what I know now...

I would not have stressed as much as I did about choosing to be a stay-at-home mom. I went back to work six weeks after our daughter was born and for the next year and a half I was a part-time mom. I was afraid we would not be able to survive the financial burden of being a single income family. And to be honest I liked my career; it was a part of who I was and I aspired to be more in the industry, hoping to one day claim a spot in the "boys' club," if you will.

That all changed one Saturday afternoon when I was attempting to comfort our daughter with a boo-boo bunny after a fall. She looked at me through her tears and sniffled, "I just want my Nana." My mother had so wonderfully been her caregiver for much of her life, but I was crushed that she didn't instinctively know to want her Mommy.

I struggled over the next several months but ultimately made the decision (with my husband's full support) to voluntarily leave my position during a company downsize. Looking back, I know without reservation that God's hand was over the decision and His faithfulness has been with us each day since.

Within a year of leaving work I was diagnosed and underwent surgery for precancer of the cervix, which would make it risky for me to carry another child. I cannot begin to imagine how much I would have missed had I not taken time to be with our daughter. I am so thankful that I listened to the promptings of my heart.

In the twenty-five years since making that decision, we may not have always had the best of everything, but we have always had enough. And I have changed my career path not once but twice; never once regretting not having climbed the corporate ladder.

The absolute treasure of having a front-row seat to moment by moment watch our daughter grow has been no sacrifice at all, and I am privileged to think that just maybe I played a supporting role in her becoming the confident, beautiful young woman she is today.

T.L. Grabowski
Mother of one
Operations Coordinator, The John Maxwell Company

40. If I knew then what I know now...

I would spend more time with my children. Those precious moments never come again. Most importantly, I would teach them the values of cultures, money, and relationships.

Farzana Kalvert
Mother of two
Grandmother of one
Director/Partner, Kalvert Group
www.kalvertgroup.com
kalvertgroup@gmail.com

41. If I knew then what I know now...

I would notice more of the behaviors that I wanted to see repeated instead of always noticing all of the behaviors that I didn't want to see. Nothing creates repetition in a child's behavior more than a parenting "noticing" it.

Loni Metter
Mother of six
Mobiletattletale
www.mobiletattletale.com
Loni.Metter@me.com

42. If I knew then what I know now...

I would make sure that my family shared one meal daily at the kitchen table, sharing tales of the day. Friends would be welcome, and openness, laughter, and generosity would prevail.

Janet Saxon
Mother of three
Grandmother of two
Retired Real Estate Agent

43. If I knew then what I know now...

I would persevere through my first marriage. Although blended families are a blessing, there is nothing compared to raising your children with their natural parents. You do not realize the effect that your selfish, young, and immature decisions have on the lives of the jewels God has entrusted into your care. I would push myself past my comfort zone to enhance the lives of future generations.

Dr. Suzette Moore
Mother of two, Stepmother of two
Grandmother of three, Stepgrandmother of seven
Associate Broker, Keller Williams Realty Atlanta Partners
suzetteg@bellsouth.net

44. If I knew then what I know now...

I would live fully in the present instead of thinking too much about the future. I recently heard the statement, "Enjoy the path, instead of living for the peak." The reality is that the peak may never be reached. If every day has been lived enjoying the path along the way, with the realization that God is guiding it, then whether or not we reach the peak will not matter so much.

Rhonda Hawkins
Mother of two
Grandmother of one
Elementary Principal, Greater Atlanta Christian School
rhawkins@greateratlantachristianschool.org

45. If I knew then what I know now...

I would be one fantastic mom! I would read the Bible to my children every day, and this holy book would be the guide and the resource they would rely on as they resolve life's issues. I would teach them by example to participate in random acts of kindness every single day. On spring breaks, holidays, and weekends, we would reach out to help those less fortunate by participating in mission trips and community service. They would learn firsthand that giving is far greater than receiving. I would guide them to have an intimate relationship with God as their source of strength and love.

My children would know every single second of every day the depth of my love for them by my actions, words, and deeds, and this love would allow them to show love and have the capacity to love others. We don't have "do-overs" in raising children, so make raising them to become healthy, spiritual, and loving people your ultimate priority in life. This is the greatest gift you can give them!

Leslie Kunkel
Mother of two
Grandmother of two on earth and one in heaven
Real Estate Consultant, Keller Williams Realty Atlanta Partners
www.kunkelsells.com
facebook.com/realtor.leslie.kunkel
twitter.com/leslieGArealtor
lesliewkunkel@gmail.com

46. If I knew then what I know now...

As a working mom, I occasionally suffered from "mommy guilt." Even though my career allowed me to be home with my children after school and during the summer, I still felt a sense they were missing out on something.

When they entered middle school, I truly began to worry I had not given them "enough." So one weekend I took an opportunity to take a long drive by myself. Praying the entire way, I begged God to give me answers in helping my children develop a healthy self-esteem. His answer was fast! "Teach them to serve others."

As a math teacher of twenty-eight years, I know the more students "teach," the more they learn. I believe God was telling me the same thing about serving. The more they serve, the more they learn their true worth in the sight of God. It is a philosophy I hold even today in leading the junior high. Teach children to love others, by teaching them to serve.

Misty Overman
Mother of three
VP of Learning Initiatives and Junior High Principal, Greater
Atlanta Christian School
www.greateratlantachristian.org
moveman@greateratlantachristian.org

47. If I knew then what I know now...

I would include but limit outside activities and focus more attention on developing my children's appreciation of reading and the many adventures a great book can bring. This is how my love of learning developed in me and created a massive curiosity and thirst for adventure. Children's imaginations will be unleashed between the covers of great books. They will never be lonely or bored there.

Susan Hubek
Mother of four
Grandmother of eight
Operating Principal, Keller Williams Realty Allen, Texas
hubek@kw.com

48. If I knew then what I know now...

I would say that your children do not remember your clean floors or material gifts. They will remember the time you spend with them, the hugs and the kisses and the songs you sing to them. My favorite was "I Love You a Bushel and a Peck." Today, my three grown sons sing this song to my six wonderful grandchildren.

Elaine Tavani
Mother of three

TILT: 7 SOLUTIONS TO BE A GUILT-FREE WORKING MOM

Grandmother of six
Office Manager, Behavioral Institute of Atlanta
"Icee" Lady, Tavani Soccer Camps
www.tavanisoccer.com

49. If I knew then what I know now…

I would take the time (that I thought I didn't have) to listen. I would understand with all my heart that no job, no person, no long list of to-dos—NOTHING—was as urgent or as important as giving my time and attention to my child. I would listen, then ask positive questions that begin with "what" and "how." Questions with a negative connotation, "why" questions, would almost never be asked.

Erica Hill
Mother of three
Grandmother of two
Keller Williams Realty Boise and L.A. Coastal Regions

50. If I knew then what I know now…

I would not change anything; however, I might have done less traveling for my job. I thank my husband, who was very supportive and very engaged in our girls' welfare, for making it easier to leave each time and for helping the feelings of guilt not be as strong, but my separation from them was heart wrenching.

I have no regrets because I do not believe in regrets; it is counter-productive. All of it, good or bad, was a part of my journey to the place I am in now—still learning, growing, being a better mother and wife, building greater relationships, and meeting new people.

Claudia Carignan
Mother of two
Realtor, Keller Williams Realty Atlanta Partners
www.carignansellsgeorgia.com
@carignan26
ccarignan26@gmail.com

51. If I knew then what I know now...

I would be thoughtful that life gives you no guarantees.

1. Savings is a MUST! Your savings must be what YOU can put away, not what anyone else might have for you (inheritance, husband, etc.). I heard Clark Howard say that if you are not saving at all, no matter your age, start by having 1 percent deducted each paycheck. In six months have an additional 1 percent deducted (2 percent total). Do this every six months, and in five years you will be saving 10 percent of EVERYTHING you earn! Go girl!

2. Long-term care is a MUST. No matter who you think might take care of you, you never know what might happen. I bought it when I turned fifty—the first year's payments were hard, and then it just became something I did not think about. By buying early I am paying a much lower premium.

Andrea A. Moore
Mother of four
Grandmother of eleven
CEO, Office Creations, Inc.
www.officecreations.net

52. If I knew then what I know now...

I would schedule time to take better care of myself (when Mom is stressed/burned out, everyone suffers). Schedule time for yourself—even if it begins with five minutes of meditation/prayer time and expands to forty-five minutes of exercise time.

I would also do a better job of following a consistent routine each day with the kids (especially morning time—getting everyone out the door to school, etc.) by planning and doing more the night before so we would have been ready to go each day!

It is important to stay involved in their school lives. Have a set day each week, or every two weeks, or one day each month that you go and have/take lunch to them (my kids loved that). That is just one little idea on that subject.

Prioritize what is most important, and always be there for kids' games/performances, et cetera. Finally, I would pray as a family each night.

Susan Frederick
Five children (blended family—with three of mine and two of my husband's)
Grandmother of two
Owner/Operating Principal and Licensed Realtor, Keller Williams Realty
Facebook.com/ Susan Cronin Frederick
susanfrederick@kw.com

53. If I knew then what I know now…

I would have given more focus daily to being my best spiritual, physical, and emotional self. Being my best *within* would enable me to be my best for my three older children. I thank God I know it now, as my precious six-year-old child, Journey, is today the recipient of my best version of me. My Lord is the giver of second chances—in my case, four chances!

Brenda Conley
Mother of four
Grandmother of two
Journey Home Team, Keller Williams Realty Atlanta Partners
www.facebook.com/journeyhomerealty
brenda@journeyhomere.com

54. If I knew then what I know now…

I would not have worried about when my child reached the next milestone. I wouldn't have cared if my child rolled over, walked, got toilet trained, et cetera, "on time," according to baby books and friends' comments. I would have known that children grow up at their own pace, and you have to let them do it their own way. And that is perfectly fine!

Sally Ponchak
Mother of two
Grandmother of one
Team Leader, Keller Williams Realty Village Square Realty,
Ridgewood, New Jersey
kwvillagesquare.yourkwoffice.com
Facebook Sally Burger Ponchak

55. If I knew then, what I know now...

We have all heard successful people from every stripe mention that many of their parents believed in them and were their biggest cheerleaders—that in fact they wouldn't be where they are now without their mom's support. That's easier said than done when we don't necessarily agree with the path our kids want to journey on—but can be critical to the child following their dreams.

A few examples:

Tiki Barber – former NFL standout:

"Ever since I was a kid, my mom has always been my biggest fan. She was always there to support me. I attribute my success in life to the moral and intellectual guidance she provided me with."

Michael Phelps – Olympic Phenom

Michael's mom was no pushover, but she let her kids take part in decision making. She never gave up on her son when others voiced concerns about his ability to do well in school due to his attention difficulties.

Albert Einstein – needs no introduction

Albert was reportedly dyslexic and had limited verbal skills for many years. His parents had to ignore the negative reports from teachers in order to succeed by finding different schools that were the best for Albert—even financially supporting those schools.

Cait Barker – My daughter

Here is where it gets personal. Cait is twenty-three now and a successful YouTube entrepreneur, with her sister Shannon (eighteen) as her business partner. They are now on the journey together, living in California following their dreams. Cait started a YouTube channel on fashion, which has now amassed over one hundred thousand subscribers, and Shannon has over sixty thousand. Cait always wanted to be in the fashion world— we just never knew that it would happen through YouTube. She dropped out of college to pursue her endeavor, and it's paying off in a big way.

She has been to London, New York, and Hawaii just in the last several months, working with big brands and magazines (BCBG, O'Neill, Brandy Melville, Ford (the car company), *Foam Magazine,* and *Teen Vogue*). With her sister at her side, they are becoming influential in the fashion/social media new world. That's all exciting—now...but it took courage for her and us as her parents to forgo the traditional path toward her vision for the future.

Cait had struggled in her very academically focused school, as her creative PASSION did not fit in well. We regularly told her we believed in her dream to have a great future in fashion, despite the Ds in algebra. Both of our daughters recognize we supported their endeavors, even though it was not popular with our friends' opinions or our family's concerns. But in our opinion, it's not about us. It's about them, "the way they should go" and who God made them to be.

I encourage anyone reading this to consider taking the time to really discover what your child's passion might be. Then learn how best to train them and support them toward their journey and vision for their lives. God's got BIG plans for them!

Maureen Barker
Mother of three

**Director of Operations, Keller Williams Realty Roseville and
Sacramento
Twitter: @maureenbarker
www.youtube.com/caitbarker
www.youtube.com/shannonbarker.com
mkbarker@kw.com**

56. If I knew then what I know now...

I would believe that I could really make my dreams come true!

Lynn Kaley
**Mother of one
Grandmother of three
Realtor, Instructor, and Stakeholder, Keller Williams Realty
Atlanta Partners
www.thesnellvillerealestatelady.com**

If You Are Being Helped,
Then Whom Are You Helping?

> "Mom, my feelings don't feel very good."
> —Elle (age 5)

We know we have a lot to learn from the wisdom of older moms. But if they are helping us on our journeys, then who are we reaching out to for giving help? This is the circle of life. When we have found some moms who will help and inspire us, the next step is to do the same for other moms. Then real, true inspiration will come back to us. Some examples of ways we might help others include:

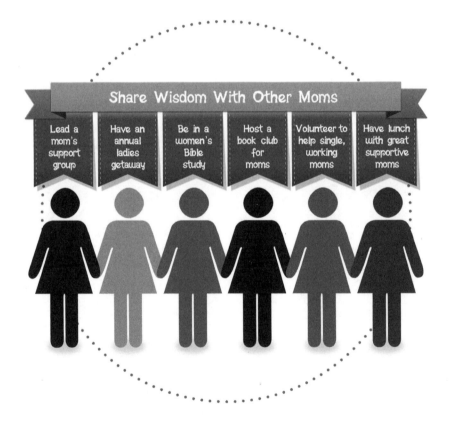

Share Wisdom With Other Moms

Lead a mom's support group | Have an annual ladies getaway | Be in a women's Bible study | Host a book club for moms | Volunteer to help single, working moms | Have lunch with great supportive moms

- Leading a mom's support group

- Having an annual ladies' getaway to rest and rejuvenate

- Participating in a women's Bible study

- Hosting a book club for moms

- Volunteering to help single working moms in our local community

- Having lunch every other month with great, supportive mom friends

Do not be discouraged if you are not involved in any of the above. I still cannot do every option I listed there. Maybe your chance to reach out will come later. If you cannot get out of the house yet due to too much baby paraphernalia and/or a fear of your child wanting to breast-feed as soon as you finally get him or her all the way into a store shopping cart to do some shopping, just know that your freedom does come back. In the meantime, you can use all the social-media tools (Twitter, Facebook, Google+, texting, e-mailing, etc.) to reach out to other moms to get, and to give, support.

We need to help each other and share our best ideas. I wish that earlier in my mom life, I had reached out to more working moms for support. It would have helped me to know that I was not the only one struggling with the life juggle and the mom guilt. Even more, it would have helped me reach out to help other moms who needed that same support.

My seventh life lesson actually came that first day our first child arrived: I could not know it all, and I did not have to reinvent the wheel. I needed to learn from those who had gone before me. Their experiences can help us answer real-life questions with practical solutions. Their wisdom can give us action steps we can take to dissolve guilt and make our lives a lot easier. Their insight into both heartache and joy can help us steer a smoother and happier path to fulfilling our mom missions. Then we have a responsibility to reach behind us to raise up the next mom who is, perhaps precariously, climbing her own *TILTed* life ladder.

Personal Profile in Mom Courage:
The Treasures of My Life

If I knew then what I know now, I would have made a tape of their laughter as children, and I would play it every day now, rain or shine, and it would be the best part of my day.

If I knew then what I know now, I wouldn't have worried so much about what college or what profession they chose; I would have just relaxed, knowing how smart and capable they are and knowing that they would succeed at whatever they chose to do, at whatever time of life they chose to do it.

As to sharing life experience as a mom, I have been made so rich by it all. The biggest wisdom I can share is that nothing else will matter in your future, so pay attention to your family now. Accept and love them for who they are. They may be crazy, but they are my kind of crazy. Laugh and love and give nothing else significance. You will get everything you give back a millionfold, so give all you have and never resent it.

In closing on this issue, I can tell you that I have always had one great attribute that I am very thankful for. I knew what I had when I had it, and I knew they were the treasures of my life and that nothing else before or after would ever matter much. I know that my life is about my family, and somehow I have gotten to live in that joy for many years. I am a lucky lady who still gets to milk the love and fun every day. I am so thankful.

Mary Tennant
Mother, Grandmother
President, Keller Williams Realty International

GUILT-FREE TIPS –
Ten Resources for Mom-Wisdom—
When in Doubt, Reach Out

1. Who are your role models? Look for working moms whose family lives are what you are striving for. Aim high and learn from them. Find them online and read about their ideas and solutions.

2. There are more mom-focused online resources than I can list! Check these out:

   a. mommytracked.com

   b. 30secondmom.com

   c. momscape.com

   d. momsgetreal.com

   e. mothersdaycentral.com

   f. babble.com

   g. workingmother.com

   h. workitmom.com

   i. workingmotherscoach.com

   j. And many more!

3. Look on Twitter at the "Lists" on my account @marcifair. I have been seeking out other great working moms as well. You will find some great ones there. Follow them! They love to share their best ideas to help you with your mom life.

4. Have lunch at least once per quarter with a working mom like yourself whom you respect and whose children are older than yours and doing well. Ask her a million questions for her best tips and tricks.

5. Check out some of the good woman-focused groups on Facebook, such Working Moms Only, Diary of a Working Mom, Working Mom Lifestyle, and TILT: 7 Solutions To Be A Guilt-Free Working Mom. "Like" them so their stream of sharing shows up in your news feed, or just go back to their pages every week or so for new news.

6. Join a working mothers association, such as Entrepreneurial Moms International (momventures.com), or a local women's group at your chamber of commerce, or a women's group at your church. Together with other working women, you can tap into ideas and resources you do not have when you are trying to figure it all out on your own!

7. Subscribe to *Working Mother* magazine (delivered right to you!) so you can read current articles and ideas to help you.

8. Consider creating a private Facebook group with fellow mom friends. It's a fun and fast way to get suggestions and support from one another when you need it.

9. Be a mentor to a mom with children who are younger than yours. Be honest about the experiences and struggles you have and you'll likely learn just as much in sharing your issues with others as you do from asking more experienced moms about theirs.

10. Read this book again (and again, in case a little person interrupted you and you missed an important idea)!

Closing Thoughts: Our Purpose Is in Our Journey

> "Wow, those new tennis shoes will make you SO fast!"
> —me to Chloe (age 6)
> "Mom, they don't make me fast—I do."
> —Chloe's response

It has taken me at least five years to find the time to write this book. In the midst of bringing so many children into this world and working on multiple businesses and our children's charity, in between the dance recitals, second-grade school programs, uncountable visits to the pediatrician's office, birthday parties, and my notoriously not–Rachael Ray dinners, I have started, stopped, started, and stopped again. Thankfully, my husband continued to encourage me, even though I did not really think many people would be interested in my personal trials and tribulations.

It was in the middle of the hardest mental trials that I knew I needed help. I knew I needed to believe my life was bigger than putting away toys that immediately unorganized themselves again, or washing dishes that magically reappeared dirty as soon I had cleaned them. I knew I had a bigger purpose, and I had to figure out what it was.

I believe we each have a big reason for being here. In some of my toughest, most *TILT*ed mom moments, my heartfelt fear was that my mom role was insignificant in its basic repetitiveness and that I was losing the professional opportunities I had worked for and trained for all my life. I wanted to pursue those and fulfill my life purpose, whatever it was supposed to be. Instead, I was woefully outnumbered by people shorter than me.

Then, slowly at first, as my momoirs unfolded, I discovered that *my purpose is in my journey*: learning, working, washing, striving, mothering, failing, giving, hurting, growing, and loving all along the way. Our purpose is in fact woven delicately and intricately through each day. It is in the early-morning kisses on the sweet cheek of a sleeping angel toddler; it is in the fulfilling connections we make with like-minded peers during the day; it is in the laughter and tears shared around the family dinner table at night. It will not be discovered only at the end of our life; it is meant to be uncovered and lived each day that we are blessed with.

"Live My Best Life and Make a Difference in the Lives of Others"

—my life mission statement

By striving to live my best life all along the way, I am teaching my children (especially my girls, who are future mothers) that I have to live my life well, even as I am here to help them live theirs.

We can and need to let go of the mistaken idea (and the accompanying guilt) that we should be in perfect balance along our journey. It might happen in small moments, but those disappear quickly. Instead, striving for balance over time and for special memories along our journey with our family and for ourselves *is the truth* of a real well-lived life.

We each have our own special light, and we need to live it. We cannot hide our light as we help our children find theirs. We will become our personal best when we shine brightly. My momoirs have helped me understand that sometimes my light might shine more brightly than others, but that is called normal and not an indication of never. I am determined to not hide my light in a closet. And I wrote this book with the hope that you will not hide yours either.

Along the way, my children have elevated me to another level that I never imagined. Rather than keeping me from accomplishing my dreams, they have helped me achieve bigger ones. I am, in fact, much better *because of them*. They challenge me to set the right example and be the best mom possible so they learn to become their best, to love my husband so they learn to love their spouses, to go after my dreams so they will never stop chasing theirs.

Did I potty train my children by age six? Well, I had hoped I would, but whether or not I was able to do that ultimately did not define me as a mom. Instead, what define my mom success are the same values that define my life success. We can demonstrate to our children that our greatest challenges are, in fact, our greatest opportunities. By pursuing our dreams, as we help our children pursue theirs, we set an example that makes words unnecessary. We teach our children that just as we are here to help them find the path to fulfill their own missions, we need to fulfill ours as well.

I believe that our impact can be awesome and inspiring. We can lead future generations to loving families and relationships; to successful businesses that impact our communities; to peaceful coexistence in this new, flat world; to spiritual fulfillment; to any form of greatness. Or not.

It is our choice, in the nucleus of our families and homes, to set the example by shining our own light, so we can love, guide, and empower those whose little lights we brought into this world.

> "Mama, I be a dansa (dancer) when I gwow up.
> What you be when you gwow up?"
> —Chloe (age 4)

Acknowledgments

For simplicity in writing this book, I often used the singular person in referring to the children as "my children" or when "I" parent. I do want to be clear that Bryan and I parent our children together. Although I might have written "my children," they are "ours." We parent together, set goals together, make mistakes together, and then laugh about the chaotic life we have created together.

Truly the only way a dream project like this comes together is by the support of many wonderful people. From my family and friends who have believed in me from the beginning, to the talented book people who helped me in the middle and finally to the moms who will chose to read this book to help themselves and their families in the end – may each of your lives be as rich as you enrich the lives of others.

Diedra Sorohan, you are such a big thinker, you listened and believed in me from our first coffee at Starbucks. Paige Powers, I know one day you will write your Benjamin story, and I will get to cheer you on. Jay Papasan believer in big goals, you met with me over a few years to guide, suggest and push me to think bigger. Gary Keller, you somehow generously found the time to review *TILT* and offer excellent advice. Rachael Bodie, you befriended me immediately - how lucky I am to have met you. Jennifer Mest and Nikki Bonds, you both listened and I learned so much on our coffee dates. My 30 Second Mom friends, you stepped up so quickly to help and support me. Mo Anderson, Mary Tennant and Dianna Kokoszka, you all so generously and immediately believed in *TILT*. Pat Hiban, you unhesitatingly shared all your best seller tips with me (7 Steps To Six Figures). Meredith Atwood (Triathlon for The Every Woman), you had not even met me, yet you shared your ideas from your success with your book. Antoinette Perez, you not only graciously met me a couple times to share your insights, you also introduced me to Trish Morrison and MomCom.

For the people who helped me construct a well written book – Sarah Zimmerman, Laura Meehan, Vickie Lukachik, Toni Robino, Ginger Moran, Karen Cherry, my awesome createspace editors, and my outstanding mom editor – Mary Nance. For Mark Schaefer (Tao of Twitter) who told me about createspace. For those who helped me make a beautiful book – Nelly Murariu and Kelly Greer.

For the talented Matt Rains, who helped me bring *TILT* alive online through all things techy - my website (guiltfreemom.com), emailing my monthly mom-inspirations, and more, even helping me find my wonderful graphics designer. For Michelle Steele whose story is a beautiful tribute to her, and whose support on all that I have had to learn on this book journey has been unfailing. For Anne Rains, who helped me with countless responsibilities in order for me to make *TILT* a reality.

For my friends who read excerpts and shared their (thankfully) wonderful and thoughtful feedback – Wendy Papasan, Eadaoin Waller, Stacy DeRogatis, Tiffany Jackson, Nikki Ubaldini, Janice Baldwin, Rhonda Polhill, Bonnie Rich, Lauren Hollier, Leslie Kunkel, Corey Ralston, and Cindy Cooksey.

For the people who taught and inspired me through their work – Renee Peterson Trudeau (The Mother's Guide To Self-Renewal), Guy Kawasaki (Enchantment and APE), Michael Alvear (Make A Killing On Kindle), and John Maxwell for his amazing example as a writer and author inspiring others to lead.

For the over eighty women who contributed their thoughts and shared a part of their hearts with us – they so deserve a very sincere thank you. They are all special and unique in their own way, each with a beautiful story to share – Mo Anderson, Beth Aldrich, Elisa All, Donna Ardolino, Janice Baldwin, Maureen Barker, Nola Belle Heald Bennitt (In Memory Of), Norma Biggs, Rachael Bodie, Nikki Bonds, Shadra Bruce, Annie Burnside, Claudia Carignan, Brenda Conley, Linda Cooke, Cindy Davidson, Adele DeMoro, Stacy DeRogatis, Jennice Doty, Kristin Ervin,

Kim Estes, Kay Evans, Linda Fair, Roxanne Formisano, Susan Frederick, Linda Gifford, Alicia Gonzalez, Tammy Grabowski, Mary Harker, Ann Hartley, Rhonda Hawkins, Patricia Hermes, Dr. Christi Hibbert, Erica Hill, Susan Hubek, Lynn Kaley, Farzana Kalvert, Dianna Kokoszka, Leslie Kunkel, Kathy Larrabee, Sherry Lewis, Tara Locke, Susan Macaulay, Christine Martinello, Patti Martinez, Linda McKissack, Jennifer Mest, Loni Metter, Andrea Moore, Suzette Moore, Danette Moss, Mary Nance, Deb Nardy, Julia Nelson, Misty Overman, Wendy Papasan, Trinita Patton, Wendy Patton, Rosemarie Pelatti, Sally Ponchak, Paige Powers, Kathy Ramos, Mary Jane Rogan, Beth Rosen, Katie Ross, Kaira Rouda, Rebekah Rivers, Marie Sapienza, Linda Sasser, Janet Saxon, Danielle Schneller, Peggy Slappey, Diedra Sorohan, Amy Sperr, Michelle Steele, Beverly Steiner, Elaine Tavani, Kathleen Teare, Mary Tennant, Leslie Thebaut, Heather Travitz, Debbie Tufts, Nikki Ubaldini, Judy Waters, and Connie Wiggins.

For anyone I inadvertently left out, please forgive me. Bringing *TILT* to life has taken years in between everything else and raising our children. I appreciate all the assistance and support I have had all along this book journey.

My deepest life appreciation goes to my amazing family. Bryan, you never let me let go of this dream. Thank you for your unfailing support and belief in me. Parker, Courtney, Chloe and Elle – you are each the true inspiration behind *TILT*. Your young, but wise insights and views of the world changed my view of it as well – and made it so much richer. My love for each of you is beyond anything words can express.

Resources

To Lift You Up

Through my years of charity work, I have seen over and over the power of giving: giving of time, giving of thoughtful attention, giving of care for those hurting, giving of donations when someone cannot take care of their needs. One of the most powerful ways to lift yourself up when you are struggling is to turn and lift up another. To find a simple, easy way to help another, I encourage you to seek out local charities or organizations that serve others. If that is hard for you to do, bake some brownies with your children and take them to the local fire or police department. Those people, who give their lives to take care of us, will greatly appreciate your care for them.

Book Clubs and Lunch and Learns

If you find this book, its practical tips and ideas interesting to you, why not start a small group around you for peer support to discuss what you are learning and how you are applying it as you move through the book? Please visit the website www.guiltfreemom.com for more ideas and suggestions on how to do this.

Questions? Comments?

Please visit my website www.guiltfreemom.com for current information and additional ideas from the book.

Notes

1 "Economic Characteristics of Families Summary—2012," Bureau of Labor Statistics, United States Department of Labor, April 26, 2013, http://www.bls.gov/news.release/famee.nr0.htm.

2 "What Moms Choose: The Working Mother Report," Working Mother Research Institute, 2011, http://www.workingmother.com/research-institute/what-moms-choose-working-mother-report.

3 "How People Shop Online—E-commerce Statistics," Lab 42 Market Research, August 27, 2012, http://www.fortune3.com/blog/2012/08/how-people-shop-online-ecommerce-statistics/.

4 Sara Radicati, PhD, and Quoc Hoang, "Email Statistics Report, 2011–2015," The Radicati Group, Inc., A Technology Market Research Firm.

5 Michael Austin, "Humility and Parenthood," *Psychology Today*, July 5, 2010, http://www.psychologytoday.com/blog/ethics-everyone/201007/humility-and-parenthood.

6 "The Perfectionist Parent," Parents.com, http://www.parents.com/parenting/better-parenting/advice/perfectionist-parent/.

7 Richard Koch, *The 80/20 Principle: The Secret to Achieving More with Less* (New York: Doubleday, 1998).

8 Trinh Tran, "Hard-Working Mothers Recognized," *Penn Current*, July 18, 2002, http://www.upenn.edu/pennnews/current/node/1742.

9 Ann Smith, "The Perils of Perfectionism in Motherhood," *Psychology Today*, May 9, 2013, http://www.psychologytoday.com/blog/healthy-connections/201305/the-perils-perfectionism-in-motherhood.

10   Todd M. Thrash, Andrew J. Elliot, Laura A. Maruskin, and Scott E. Cassidy, "Inspiration and the Promotion of Well-Being: Tests of Causality and Mediation," *Journal of Personality and Social Psychology* 98, no. 3 (2010).

11   Kaihan Krippendorff, "Where to Find Inspiration When the World Tells You to Give Up," *Fast Company,* February 1, 2012, http://www.fastcompany.com/1812897/where-find-inspiration-when-world-tells-you-give.

12   Mayo Clinic Staff, "Positive Thinking: Reduce Stress by Eliminating Negative Self-Talk," Mayo Foundation for Medical Education and Research, May 28, 2011, http://www.mayoclinic.com/health/positive-thinking/SR00009.

13   Ellen Gibson, "3 Smart New Ways to Kick Pessimism to the Curb," *O, The Oprah Magazine,* March 2012, http://www.oprah.com/spirit/How-to-Be-Optimistic-Focus-on-the-Positive#ixzz2Umyw3kLm.

14   Ira J. Chasnoff, "Catch 'em Being Good!," *Psychology Today,* May 27, 2011, http://www.psychologytoday.com/blog/aristotles-child/201105/catch-em-being-good-0.

15   Judith A. Myers-Walls and Rajeswari Natrajan, "Positive Reinforcement and Rewards," Purdue Extension Knowledge to Go, School of Consumer and Family Sciences Department of Child Development and Family Studies, http://www.extension.purdue.edu/providerparent/PDF%20Links/PositiveReinfRewards.pdf.

16   Carolyn Williams, "The Importance of Giving Children Boundaries," Livestrong.com, August 18, 2011, http://www.livestrong.com/article/516853-the-importance-of-giving-children-boundaries/.

17   Claire Winter, "Boundaries—Kids Will Always Test Them," BBC, March 12, 2011, http://www.bbc.co.uk/blogs/parents/2011/03/boundaries—kids-will-always.shtml.

TILT - 7 Solutions To Be A Guilt-free Working Mom
Marci Fair

Published by createspace, a division of Amazon Publishing
Copyright @2013 Marci Fair, Pacochel Press LLC
All rights reserved.
Printed in the United States of America

Grateful appreciation is made for the thoughts and ideas of many others, whom I have acknowledged throughout the book.

Ordering Information
For additional copies contact your favorite bookstore, online store, or email info@guiltfreemom. com. Special offers for large orders are available.

ISBN: 0615859895
ISBN 13: 9780615859897

First Edition
First printing: January 2014